IMMOMENT TOYS

IMMOMENT TOYS

*A Survey of Light Entertainment
on the London Stage, 1920-1943*

by

JAMES AGATE

'Say, good Cæsar,
That I some lady trifles have reserved,
Immoment toys . . . '
            Antony and Cleopatra, Act V, Sc. 2

BENJAMIN BLOM  New York/London

First Published 1945
Reissued 1969 by
Benjamin Blom, Inc., Bronx, New York 10452
and 56 Doughty Street, London, W.C. 1

Library of Congress Catalog Card Number 77-86884

Printed in U.S.A. by
NOBLE OFFSET PRINTERS, INC.
NEW YORK 3, N. Y.

CONTENTS

MUSICAL PLAYS

5

CONTENTS

CONTENTS

CONTENTS

CONTENTS

CONTENTS

CONTENTS

CONTENTS

CONTENTS

13

CONTENTS

ACKNOWLEDGMENTS

My thanks are due to the proprietors of the *Sunday Times*, in whose columns nineteen-twentieths of the matter in this book originally appeared, for their courteous permission to reproduce that matter here.

Also to Messrs. W. Collins, Sons & Co., Ltd. (*Buzz, Buzz!* and *Fantasies and Impromptus*), Chapman & Hall (*The Contemporary Theatre, 1923, 1924* and *1926*), Victor Gollancz Ltd. (*More First Nights*), George G. Harrap & Co., Ltd. (*The Amazing Theatre* and *Here's Richness!*).

DEDICATORY LETTER
TO
ALAN DENT

MY DEAR ALAN,

I began the second of my Dedicatory Letters to you with the sentence: 'I am not a believer in doing things by halves.' Neither am I a believer in doing things by two-thirds. This is why I offer to you *Immoment Toys* which, with *Brief Chronicles* and *Red Letter Nights*, completes my survey of the London stage during the years 1920-1943.

I have divided the book into four sections: Musical Plays, Revues, Silhouettes — these are portraits of great music-hall artists — and Pantomimes. You will not find everything here, of course. The book runs to some 100,000 words, as against the million or so which I must have written about light entertainments of various kinds. I admit, sorrowfully, to one or two obvious gaps. It would seem that I have never had occasion to write at length about, for example, those two great performers, Nellie Wallace and Harry Tate. And I refuse to make up something now and pretend that it is not new.

You may ask me whether the material justifies reproduction? If you do, I shall say that A. B. Walkley held it to be not beneath his dignity to write one of his best essays about a clown. I hold that if you have anything worth-while to say about Shakespeare or Congreve, Shaw or Eugene O'Neill, it doesn't matter very much how you say it, since the stuff will carry the style. But that when your material is the 'lady trifles' of a Sophie Tucker or a Nervo and Knox, the words you choose, and their order, are of the first importance.

I hope, my dear Alan, that as you read you will detect some glimmer of that 'scholarship, perceptivity, wit and love of the theatre' with which, on the last occasion, I credited YOU!

London

July 22, 1944

JAMES AGATE

16

MUSICAL PLAYS

THE BEGGAR'S OPERA

BY JOHN GAY. MUSIC BY LINLEY

(Lyric, Hammersmith)

'HANG the age! I will write for antiquity!' cried a fastidious spirit. 'Hang the age!' Mr. Nigel Playfair exclaims, 'I will revive for antiquity!' and so saying pulls out the old *Beggar's Opera* and enlists a popular author to help in the text revisions. The opera is an enchanting affair, a perfect combination of 'those two good things, sense and sound'. Spontini, Cherubini, Bellini, Rossini, Puccini — the whole 'ini' family have done nothing more fragrant than this bouquet of homely melodies. Of the first author and producer of this play it is possible to be handsomely ignorant.

> Of Doctor Pepusch old Queen Dido
> Knew just as much, God knows, as I do.

Since four hours is too much of a good thing for modern audiences, and taste has degenerated, let me, poetizing in turn, imagine Mr. Playfair in soliloquy, confronted with these two-fold difficulties of space-time and century-taste.

> If cut I must this be my tenet,
> The cutter shall be Arnold Bennett,
> And Pepusch' spirit won't be lost in
> Sympathetic Frederick Austin;
> Whilst how to act the tribe of Peachum
> It's up to Nigel P. to teach 'em.

A curious adventure to find the perfect entertainment in this modest Hammersmith playhouse. You leave the unfashionable street to mix with a crowd of shiny-faced enthusiasts who have

17

not thought it necessary to bare their backs and tire their heads in order to hear better. And what a world of romance greets you on the stage, the world of the High-toby-crack, and the Ordinary, the bridle-cull, the clay-faker, the buttock-and-file! A world of scoundrels undismayed, of rogues with a sense of style, doxies and wives, soon to be hempen widows, gazing tearless upon the heroic turning off. Polly was of gentler mould. The picture she makes of her lover going to the gallows is of the most touching simplicity. 'I see him sweeter than the nosegay in his hand; the admiring crowd lament that so lovely a youth should come to an untimely end; even butchers weep, and Jack Ketch refuses his fee rather than consent to tie the fatal knot.' All, it would appear, were exquisites who came to this tree. 'He was but sixteen,' says the biographer of Roderick Audrey. 'He went very decent to the gallows, being in a white waistcoat, clean napkin, white gloves, and an orange in his hand.'

The Beggar's Opera was Hazlitt's favourite satire. Plentiful references to it abound throughout the essays, which contain two full-dress descriptions of the plot, and the lessons in morality to be drawn therefrom. In both Hazlitt stresses the vulgar error which would call this a vulgar play, and harks back to that 'happy alchemy of mind' which can extract the essence of refinement from the dregs of life. He is full of the 'justice to nature'. It is because America has no history that she has never been able to appreciate the play. 'And in America — that Van Diemen's Land of letters — this sterling satire is hooted off the stage, because, fortunately, they have no such state of manners as it describes before their eyes; and because, unfortunately, they have no conception of anything but what they see. America is singularly and awkwardly situated in this respect. It is a new country with an old language; and while everything about them is of a day's growth, they are constantly applying to us to know what to think of it, and taking their opinions from our books and newspapers with a strange mixture of servility and of the spirit of contradiction.' This was written in 1827 and it is curious that when, in 1921, in consequence of the tremendous success of the revival over here, the play was once more tried in America, it was again a dismal failure. The Yankees appear to have made up their minds on both occasions without applying to our books and newspapers to know what to think.

The vicissitudes which *The Beggar's Opera* has undergone in its own country should explain the lack of appreciation abroad. Already, in 1828, we find the essayist deploring the degeneracy of the age. 'It is not that there are not plenty of rogues and pick-pockets at present; but the Muse is averse to look that way; the imagination has taken a higher flight; wit and humour do not flow in that dirty channel, picking the grains of gold out of it. Instead of descending, we aspire; and the age has a sublime front given to it to contemplate the heaven of drawing-rooms and the milky-way of passion.' Even the players had begun to forsake truth for gentility. The Lucy of that year 'put a negative on an encore that was likely to detain her five minutes longer in New-gate'. Polly 'was frightened at the interest she might inspire and was loth to waste her sweetness on a blackguard air'. How then shall we account for the enormous success of the present revival in an age of fashionable comedy raised to the seventh heaven of inanity? Shall I submit a revulsion from those drawing-room games of Blind Man's Buff or the King's Proctor Hoodwinked, Hunt the Slipper, or The Maid's Shift? Shall I say that these days of terrorism and unwritten laws are a sign that we are no longer degenerate, but reborn? I am afraid that neither plea will hold. The success of *The Beggar's Opera* is, alas! not more than a success of antiquity; it pleases like a chair of some good period which it is delightful to gaze upon and to handle, but which one would not dream of using. The satire of the past has lost its sting.

And this brings me to a very nice point. What, exactly, do we expect in a performance of *The Beggar's Opera*? Let me pay all possible tribute to a production of charm, taste and wit. The artists act well enough, and sing tunably; the stage-pictures are a delight to the eye, the ground-swell of the musicians is a solace to the ear. All that can humanly be asked is performed, and yet the thing is not the Beggar's Opera of our dreams. This is a matter worthy of some discussion, since the whole function of the theatre is here called in question. Can life be put upon the stage at all? Was that slice of life which is *The Beggar's Opera* ever played to any perfection save in the spectator's brain? And is not something more demanded from the spectator than mere corroboration, an essential eking out of the all too insufficient actor's art? It is the case of the blackamoor in a temper all over again. The quintessence of the Moor is not to be acted. Read *Othello*, and the map of a noble character is spread before you like some fair country, of which jealousy is an accidental scarp. But in the theatre the spectator's nose is to the quarry-face; he too is blinded by a single passion. In the theatre you are allowed to take nothing for granted; the sawing of the lip, the frenzied rolling of the eye are 'effects' to be brought off to satisfy the dullards. So, too, Falstaff's paunch may never be taken for granted. The actor must, at all costs, inflict upon you the well-oiled machinery of ventripotence, whereas, to the reader, it is his mind which drips fatness. Who will say that that stoutish, middle-aged, bald-headed figure in the limelight, clad though he be in brown surtout and imposing shirt-collar, with a roll in the voice and indescribable, genteel air, is really Micawber as we know him who have lived with him? These, the externals of the man which the reader takes for granted, are on the stage stressed beyond endurance, lest, peradventure, we mistake the fellow for Ally Sloper. Peachum and Macheath are alike unactable. They shall be pictures to fright and to please the eye of childhood, villainy lined roughly and gallantry daubed after the fashion of a Christmas Number. The fault is not in the actors but in their art which, of itself, can go only such a little way towards creation. In the theatre the brain of a spectator must prove the female to the actor's; in no other way can life be begot. The poorest printed page is, by itself, nearer creation than the actor's unaided flesh and blood.

Apply this to the work before us. *The Beggar's Opera* was written some twenty years before *Jonathan Wild*, but it is from Fielding that these immortal rogues look out upon their time and upon us. Where Gay writes Peachum, Lockit and Polly we must read Jonathan, Blueskin and Laetitia Snap. Listen once again to Fielding's description of Miss Tishy: 'Her lovely hair hung wantonly over her forehead, being neither white with, nor yet free from, powder; a neat double clout, which seemed to have been worn a few weeks only, was pinned under her chin; some remains of that art with which ladies improve nature, shone upon her cheeks; her body was loosely attired, without stays or jumps; so that her breasts had uncontrolled liberty to display their beauteous orbs, which they did as low as her girdle; a thin covering of a rumpled muslin handkerchief almost hid them from our eyes, save in a few parts where a good-natured hole gave opportunity to the naked breast to appear. Her gown was a satin of a whitish colour, with about a dozen little silver spots on it, so artificially interwoven at great distance, that they looked as if they had fallen there by chance. This, flying open, discovered a fine yellow petticoat, beautifully edged round the bottom with a narrow piece of half-gold lace, which was now almost become fringe; beneath this appeared another petticoat stiffened with whalebone, vulgarly called a hoop, which hung six inches at least below the other; and under this again appeared an under garment of that colour which Ovid intends when he says,

Qui color albus erat nunc est contrarius albo.

She likewise displayed two pretty feet, covered with silk and adorned with lace, and tied, the right with a handsome piece of blue riband; the left, as more unworthy, with a piece of yellow stuff which seemed to have been a strip of her upper-petticoat.'

Who, with this picture in his mind, can quite have reconciled himself to the ladies at the Lyric, those immaculate and silver fountains? And then there is the difficulty of Polly, who was played as though she were Patience. Alas! that we cannot know from observation how Miss Stephens or Miss Nash used to play the part. We read: 'The acting of Miss Stephens throughout was simple, unaffected and graceful and full of tenderness. There is a severity of feeling and a plaintive sadness, both in the words and music of the songs in this opera, on which too much stress cannot be laid.' Neither Miss Nelis nor Miss Arkandy had tenderness; they were neither plaintive nor sad, nor unaffected. They took refuge from anything resembling severity of feeling in the highly artificial, conscious artlessness of Gilbert's milkmaid. They were china figures, and delectable, but unreal. Peachum erred on the side of gentility. He should be 'an old rogue'. So is not Mr. Frederick Austin. He should have looked like 'Phiz's' illustrations, his face all bubukles and whelks and flames of fire. Whereas there was something *moral* about Mr. Austin, something of Matthew Arnold in's aspect, a dash of the disconcerting debonair, a hint of Escamillo. You could not imagine him cutting up lives and booty. The Mrs. Peachum of Miss Elsie French was excellent in intention, but a trifle lacking in gusto. Not the cleverest actress can, by taking thought, add *richness* to her personality, and I do not think it lay in Miss French's physical powers to play the part other than as she did. Nevertheless, Mrs. Peachum was too shrill and shrewish, too much the harridan, the secret, black and midnight hag. Chambering and strong waters called for a more generous habit; she did not warm to her villainies. Where there should have been the rump-fed ronyon there was the ghoul. The Lucy of Miss Violet Marquesita was an admirable spitfire, and Lockit most excellently cut out in cardboard. His hypocrisy had just the proper touch.

'Tis thus the crocodile his grief displays,
Sheds the false tear, and, whilst he weeps, betrays.

The scuffle between Peachum and Lockit was well done and we should not have been surprised to hear an old gentleman in the pit shout, as on an earlier occasion: 'Hogarth, by God!' But the performance, as any performance of this opera must, stands or falls by Macheath. Upon this part Hazlitt expends all the wealth of his discernment. Macheath, he says, is not a gentleman but a 'fine gentleman'. His manners should resemble those of this kidney as closely as the dresses of the ladies in the private boxes resemble those of the ladies in the boxes which are not private. He is to be one of God Almighty's gentlemen, not a

gentleman of the black rod. 'His gallantry and good breeding
should arise from impulse, not from rule; not from the trammels of
education, but from a soul generous, courageous, good-natured,
aspiring, amorous. The class of the character is very difficult to
hit. It is something between gusto and slang, like port wine and
brandy mixed. It is not the mere gentleman that should be represented but the blackguard sublimated into the gentleman.' Hazlitt
could find no one on the stage of his day to play the part as he
conceived it. The elder Kemble might have done, but he was
no singer. Mr. Kean might have made the experiment, but he
would not have succeeded. Incledon was not sufficient of a gentleman, Davies did not sing well enough, Sinclair was too finical,
Cooke without title for the part.

Mr. Frederick Ranalow, then, had in Macheath a sufficiently
challenging part from the point of view of tradition. We may say
at once that he was good-looking, gallant, debonair, vocal. Perhaps he was a trifle over-wigged, which makes Macheath something less than the 'pretty fellow' of Madame Vestris. Whilst his
gentility was exactly right — and we can imagine the page of
purple our essayist would have given to the nicety of his hitting-
off — we did not quite believe in his scoundrelism. He was the
sentimental philanderer of our own day, and not the trusser of
women. This small discrepancy apart, Mr. Ranalow was admirable. No praise could have been too high for the perfection of his
diction, the wit of his 'Before the Barn-Door Crowing', the pathos of
'The Charge is Prepared', the finesse of 'How Happy could I be
with Either'. He is a most accomplished singer, and an actor to his
finger-tips. Still, the only part in the present production which I
take to be entirely in accordance with the old spirit is Filch.
Filch is a serious, contemplative, *conscientious* character. He is to
sing ''Tis Woman that seduces all Mankind', as if he had a pretty
girl in one eye and the gallows in the other. The actor is not to
make a joke of the part. By being sober, honest and industrious he
hopes to escape Tyburn by way of Transportation. The Filch of
Mr. Frederick Davies was exactly in this key. His gesture at the
words 'Pox take the Tailors for making the Fobs so deep and

narrow' was the one *canaillerie* in the play. Here we come again at our point. The characters in the Opera are to have but a superficial air of gallantry and romance; there should be something hangdog about them. All the gallants in the revival could ogle a wench; not one of them save Filch had the gallows in his composition. The shadow of the gibbet was not here; you would have unhesitatingly invited them to sup at your own house. Even the women of the town were, you feel, only pretending. An old French critic singled out among the many excellencies of the comedy, 'the differentiation the author makes between the jades, how each has her separate character, her peculiar traits, her peculiar modes of expression, which give her a marked distinction from her companions'. Whereas each of the hussies personified at the Lyric was qualified to mate with an earl. There was nothing of a distinguishing tawdriness about them except their styles and titles.

June 5, 1920

MOZART

BY SACHA GUITRY

(Gaiety)

NOT the composer of music 'all breathing human passion far above', and presiding spirit of the most lenitive art the world has ever known. Not the supreme melodist whose quality of spiritual detachment was summed up by Amiel in the single word 'disinterestedness'. Neither the despised protégé of the Archbishop of Salzburg, nor an Emperor's employé passing rich on eighty pounds a year. Neither the husband of commonplace Constanze Weber, the dapper little courtier, fond of punch and billiards and proud of his hair, nor the man of genius hurried into a pauper's grave with his five so-called friends scuttling away from the cemetery in the rain. M. Guitry has cared to write about none of these

24

things, which can all be proved. Nor yet for him the chromo-lithograph, historical drama's illustrated supplement, in which a Chopin drowses over the keyboard to the nocturnal dancing of nineteen strapping wenches, or a Beethoven, face-scratched by a cook and soul-slapped by a nephew, crashes out a vengeance in the walloping opening chords of Opus something-or-other.

M. Guitry has chosen his hero's twentieth year, and to embellish that year with incidents which, as he charmingly put it on the first night, cannot be disproved. The time is 1775, the place Paris (actually Mozart did not revisit France till 1778, but no matter). The curtain rises on the drawing-room of Madame d'Epinay, surely one of the most skilfully devised 'sets' ever seen on the stage. On the spectator's left are folding doors which, being opened, reveal an ante-chamber where minor personages not concerned in the immediate traffic of the play may yet continue their elegant existence. At the back a flight of low stairs leads to a raised land-ing, ostensibly the hall of the mansion, actually the pedestal from which the little god is to descend into the common heart.

At the beginning the piece moves slowly, and we are grateful since the eye is thereby given leisure to renew acquaintance with a delicious epoch. Those engravings, each with its coquetry of blue ribbon, can only be after the little painters of the *grand siècle*, the spinet must have tinkled its accompaniment to Orfeo's 'Che farò' the very furniture prates of great ladies lancing discreet œillades and *petites marquises* making fluttering confession behind their fans. Two such fair vessels are here becalmed on the tender sea. That well-found frigate, Madame d'Epinay, has hoisted full sail to catch the Baron Grimm's ardour, which no longer blows in her direction; that fast cutter which is her god-daughter discusses a convenient match. Her gallant chatters about passion, fidelity and the like, idly enough to give you time to reflect what your thoughts had been on seeing your first Molière play, or on turning the first pages of Choderlos De Laclos's *Les Liaisons Dangereuses*.

The Baron Grimm brings you back to decorum with some ob-servations as to the value of criticism and the worth to his century of Jean Jacques Rousseau. He takes up a manuscript which is lying on the spinet and handles it with all the reverence which the French use towards genius and wit. What is this manuscript? Why, what else could it be but Beaumarchais's *The Barber of Seville*, which — oh, cunning Sacha! — we remember to have been produced in the very year which the characters are now living. Perhaps we recollect also that this work was as much a disastrous failure at its first performance as Gluck's *Alceste*. Then, bethinking ourselves of Rousseau's 'Certainly this opera fell, but it fell from the skies!' we attain realization that M. Guitry, half by virtue of his own quality of *marivaudage*, and still more by the leave he has given us to think for ourselves, has reconstituted the world when it was most polite.

And perhaps it was time, at least for those who are impatient of the cackle which dates the action of a play, and long for the prancing and curveting of the 'osses. Every theatre-goer has experienced moments of emotion, for the justification of which he must search his intelligence in vain. Duse gave him many such, and I remember one of the sort in Bernhardt's scene of tender banter in the church in *La Tosca*, and one when Armand asked how long before the flower must fade, and Marguerite replied: 'Mais ce qu'il faut à toute fleur pour se faner, l'espace d'un soir ou d'un matin.' It is not exaggerating to say that on Monday evening people were observed to cry, and by that I mean shed tears, when Music's heavenly child appeared at the top of the stairs and came down them to kneel at Mme. d'Epinay's feet. Those who like to resolve a theatrical emotion into its component parts may find here something of the stirring of the sensibilities always occasioned by radiant happiness in conjunction with youth, something of their own unceasing wonder at that genius whose pure loveliness in achievement has never been surpassed, something of that sympathy which a certain quality of magnetism in certain players can evoke before a word has been uttered, something of recognition that the piece which M. Guitry has written to Mlle. Printemps should be so obviously an act of adoration. At the moment of her entrance this exquisite artist made conquest of the house, and subsequently held it in thrall until the final curtain.

As a piece of play-making the piece is of the slightest. Mozart blushes, stammers, and must have recourse to the spinet to express in song the gratitude he cannot utter in speech. The idiom which he uses is not his, but M. Reynaldo Hahn's, and later by a century and a half. And confidently we ask ourselves what are two worlds worth if the playgoer is not to make the best of both of them. The act-drop falls on the boy's resolve to set the story of Don Juan to music. In the second act we have the unspoken plea that no man can write a grand opera of the passions without having made the grand tour of the sentiments. Will Mme. d'Epinay be Mozart's guide? She will, and readily. Willing mentors are also found in the marriageable young lady, a serving maid, and a dancer. The second act closes on the reading of a letter from Mozart's homely fiancée. This little scene, which is the best in the play, also gives us the best of M. Hahn's music, and proves once more the French genius for idealizing the *facteur*. The postman is the most sensitive personage in French opera, so much so that in his presence even a Massenet can desist from nauseating and content himself with being merely cloying. Our visitors are great artists in this, that having provided a good thing they take care not to give too much of it. In both acts the curtain came down ten minutes too soon — in other words, it fell at exactly the right moment. The third act did not quite come up to the level of the others. In it M. Guitry dissented from the Tennysonian view as to the propriety of loving one woman only, cleaving to her, and worshipping her through years of operatic scores. At the end Mozart drew up his mistresses in revue order, and bade farewell to the assembled troop with a particular inflection which each of the fair might take to herself.

It would be impossible to praise too highly the perfection and finesse of Mlle. Printemps's acting as the young Mozart. She does not entirely divest herself of her own personal charm, but she sees and presents all the wayward pathos of immature genius, and her manner is reasonably boyish. She sings, if one may say so, quite as well as need be, and spares us the airs and graces of the prima donna. There is none of that operatic nonsense which breaks a mood, launches into some formidable aria, and then resumes existence where the singer left off. Mlle. Printemps uses song and speech indifferently, changing almost imperceptibly from one to the other. But the most significant thing about the performance is the way in which we are made to feel that we are in the presence of genius. It is credible that behind the pretty boy who walks Mme. d'Epinay's boudoir in adolescent trepidation, behind the inessential Mozart there should be the happy jeweller of pure sound. Credit should always be given to the artist for having implied that which we infer, and exquisite, therefore, must be the artist who to her remorseless little realists of drawing-room and gutter can add the spirit of the composer speaking through the mouth of his own Cherubino. M. Guitry plays the Baron with verve and brilliance whenever Mlle. Printemps's occasional absences from the scene call for such display. At other times he stands apart, rapt like one who has accomplished a marvel. And we in the audience perfectly understand the reason for that rapture.

June 27, 1926

MARIETTE

BY SACHA GUITRY. MUSIC BY OSCAR STRAUS

(His Majesty's)

'AN two men ride on a horse, one must ride behind', is as near the quotation as makes no matter. But what would Dogberry have said if he had been judge at a horse show? Would he have laid it down that of two equal exhibits one must be put behind the other? A phrase has been coined to meet the difficulty: the judge in such cases 'cannot separate them'. So, too, I cannot separate the lovely performances of this week's two teams of visitors.

But then, I don't particularly want to separate them, for both achieve the same kind of merit, or even kinds of merit. Both are conquests over dullness, keeping the spectator agog with excite-

28

ment, and alive with that happy expectation which is the mark of true enjoyment in the theatre. Both have banished boredom so that it is not even in the offing. Both are true theatre, in that both convey a quality of delight which could not be had elsewhere. It is unimaginable that either Guitry's comedy or Sil-Vara's *Caprice* should, as they say, read well. Both plays have sparkle, though neither is good in the stodgy English sense — in the way in which, in Mr. Bennett's novel, Mrs. Baines's furniture was 'good'. On leaving both theatres we are not the richer except intellectually and aesthetically; and this, as Shelley long ago pointed out, is the only profit with which works of art are concerned. The piece about Prince Louis Napoleon and Mariette takes it for granted that the spectator's literary taste leans more to Mr. Philip Guedalla than to the penny-a-liner's babblings about uncrowned queens. The play about the American lawyer and his mistress suggests that Balzac was right when he laid it down that Nature made the female but that Civilization created woman. Both plays, let it be said, move in the same world, though in different centuries. The one world is still exquisite, while the other contrives to remain polite. Both, finally, call for a sophisticated audience. The French piece, albeit no more than an operette, has something of the footnote to history, and though its texture is of the lightest you feel that it is strong enough to bear the weight of pathos and of irony. M. Guitry's writing, though it may be nothing to read, has on the stage all that non-seeming strength which is the proper quality of gossamer. You must bring your mind to it. The Viennese play makes other demands upon the spectator hearing it performed by American actors. It demands that we shall abjure the childishness of believing an English accent to be nearer the Viennese than an American. It has been objected, too, that these American players talk too often against one another, that is at the same time. Quite. If two people converse in a room, two will often be talking at once. But the producer of this play is not an ass, and has in no instance allowed his actors to rage together when it was necessary that we should bring our single mind to what any one actor was singly saying.

29

MUSICAL PLAYS

What a lovely thing it is to sit once more in a theatre which could
never be mistaken for a schoolroom or a lecture hall and watch
actors who could never be mistaken for barristers or tax-gatherers
out of their vocation! The theatre is in every Frenchman's blood:
it is a part of his consciousness whereas it is an imposition upon
ours. The French are a nation of actors in the best sense, by which
one means that their temperament is more fluid. 'I am, therefore
I act', is the French dictum. A moderately clever dramatist could
have given us that first act of *Mariette,* the stage of a provincial
opera-house seen from the back, with the singers hurling their
dithyrambs in grand, nonsensical gestures at the yawning,
shrouded cavern which is the auditorium. But only a great actor
could have sat in that box and by his half-bovine, half-imperial
impassivity and a few portentous claps of his heavily kid-gloved
hands conveyed so much of reality. All great comedians live with
the intensity of puppets, and it is the highest compliment to
M. Guitry to say that that motionless figure in the box was as much
alive as the pianist in the little wooden concert-party we saw
recently at the Scala. In the scene in the foyer the figure began
to take more particular shape, and, helped by a hat which
Gavarni might have drawn, an air of semi-majesty and faint self-
mockery, the habit of adjusting the hair at the side of the head,
and the whispered phrase: 'Il faut tâcher de ne pas être ridicule!' —
by these things we were made to feel that we were in the presence
of the third Napoleon. Is it possible that Mlle. Yvonne Printemps
a little overstresses the *gaucherie* of Mariette, just as she holds on a
little too long to her top notes, and a little over-does the intimacy
of her curtains at the end of each act? I strew ashes on my head
for writing this sentence: but it must remain. For the rest this
delicious artist's fun, high spirits, charm, delicacy, and suggestion
of pathos remain the miracles of deftness that they always were.
In my view the epilogue or last act is a mistake. It has only
one point — that at a hundred the memory is shaky. But to show
Mariette and Mlle. Printemps in the winter of life is to exchange
nostalgia and faint melancholy for the bleak horrors of a realism
which I personally find unbearable. Here the piece changes key,

30

and it is as though Maupassant's exquisite *Menuet* has been re-written by a Zola, or a Fragonard redrawn by a Goerg. It remains only to say that Oscar Straus's music is charming.

June 3, 1929

MERELY MOLLY

BY JOHN HASTINGS TURNER. MUSIC BY HERMAN
FINCK AND JOSEPH MEYER

(Adelphi)

IT was on my mind as I sat watching this jolly piece that it was all very like a book which everybody was reading some thirty years ago. For who was Henry, Duke of Wynninghame, marrying for her reputation's sake Molly Shine, the Stepney workgirl, and leaving her immediately after the ceremony, except one Prosper le Gai contracting for her soul's sake a virgin marriage with Isoult? It took Maurice Hewlett some three hundred pages to transform Isoult la Desirous into Isoult la Desirée, and Mr. Hastings Turner uses three long acts to work the same transformation in Molly's lover. The hypercritical may object that Dock Lane, Stepney, is not the Forest of Morgraunt. To which I would answer that London Fields and Hackney Downs — flowery meads both — are Stepney's next-door neighbours.

At home that night I turned up an old copy of *The Forest Lovers*. The page at which the book opened contained these words: 'She must woo, she saw; dare she trail this steel-armed lord of battles, this grim executant, this trumpet of God, as a led child by her girdle-ribbons?' Here, for all time, has surely been set down Mr. Godfrey Tearle, tragedian. Which brings me to the question as to whether a tragic actor should bemean himself by descending to a lower sphere. Now I suggest that we should free ourselves from cant. It is possible that the age of Macready would not have

31

tolerated any such degradation; but it is probable that it would have shown its intolerance in the best possible way — by flocking to see Macready when he was magnoperating. Or we may argue along Mrs. Micawber's lines. We may admit the conviction that Mr. Tearle's abilities peculiarly qualify him for the tragic business, and ask 'if the public refuses to avail itself of those abilities, or receives the offer of them with contumely, what is the use of dwelling on *that* idea?' Are we wrong in saying that a tragic actor must live? Now I am not going to pretend that I derive the same amount or quality of pleasure from Mr. Tearle's Duke of Wynning-hame that I do from his Othello; but I am not going to deny that his performance is very delightful in its way. The actor accomplishes the climb-down with all possible dignity. A neo-Georgian Mæcenas confided to me in his brittle porcelain whisper that he was 'revolted by the inherent improbability of the whole conception' — a criticism which might serve equally for Bottom or Malvolio. Mr. Tearle quite rightly made no precious bones about the matter of his part, but loyally accepted his author's premises and abode by them to the end.

The piece opened admirably, almost at once taking the plunge beloved of our slum novelists. Dock Lane, Stepney, was a setting of most excellent realism, including door-numbers of the correct shape and imitation silk stockings, with authentic cotton tops and trade-marks unobliterated by the laundry. It was a pity, one thinks, not to complete the observance of verisimilitude by an invitation to the Stepney roughs to discard their massive gold signet rings. Mr. Ben Field gave an excellent portrait of a rascally patriarch who peddles in his family honour. A newcomer to London, Mr. Max Wall, began what looked like being a perfectly observed study of the bantam-weight boxer's strut and dart and poise. Miss Pollie Emery let loose a virago redolent of gin. In fact, the whole of the first act went very well. The roughs unanimously scouted the idea of a toff sending a straight girl five pounds a week, unless, of course, he was barmy; the bevy of local beauties openly declared Molly to be a baggage; Molly herself, hosed symbolically in black worsted, fluted and carolled

32

her innocence. Presently there stepped out of a Max Beerbohm cartoon and into the riot Mr. Morton Selten, *homme du monde* in the old Edwardian way. Ultimately Mr. Tearle strolled in, ducal and *distrait*, protesting that if the manners of the time were such that a girl could not blamelessly accept a pittance with which to buy books, why then, by his escutcheon, he would marry her.

When in the second act the scene was transferred to Wynning-hame Towers the comedy rose in the social, but dropped in the aesthetic, scale. As the Lady Octavia, ready, like her Roman namesake, to plough the adventuress's visage up with her prepared nails, Miss Helen Haye rightly abated no jot of her accustomed superbity; and as a dragonsome figure in a wheel-chair Miss Marie Ault was properly terrifying. But the scene was too long and too talky-talky, and the device of the heartbroken goose pretending to be a vamp is worn a little too thin. Mr. Wall, alas! had fallen to the state of the acrobatic dancer, and in the meantime our Stepney friends had put on immaculacy and taken to the dreary round of guests at a house-party. The third act was better. There was a good first scene on board a yacht, and an excellent second scene in which the Isle of Wight was deployed at very nearly full extent. It was here that Molly 'knew that she must beguile her husband now for his soul's ease and her own'. And this she did very prettily, first in a pair of borrowed ducal trousers and then in a confection of molten gold. And so green Morgraunt, or rather the downs at Freshwater, made these lovers' bed.

Several things charmed me in this little piece. There was the excellent, perhaps too witty, dialogue; there was the absence of the industrious, unfunny comedian; there was the steady refusal of Messrs. Herman Finck and Joseph Meyer to pander to the epileptic or negroid strain. I have known catchier music, but at least we were spared the abomination of derivative jazz. The real thing is first-rate: that is to say, it is at least the natural expression of the negro mind. Nobody with any sense wants to see a coal-black Lohengrin or a melon-sucking Parsifal. But that is not to say that one wants to see white people shuffling about as if they kept their brains in their shin-bones. And so I welcome the

33

absence of jazz in this purely English musical comedy just as strongly as I acclaim it elsewhere.

I have left Miss Evelyn Laye for the last because that is the place of honour. I want to say how heartening it is to see an actress abandon the entire caboodle of artificiality and mannerism for the altogether more sensible business of acting. That Miss Laye must have been working very hard is shown by the improvement in her singing. But there are plenty of signs that she is also becoming a good actress — witness the entirely natural way in which she rounded on sceptical Lady Octavia and demanded to know whether she took her and the Duke for 'a couple of ruddy liars'. The delivery of this was a model of aplomb and perfect timing. Really it looks very much as though Miss Edna Best were going to have a companion in the arduous task of using popularity as a stepping-stone to something better. This piece, in favour of which I give my wholehearted vote, had something of a mixed reception. I do not expect my views to be shared by everybody. Musical comedy 'fans' will doubtless rejoice that I have seen the light at last. Others will probably shake their heads.

September 26, 1926

LIDO LADY

BY RONALD JEANS. MUSIC BY RICHARD RODGERS

(Gaiety)

HAPPY is the country which has no history, and happier still is that musical comedy about which one can find nothing to say. Thrice is he armed who hath his quarrel just, and three times is that musical piece insured against disaster which has no plot to speak of, no lyrics that count, and no music unduly to strain the musical sense. *Lido Lady* is an admirable title because it is about the Lido and a lady. Whether it is the lady who goes to the Lido or the Lido which comes to the lady does not really matter. One would choose the second alternative for the simple reason that this is a Venice innocent of gondolas, gondoliers, doges, dukes grand or small, merchants successful or otherwise. As soon as the curtain goes up we know that the back-cloth is so much elegant pretence, and when the familiar artists appear we know that we are where the poet tells us he fain wad be. Which is Hame, Hame, Hame.

Surely if John of Gaunt could have foreseen Miss Phyllis Dare he would have included her in his tumultuous imagery as to the perfections of this sceptred isle. Every musical comedy in which she appears becomes at once another Eden, demi-paradise. She is the precious stone set in this medium's silver sea, and thus serving our native genius against the envy of what the poet so ungrammatically calls 'less happier lands'. In plain English, Miss Dare is jolly good. But I think she has some right of quarrel with a lyrist who should commit her to such English as:

> Here in my arms it's adorabull;
> It's deplorabull that you were never there!

and then go on to ask why it is not permissibull to demand a share in lips so kissabull. The melodic accent falling on the last syllable of these dreadful words, the singer has to take the choice of pronouncing them properly and ineffectively or effectively and ridiculously.

There are those for whom Mr. Hulbert's fascination lies in his dancing, and one would agree that if the little hills are privileged to skip there is no reason why this six foot of long, lean athlete should not bemean himself to the business of heel and toe. For myself I always regard the time which Mr. Hulbert spends in dancing as so many golden moments stolen from his distinguished gift of comicality. Can any man so put on the rapture of an invoice clerk? Or the despondency of a plumber who, calling to mend a leak, finds that he can stop it on the same day? Can any light comedian so simulate the Cyrano who is at the heart of every

35

humble lover, take rebuffs with so high a spirit, or so gallantly return unto the breach? Mr. Hulbert is optimist *par excellence*, or you might put it that he is all silver lining and no cloud. In the present play it is postulated that before he wins the hand of his lady-love he must knock out the world's welter-weight boxing champion. Here the actor's face radiates as that which should say: 'Weltering's my game, whether in gore or glory.' He will go into training at once and do such things — he knows not what — but they shall be the terrors of the earth. Complementary to Mr. Hulbert is Miss Cicely Courtneidge in the captivating situation of a film-star who would give her soul for publicity and can't get any.

December 12, 1926

THE BLUE TRAIN

BY REGINALD ARKELL AND DION TITHERADGE
MUSIC BY ROBERT STOLZ

(Prince of Wales)

THE 'Supper Song', which concludes the second act of this musical comedy, is written round the lyric:

> I'll be back inside a minute
> With a taxi — you'll be in it,
> And we'll seek some cosy place in which to dine.

Be It Cosiness might, with apologies to Mr. Max Beerbohm, be the title of this very charming, very intimate little piece of which the recipe is the familiar one of an extremely improbable story wedded to extremely probable music. Eileen Mayne, enamoured of Lord Antony Stowe, threw over her lover in a tiff, and after some three years repented. Obviously, if she had taken the straight way of telling his lordship so, or if, alternatively, that austere young man had not become more difficult of trapping

36

than a Trappist, there would have been no musical comedy. So Eileen, like Sentimental Tommy, had to find a way, and the way she found was this: She spun a yarn to the effect that she was in love with a young man called Freddy, but that as she had inveigled an uncle (Australian and non-existent) into lending her thousands of pounds on the strength of her being Lady Antony (which she wasn't), she couldn't marry Freddy (which she didn't want to) unless Lord Antony would oblige by making her his wife, for a month and in name only, as the preliminary to divorce proceedings. These convolutions, than which nothing more fantastic is to be found even in the comedies of Shakespeare, attained their maximum complication on the upper slopes of the Wetterhorn, and were straightened out, after a journey in the Blue Train, in an expensive restaurant on the Côte d'Azur. For people who have dined cosily this is indeed the cosiest of entertainments. Authors, composer, contributors of lyrics and additional numbers — all have combined to make us feel snug. Cosy, so to speak, *fan tutti*.

I will not conjecture what the show would be like without Miss Lily Elsie, who, having dwelt too long among untrodden ways and hidden from the eye, returns fair as a star when only one is shining in the sky. This, of course, is pure parodic licence. This charming artist would still possess her particular radiance if the theatrical firmament were raining musical-comedy stars, which it isn't. Her beauty is as serene as ever, her voice as touching, and her motions as graceful. She dances with exquisite melancholy, and we reflect that Venus, unyoking at Paphos her silver doves, must have trod some such measure. Mr. Arthur Margetson, as a younger son turned misogynist, bore himself befittingly and moved to the comedy's final catastrophe as a gentleman should. There was some admirable acrobatic dancing by Mr. Sid Tracey and Miss Bessie Hay. Mr. Bobbie Howes and Miss Cicely Debenham gambolled and frisked, and at the end Covent Garden showered its blooms as it had rained geraniums, cinerarias, odontoglossums, parallelopipeds, glubjullahs, damphobias, and the entire flora of Miss Draper's inventive genius.

May 22, 1927

MUSICAL PLAYS

OH, KAY!

BY GUY BOLTON AND P. G. WODEHOUSE
MUSIC BY GEORGE GERSHWIN

(His Majesty's)

In so far as I can make anything of the imbroglio of this piece it concerns a cretinous earl so harassed by the super-tax that he is reduced to rum-running in his last remaining possession, his yacht. With him is his sister, who is apparently called Kay. Kay, clothed in a mackintosh, makes a burglarious midnight entry into the house of one Jimmy Winter, whom she has previously saved from drowning. Jimmy, who is arranging to marry a second wife before completely divorcing the first, now falls in love with Kay. It also happens that another rum-runner, one 'Shorty' McGee, has also chosen Winter's house in which to store without permission his stock of illicit liquor. The establishment possesses forty unexplained housemaids and a baker's dozen of inexplicable footmen, who from time to time interrupt such action as there is. This is the entire story, and I can frankly say that I have known nothing in the musical-comedy line of greater melancholy.

The book is by Messrs. Guy Bolton and P. G. Wodehouse. Of Mr. Bolton I am not privileged to know anything. But *Who's Who in the Theatre* informs me that he is the author of thirty-nine plays, of which twenty-eight have been written in collaboration with eleven collaborators, Mr. Wodehouse functioning on eight occasions. Of Mr. Wodehouse little need be said except that temperate admirers of his work are non-existent. Like O. Henry, this writer apparently divides the world into two classes — those who cannot read his books and those who can read no others.

Mr. Wodehouse, I learn from *Who's Who*, is also part-author of twenty plays. Surely there are reasonable grounds for supposing that so experienced a writer would salt with his wit so dull and sad a plot as that outlined above? Not a bit of it. Listening with maximum intentness and a desperate anxiety to be amused, I

38

could not find in the entire work one single spark of wit or even humour with which to credit either of the authors. 'What is a *Poltergeist?* A ghost that palters', and 'He's a topping bishop. What's that? A bishop who plays. golf' — these represent fairly the best of the writing. But 'What sort of flowers does your fiancée fancy?' and 'I shall act accordion, I mean according', represent, I think also fairly, the general level of this libretto. I am not to be persuaded that Mr. Wodehouse, whose stories notoriously banish melancholy from our Universities, cannot do better than this.

Musical-comedy 'fans' tell me that to enjoy this particular form of art one should leave at home not only one's play-going intelligence, but one's revue brains. Now, in revue it is unlikely that one will be perpetually bored; the themes are continually changing, and the actors, not chained to a particular personality, are continually given the chance to show that they can act. Mr. John Kirby, for example, is a magnificent character actor, as those know who remember his study of a taxi-driver; and there is no doubt that he could be amusing in a score, of different ways. In the present piece he must as a butler continue to resemble the Fat Boy as Gainsborough might have painted him. It says a great deal for Mr. Kirby's comic gifts that he should be able to keep us entertained as consistently as he does. But do not musical comedy 'fans' see that confining Mr. Kirby to one character is like engaging a great pianist to play the same piece twelve times over?

Miss Gertrude Lawrence is, within definite limits, a very considerable artist. She will not, I think, claim to be a dancer, and she has hardly any singing voice. In fact, of her last number I could not, sitting in the sixth row of the stalls, make out one single word. But Miss Lawrence, considered as actress and *diseuse*, shows astonishing command of character and power of mimicry. In quick succession, without any alteration of pose, and by the mere expression of her face and inflection of her voice, she will present to you a scullery-maid, amorous or dejected, or a heroine from one of Mr. Lonsdale's comedies, *insouciante*, challenging and deliciously over-mannered. Or she will take up a doll and by

39

holding it to her breast and crooning to it, take you straight into the infantile heart of woman, and in the next moment, holding the wretched thing by the ankle, plunge you into a world of mockery from which sentiment and sentimentality have been banished.

Miss Lawrence gives a brilliant edge to everything that she does; her line is firm and purposeful, and we know exactly what it means. Then why chain her down to portray that nothingness which every heroine of musical comedy must be? It has been said that she clowns too much. In my view she does not clown nearly enough, for it is when she is being most wilfully absurd that one admires her most. Clowning, of course, is the wrong word. Miss Lawrence is a mistress of that sharp realization of the ridiculous in character which is burlesque. Is it not, then, monstrous to crib, cabin, and confine her to the portrayal of nothing at all? When she and Mr. Kirby stick to their book they achieve little; when they break away from it they are delicious, and the oftener and the further they break away the more delicious. Both artists succeed in musical comedy in proportion as they throw over that medium.

When neither of these shining ones was on the stage a darkness fell which was almost palpable. Mr. Harold French, who would not pretend either to sing or dance, went about the lawful occasions of a leading man not more than pleasantly, the Misses Dodge went through steps, gyrations, and contortions with skill, and Mr. Claude Hulbert made familiar exploration of the inane. Then there was Mr. Gershwin's music, which was well orchestrated. One saw, and occasionally heard, a harp. But as far as I can judge, Mr. Gershwin's score was largely made up of two tunes, one of which was plugged at least fourteen times. Shade of Sullivan! What should we have thought in the 'eighties of a composer or an audience if it had been judged necessary to repeat 'Take a Pair of Sparkling Eyes' or 'The Flowers That Bloom in the Spring' fourteen times? Sullivan did plug one tune, 'I Have a Song to Sing-O', but the value of that *reprise* lay in the discreet use which was made of it. Mr. Gershwin's over-insistence first amuses and then wearies; one can have too much of a commonplace monotony.

September 21, 1927

LADY MARY

BY FREDERICK LONSDALE AND JOHN HASTINGS TURNER
MUSIC BY ALBERT SIRMAY AND PHILIP CHARIG

(Daly's)

I DO not know the maximum amount of rightness contained in a trivet, but the new show at Daly's demands for comparison a trivet of maximum endowment. Nor do I know how right rain may be, but *Lady Mary* is as right as the wettest day in any of Meredith's novels. One imagines this piece striding out for a twelve-months' run, proof against the elements, straight rains, tiger skies, and all the rest of it. The fiddle is also a symbol of fitness, and in Messrs. Frederick Lonsdale and John Hastings Turner, who have done the book, Captain Harry Graham, who has done the lyrics, and Mr. Albert Sirmay, who has done the music, *Lady Mary* may be said to have four good strings to her bow, one of which, the musical, was, perhaps, only goodish. Ninepence, if I mistake not, has some connotation of felicity. But these extravagances grow tedious. Summing up this musical comedy in the jargon beloved of musical-comedy fans, *Lady Mary* is topping.

In a silence so taut that you might imagine the audience held in thrall to one who had loved not wisely but too well, the first-act curtain fell upon a young gentleman who was the rightful heir to untold wealth, but who refused to disclose his identity because if he did, Lady Mary, who was in possession, would have had to disburse and become a nursery governess or something. The young gentleman loved well enough, but apparently not too wisely, since Lady Mary was engaged to a detrimental who wanted her for her money. There was not a dry eye in the audience as Daly's voluptuous folds descended upon the Australian Bush in which these credible things were taking place. Could, indeed, anything have been more topping?

Then for an hour came intermission, while bevies of pretty

41

ladies and pretty gentlemen assembling in the drawing-room of
Lady Mary's country house in England went through those
dancing rites which are our dusky brothers' contribution to pale
culture. To invert Strephon, one might say that all these delightful people were mortal down to the waist, but that their legs were
fairy. They certainly danced very well. From time to time Mr.
George Grossmith interrupted the dancers to deliver, and deliver
very comically, such jocosities as occurred to him or had previously
occurred to his authors. Or Mr. Herbert Mundin would descant
with riotous effect upon the rigours of English evening dress. Or
Mr. Richard Dolman, incredibly moustached, would let loose a
song with the refrain:

> Say, guys,
> I'm puttin' you wise,
> You can't have My Sugar for tea —

Or Miss Dorothy Field would sing something equally unex-
ceptionable. Or Miss Helen Gilliland, shy as a squirrel and wayward as the swallow, would trill ditties expressive of shyness and
waywardness. Wet once more was every eye as she and her money-
seeking fiancé fluted to one another that:

> When the one that you care for
> Takes care of you,
> You'll be happy and therefore
> He'll be happy too —

Or *vice versa*. This, again, was topping. A little later somebody
else, hymning the fragrant innocence of Lady Mary, sang at her
and at point-blank range:

> Your heart you surrender,
> You don't ask why —

Bless Lady Mary and her naïve creators who had agreed to
ignore Ann Whitefield and the Life Force! However, it was getting
late, and round about eleven o'clock it is proper that the heart of

any musical-comedy heroine should be had for the asking. So the abnegatory fellow got sweetheart and inheritance in one fell swoop, and the fortune-hunter paired off with somebody else, who, for some reason or other, had just had fifty thousand pounds poured into her lap. Which is a topping thing to have happen to one. The hero of the piece was, if I remember rightly, an earl; and Mr. Paul Cavanagh delighted us all by playing the strong, silent, renunciatory nobleman exactly as he plays strong, silent, renunciatory chauffeurs. The piece should run a year. It is topping. The actors are topping. But the chorus is the toppingest.

February 23, 1928

LUMBER LOVE

BY LESLIE STILES. MUSIC BY BERTE AND EMMETT ADAMS

(Lyceum)

THE ways of theatre-managers are beyond all calculating. *Lumber Love* has been touring the provinces for weeks, so that those responsible for it must have known the length to which it has been running. Provincial audiences like the theatre-curtain to go up at half-past seven and to remain up until as near eleven o'clock as makes no matter. That is three hours and a half. At the Lyceum they rang up at a quarter-past eight, and must have known that the show could not be over until a quarter to twelve. This was bad policy, and if persisted in may prove bad business. Everybody must have known about that exceedingly weak third act made up of tedious explanations which explained nothing and which nobody wanted. The proper thing was to have brought the curtain down on the very remarkable Tiller Girls and cut the imbroglio short wherever it happened to be. Instead of which, at

43

a quarter-past eleven of the clock, they brought on a table and some lawyers and started a judicial inquiry.

To suggest that *Lumber Love* would please a sophisticated audience would be to suggest nonsense. The show is nowhere and in nothing, except the Tiller Girls and one male chorus, slick and spry, and it is never marvellously on its toes like the best American essays in this kind. I watched the first act from the back of the Circle, and have pleasure in testifying to the show's one supreme merit — its audibility. But the stage-picture, considered from that altitude, was a sorry business. The word 'tawdry' comports a certain soiled magnificence; the first stage-set had not even that. But the scenery throughout was like the scenery in provincial pantomimes before the days of Hawes Craven. A silly little drain-pipe announced itself as a rivulet, and frankly I have never seen representational scenery so utterly beggared of imagination. The plot was of a fatuity which one would call incredible but for the fact that one is asked to believe in it about five times in every musical-comedy season. A young woman buys a lumber forest for two hundred and fifty thousand dollars, and, because of a hitch in the deal, must marry the only man in the Canadian Rockies she cannot abide. A previous lyric had run:

> Some day perhaps you'll
> Change your mind,
> And see my point
> Of view.

And now we had a long dramatic recitative which went something as follows: 'What's this I hear? The cheque with which you were to have paid for two hundred and fifty thousand acres of lumber, at a dollar an acre or thereabouts, has not materialized? Then my previous option holds good. What have you to say to that?'

What I have to say is that the composers of *Jephtha*, *Don Giovanni*, and *St. Paul*, putting their heads together, could not have coped with these words, nor could Rubini, Garcia, and Lablache, singing as one man, have delivered them satisfactorily. The piece

44

abounded in gems of unconscious humour, as when the hero turned to a number of guests at a Montreal evening-party and bade them:

Prate not to me
Of the open sea —

There was another delicious moment when the heroine entered veiled in elephant-breath tulle, and the sun was so shocked that it at once set behind the rockies to harps and clarinets. On one other occasion was the spirit unexpectedly refreshed, and that was when Mr. Basil Howes, blanketing his loins and elfing his hair in knots — as a dramatist who was before Mr. Stiles put it — gave a very reasonable imitation of Poor Tom, and said wistfully, 'I'm just a story that didn't come true!' And since his interlocutor didn't seize on to this, the actor had to say, 'I'm just bug-house, you can tell the world!' No, this was certainly not an entertainment for the sophisticated.

Lumber Love is a musical-comedy counterpart to those stirring melodramas in which young women who had been 'put upon' by fate are penultimately withdrawn from beneath steam-rollers. A real flesh-and-blood film-star descends from a real horse, and skipping over the real drain-pipe with the real water delivers a song of real sentiment in real riding-breeches. Miss Joan Lockton has a real voice and plenty of it, and as her songs are provided with lashings of top-notes all is well. It is a pity that she should apostrophize her hands so steadily while singing, and she should certainly avoid accompanying her repeated encores with gestures which have obviously been got by heart. Mr. Jamieson Dodds shows a manly presence and a manly voice. The success of this piece — and nothing that one may have objected is to prevent it from being deemed an immense success of its kind and in its place — is due to two things. These are the music and Mr. Fred Kitchen. The tunes in *Lumber Love* are excellent, and have been excellent ever since ballad concerts and musical comedies were. Every note foretells the next, and it is a sure sign of felicity in an audience when it can read a composer's mind at least a bar ahead.

It is only the finical and the precious who will complain of the complete absence of musical interest, and even the musical as distinct from the music-loving must admit that 'Rolling the Log' provides a rousing male chorus, and that 'The Mountains of My Home' is pleasantly sentimental.

For the rest, the piece is good only when it stops being a piece and allows Mr. Fred Kitchen to come on and be funny. There is this much to be said for the provinces, that they will not be put off with the gadgets and appurtenances of the professional funny fellow, but insist upon the body of fun itself. Lancashire, for example, has no use for the comedian who is unfunny, and the clown who can make Lancashire laugh to-day can be sure of making London laugh for any number of to-morrows. But Mr. Kitchen, beloved of Lancashire and the North, though he content himself in this piece with mere clowning, is ever so much more than a buffoon. He is an actor, an actor possessed, moreover, of an extraordinary gift of pathos; and it should be written over every comedian's door that only the player who at a pinch can make an audience cry can make an audience laugh.

March 15, 1928

SHOW BOAT

BY OSCAR HAMMERSTEIN 2ND. MUSIC BY JEROME KERN

(Drury Lane)

'SHOW BOAT' turned out to be a stupendous thing not unlike the Wembley Exhibition, and one had the same sort of feeling of being exhaustively entertained without ever quite getting to the heart of the entertainment. Miss Ferber's novel may or may not be a masterpiece — I have not read it — but at least it is something, and one had the conviction that that something was being missed.

May I hazard the conjecture that Miss Ferber does for the senti-mental side of American life what Mr. Dreiser achieves for its tragic side, that she says a great deal and says it charmingly? Mr. Oscar Hammerstein 2nd contrives, in the version presented at Drury Lane, to say nothing whatever, and I doubt whether a whole dynasty of Hammersteins could have said less.

As a piece of story-telling *Show Boat* is as inept and clumsy as anything I have ever seen on any stage. It is not that the story is jettisoned — nobody minds that. One need not be a stickler for pure story, and if an author has something more engaging to say, let him get on with it, and good luck to him! But it was obvious that the whole pith and essence of *Show Boat* was the story, and it was distressing to see the story frittered away. You were left to guess at the main structure of the tale while attention was focused upon the unimportant and inessential. The result was rather like living in a house which is complete with sun-blinds, flower-boxes, and ornamental door-knocker, but lacks stairs and a roof.

Miss Ferber's story, I have said, is something: How do I, not having read it, know this? Quite simply. Sailors sense land even when they cannot see it, and one can always sense a good story, howsoever it be mishandled. Though Mr. Oscar Hammerstein 2nd tried his very, very hardest he could not quite prevent one from realizing that Miss Ferber must have delicious things to say about the plantation folk in the eighteen-eighties. One deduced many pages of sunlit melancholy and possibly a recapture of that spirit of nostalgia enshrined in George W. Cable's volume of lovely stories called *Old Creole Days*. Old Mississippi days surely were behind Mr. Paul Robeson's singing of 'Old Man River'; and behind those sad phalanxes of brown humanity. Behind, too, the melodramatic incident in which a husband, married to a woman in whose veins ran negro blood, stabs his wife's hand and drinks at the wound so that he may make declaration that negro blood is in him also. This preposterous incident aroused no unseemly smiles in an audience obviously familiar with Miss Ferber's book, which of a surety must have something tender and pathetic and sensible to say on racial questions.

As the woman of colour Miss Marie Burke acted with a great deal of plaintive beauty; in fact, she and Mr. Paul Robeson towered above everybody else on the stage in their suggestions of character and atmosphere. It is typical of this piece that Mr. Robeson, magnificent actor, exquisite singer, and a man cut out in such pattern as Michael Angelo might have designed, should be given nothing whatever to do except dodder about with a duster. It is typical of this piece, which is to enrol a woman's life from 1887 to 1927, that it should take two hours to arrive at her marriage in 1893 — the point, one presumes, at which the real story begins. I deduce that Miss Ferber's Gaylord Ravenal was a character of distinction. In this musical version he is like some caricature which a witty foreigner might make of the English musical-comedy fan's beau-ideal — a scented mannikin *genre coiffeur*, all smirks, charm, and pomatum. It is convenient to explain here that the part of Magnolia is entrusted to Miss Edith Day.

During the interval I found an American lady in tears. Drying her eyes, she explained to me that as an Englishman I could not be expected to appreciate the exquisite pathos of the scene upon which the curtain had just fallen. The poor blacks, it appears, would not be allowed to look on at Magnolia's wedding, Magnolia being — as the familiar song used to put it — whiter than the white-wash on the wall. It was evident, then, that for one spectator the piece was succeeding entirely. So one went back into the theatre, and, after marvelling at a view of Chicago World's Fair, 1893, and being present at a rehearsal 'about five p.m. in 1904', learned that Magnolia, now become an actress, had been deserted by her husband, who was in the habit of going in a white wig to St. Agatha's Convent to see his little daughter during the tolling of the vesper bell.

Hereabouts Magnolia got her chance at the Trocadero Music Hall. Being put to the cabaret touch, her voice failed her, and there would have been a fiasco if among the suppers she had not espied her father, at sight of whom she burst into full-throated ease. Thirteen years then passed in which apparently nothing happened; and, lastly, we assembled again on the deck of the Show Boat. Magnolia, whose daughter had left St. Agatha's Convent to become a musical-comedy star, consented to emerge from obscurity to sing on the wireless, and, as it was eleven o'clock, she made it up with her husband of the contrite manner and the frosty pow.

Time, one noted, dealt in unequal fashion with people in this play. Mr. Cedric Hardwicke, for example, who played the owner of this American Show Boat in his well-known Devonshire manner, was so old to start with that forty years couldn't make him any older. His wife, however, changed from ripe middle age to palsied eld. And we have seen that Gaylord Ravenal became so old that he nearly became human. Alone Miss Edith Day held out against the wrackful siege of battering days. Her locks were like the raven when we were first acquent, and remained so to the end — a very creditable achievement for a character who, from the play's chronology, must have been at least sixty.

Yet my impression remains that this inane play had been carved out of something which in itself was not inane. Obviously, the aim of the piece was to do on an elephantine scale for the American 'eighties what Mr. Cochran at the London Pavilion does so deliciously for the Viennese 'sixties. Alas, the touch of wizardry was absent. You cannot get atmosphere merely by dressing up a coffee-coloured horde and shoving it about the stage like a fledgling officer drilling his first platoon, nor yet by spending a small fortune upon paint and canvas and electric light. Criticism should be constructive, so let me suggest that half an hour should be cut out of the show and filled in by Mr. Robeson with his 'Steal Away', 'Water Boy', and other negro spirituals. It must be said in fairness that Miss Day, Mr. Hardwicke, and, indeed, all the cast worked extremely hard. But they were so smothered in straw that they couldn't make any bricks.

May 3, 1928

THE NEW MOON

BY OSCAR HAMMERSTEIN 2ND, FRANK MANDEL
AND LAURENCE SCHWAB. MUSIC BY SIGMUND
ROMBERG

(Drury Lane)

ROUND about a quarter of a century ago Mr. Max Beerbohm coined the verb 'to bouch', ascribing derivation to an actor of the period. Let me, like Max, modestly rise, clear my throat, and propose the verb 'to balfe', acknowledging that it harks back to the Irish composer and fourth member of the well-known group of statues in the foyer of Drury Lane. The other three figures, as everybody knows, are those of Shakespeare, Garrick and Kean. To balfe, then, means to confound values generally, in the theatrical sense to elevate something to a position which it is not entitled to hold. Filling what was once our national theatre with a glorified musical comedy is a first-class example of balfing. To pay that respect to a semi-serious, semi-comic, and demi-semi-musical entertainment which the musical foreigner pays to an opera by Strauss or a production by Reinhardt, to raise the show to the rank of a social event, to dress and dine elaborately for it, to discuss it, and, in fine, do anything but dismiss it as a high-spirited lark, is also balfing. The word, you see, is needed so badly, for it sums up so perfectly the national attitude towards the theatre. If we really needed a National Theatre for the housing and presentation of the world's greatest dramatic literature Drury Lane is, as it always has been, the very ticket. But no sane person will contend that we want a National Theatre in the way in which the Germans and the French not only want but insist upon having one, and we want and insist upon having a stadium for our English Cup Final. The matter has been tried with the result that we know. We are proud of Shakespeare, Marlowe, Jonson, Webster, Congreve, Sheridan, Goldsmith, and the rest, but our pride does not go the length of practice. We will not go to see our great works played. What we will go to see played, and go in our hundreds of thousands, is drama of the *Rose Marie, Desert Song, Show Boat, New Moon* order, the kind of thing which the French put on at the Châtelet readily enough but which will not see production at the Français until all moons, new and old, are made of green cheese. Balfing, I submit, is more than an English national habit: it is an English character-istic. I look forward, then, to the time when in every dictionary there shall be, between the explanations of 'Balefulness' and 'Balisaur', 'Balfe, *v.i.* To talk of anything with respect beyond its category. (*Deriv.:* Balfe, a statue of unhappy contiguity.) Balfer, *s.* One who balfes.'

Is this attitude 'superior'? If it is I can't help it. Try as I will, I cannot see that these Druriological orgies have anything more to do with the drama than the circus has. Now criticism of the circus can obviously have only one end, which is to propound and answer the question: Is it a good circus? Following this method, one can only ask whether *The New Moon* is as good Druriology as *The Silver Sickle* or *The Gibbous Girl*, and other precedent lunar phenomena. Perhaps before estimating how good a thing is, one should decide in one's mind how good such a thing may be. What are the essential elements of Druriology? An intelligent plot? On the whole, one thinks not. Have we not seen a Captain in the regular army filling in the time between parades by leading the Arab tribes against which his regiment is at war? An audience which could stomach and even approve that would stomach and approve anything. There can be no pre-emptive absurdity, then, in a manacled French count singing love-songs on the deck of a man-of-war to the blessed stars above and what Coleridge called the silly buckets below. Nor can there be absurdity in the admir-ing group which listens to him, consisting of the heroine in un-spotted muslin, the head of the French detective service, and the vessel's captain who has been warned that an attack by pirates is imminent. After all June is June, the night and the Gulf of Mexico are still, and if pirates come they come. From the cap-tain's point of view, the readiness is all. That captain's confidence in his crew and their readiness was justified. Immediately upon the conclusion of Mr. Howett Worster's love ditty and Miss Evelyn Laye's suitable reply there glided past the backcloth a pirate bowsprit to which, armed to the teeth, clung desperadoes in an attitude which one confidently took to be that of a boarding-party. In a trice, jiffy, or other atomy of time, twenty heads emerged from hatchways and twenty cutlasses met twenty grappling irons, or whatever it is that boarding-parties use. One found no absurdity in Mr. Worster's discovery that the pirate-captain was his boyhood's playmate, or in the way in which the two crews immediately fell to fraternizing in a hornpipe of the period, wherein they were presently joined by a number of female pirates as prettily garbed as attendants at a picture palace. After which everybody decided to lead a communal existence on an island in the Caribbean Sea, a decision which prompted Miss Laye to some stateswomanly utterances on Man's need of submission to government. But it was eleven o'clock, and the digression could not be pursued. Instead, we were landed on an island beach and admired the handsome way in which the lady-sailors transformed themselves into Mexican beauties and enlivened the local mango-swamp with white organdie and dancing pumps. At about eleven-twenty the French Revolution, with which I ought to say that the story is intimately connected, hove in sight, and the necessity for further vigil was at an end.

If then plot is not the thing, what is? The music? Mr. Sigmund Romberg's score is as hearteningly reminiscent as the fans of Druriology can reasonably demand. It was a pretty tune in *No No Nanette* of which 'One Kiss' is a version in another rhythm. If another tristful ditty is only Tschaikowsky's Barcarolle all over again, it can be argued that the Russian is an excellent model. Did he not in an early theme in the Pathetic Symphony do for the opening phrase of Beethoven's Sonata Pathétique what Mr. Romberg did for the *No No Nanette* tune? There should be give and take in these matters, and the time-dimension being what it is, it must be the ancients who give and the moderns who take. The odd thing about it all appears to be that these echoes are doubtless

unconscious; doubtless Mr. Romberg, who conducted with great
zest, did his filchings in the blissful illusion of complete originality.
But if, finally, spectacle be the essence of the business then let
me say that *The New Moon* does very well. The mounting is
superb, and if the dresses have not very much to do with one
another they are costly enough to afford to be stand-offish. The
playing? Perhaps that is the rub in this particular production.
Mr. Worster acts agreeably and has a fine presence, but I doubt
whether he would claim to be a singer. To supply the deficiency
and do the necessary roof-lifting a *pukka* operatic tenor is brought
in; and as Mr. Ben Williams is content to play no acting part
worth mentioning, the pair put up an admirable Tweedledee-and-
Dummish performance. Mr. Edmund Willard brings to the
French sleuth a well-proven assortment of villainies, smiling
grimly whenever anyone addresses him as 'Mossoo'; and Mr.
Gene Gerrard is to be complimented on making quite a handful
of bricks out of no visible straw. In the matter of the ladies Miss
Dolores Farris performs with incredible virtuosity a dance as
exacting as it is ungainly; Miss Vera Pearce, that clever actress,
is as usual steadily wasted; Miss Laye, fragrant as ever, takes the
quarter-deck with the grace of an Austin Dobson marquise. It
should not need saying that there is good balfing as well as bad.
I take this to be, on the whole, good, though how many times
this moon will wax and wane before she is worn out it is not for
me to predict with any accuracy. Let me make a shot and say
a year, or whatever time is necessary to engender another and
similar entertainment.

April 4, 1929

FOLLOW THROUGH

BY LAURENCE SCHWAB AND B. G. DE SYLVA
MUSIC BY ALFRED GOODMAN

(Dominion)

For a long time it looked as though the authors and composers of *Follow Through* had completely fluffed their shot. One does not expect sense in a musical comedy, still less wit. What one does expect is lively and agreeable nonsense, jesting by the yard, and buffoonery by the bucketful; and unfortunately this piece seemed destitute of all these things. Nor, though one listened with. all one's ears, was there any approach to that catching, haunting, musical nonsense which it is the genius of these affairs to supply. The most rousing tune was almost brazenly reminiscent. But for three items the entertainment must indeed have been reckoned a sorry failure. Three swallows, however, begin to look like summer; and the piece ended in looking like a success.

The first good thing was the manifest virtuosity of the new comédienne, Miss Ada May. You are to imagine a bit of Dresden china, the size of nothing at all, attired in a pair of those overalls which Kate Greenaway ordained for her little boys and which boiler-scrapers and Jackie Coogan affect to-day. Only you must imagine the overalls built out of such stuff as dreams are made on, and of a colour which ought to be known as tiger's maw. It does not matter that you hear only with difficulty what this little American actress says or sings, and that when you do hear the difficulty is transferred to the understanding. You do not expect dissertations from a flung moonbeam, and fling is the only word to describe those dancing removals from the place in which you thought you last saw her. She is as much all over the stage as a kitten is over the hearth-rug or a lamb over the Botticellian field; she declines to be pinned to any particular board, and hardly to the gross earth. In the later reaches of the piece she puts off man's

54

attire, and if we feel disappointment it is only of the kind which every Rosalind must occasion.

Next — if there can be question of next where this glorious fun-maker is concerned — comes Mr. Leslie Henson. Like Munden, Mr. Henson is a great maker of faces: 'When you think he has exhausted his battery of looks, in unaccountable warfare with your gravity, suddenly he sprouts out an entirely new set of features, like Hydra.' Only they are not human features. He will, in moments of ecstasy, look at you out of eyes bulging like those of a moth which has eaten too much tapestry. Or, in the matter of indignant denial, shoot his head with the scowl of a tortoise accused of being born yesterday. Or, thrown by the passions, expire like Mrs. Leo Hunter's frog. Or, when the mood is abstract, crumple up his visage like a monkey contemplating the folly and ugliness of his keeper. And then there is Mr. Henson in riot, when every part of him speaks, and his very waistcoat strap is eloquent. To watch him disguised as a plumber and, in partnership with .Mr. Mark Lester, couched upon the lockers in the ladies' dressing-room at a highly problematical golf club — to view this is to know all that the Spirit of Buffoonery has invented, or that we could desire her to invent.

The third good thing is the chorus, which is lively and excellent. For the rest, one may perhaps be forgiven for holding that the new house is a little too big for Miss Ivy Tresmand, and excused for waiting to praise Miss Elsie Randolph until she is better cast, and Mr. Harry Pélissier until he has worked off a little more of his apprenticeship.

October 3, 1929

MUSICAL PLAYS

THREE SISTERS

BY OSCAR HAMMERSTEIN 2ND. MUSIC BY JEROME
KERN

(Drury Lane)

> First — to each living thing, whate'er its kind,
> Some lot, some part, some station is assign'd.
> The feather'd race with pinions skim the air —
> Not so the mackerel, and still less the bear.
> — *The Progress of Man*, by GEORGE CANNING.

WHAT lot, part, or station is assigned to the providers of books for musical plays? Obviously, that of amusing the British public. Or shall we say persuading it to sit the piece through to the bitter end in the attitude of a public which is amused? I defy anybody to fault my argument so far as it has gone, unless he happens on the notion that it is wrong *in toto*. For it *is* wrong — lock, stock, and barrel, fore and aft, hip and thigh — and by this last token apt to be found fault with and even smitten. The British public does not go to a musical play to be amused in the sense that if it is not amused it stops away. If it goes to a musical comedy and is amused, all well and good: the amusement is gratuitous, thrown in, buckshee, money for jam. The plain truth is that the British public just goes to musical comedy:

> While the moved *critics* sit in dumb despair,
> Like Hottentots, and at each other stare.

The author of this good parody has appended the following foot-note to this passage: 'A beautiful figure of German literature. The Hottentots remarkable for staring at each other — God knows why.' But the critics know why they stare. It is to ask each other how long Drury Lane is to be the asylum for American inanity. The answer is: For ever, dear heart!

A friend of mine was once tutor in the family of an English squire who looked like Mr. Rochester and had a mansion in the

Peak district of Derbyshire. The squire insisted upon dressing for dinner, though the nearest house where anybody else did this was Chatsworth, forty miles away, and every night he would rise from a meal of utter solemnity saying: 'Shall we go and see about that fire in the library?' The formula never varied. But people cast in the mould of this fireside fetishist have to be entertained, and only inanity will entertain them. They are also the backbone of the nation, which backbone when it is in town flies instantly to Drury Lane! This explains Mr. Oscar Hammerstein 2nd, who has given the present production its words and stage shape.

Now the same questions are to be asked of a musical play as of the Cosmogony:

> Whether some great, supreme o'er-ruling Power
> Stretch'd forth its arm at Nature's natal hour,
> Composed this mighty whole with plastic skill,
> Wielding the jarring elements at will?
> Or whether sprung from Chaos' mingling storm,
> The mass of matter started into form?

There is, of course, the alternative view:

> Whether material substance unrefined
> Owns the strong impulse of instinctive mind,
> Which to one centre points diverging lines,
> Confounds, refracts, invig'rates, and combines?

In the matter of the Cosmogony my views are tempered by what I remember of Sanconiathon, Manetho, Berosus, and Ocellus Lucanus. But in the matter of the musical play I must plump for the strong impulse and instinctive mind of Mr. Hammerstein. Nobody else has so firm and assured a drive in the matter of witlessness.

Mesdames Charlotte M. Yonge, Emma Jane Worboise, and the distinguished authors of *St. Elmo* and *Barriers Burned Away* could have put their heads together without equalling the lambent innocuousness of these three daughters of a travelling photographer at whom we belatedly arrive. The youngest (Miss

57

Victoria Hopper) was deserted on her wedding night by her gipsy husband (Mr. Esmond Knight) because he preferred the company of a circus busker (Mr. Albert Burdon) and the joys of the road. In cold blood one thinks there must have been some other reason having to do with unfounded jealousy, though at the time one did not detect it, perhaps because the first act had been so full of lullabying, cradle-singing, and asking who wants to go to sleep, to which one playgoer at least responded affirmatively. The second daughter (Miss Adèle Dixon) married into the peerage (Mr. Richard Dolman), while the eldest (Miss Charlotte Greenwood) espoused a village policeman (Mr. Stanley Holloway). Presently the three husbands met in the War, and years after they and their wives and their families made whoopee at Boulter's Lock. 'The way you describe me I don't seem very exciting to myself,' says one of the characters. But what is a deficiency in a person may be, as has already been demonstrated, a virtue in a musical-comedy plot, and I see no reason why on this score this production should fail.

What, then, of the acting? There isn't any, because nobody has a chance to act except Mr. Knight, who manages to give a thunder-and-lightning quality to the little gipsy. That Mr. Burdon can be a brilliant comedian cannot even be guessed, and we have to hark back to the films to appreciate how much ecstasy and riot there can be in Miss Greenwood. Fortunately she is allowed one of those dances in which her high, effortless kicking resembles the raising of the Tower Bridge. There are some charming numbers by the chorus, and both Mr. Kern's music and Mrs. Calthrop's settings are exquisite. Probably there is no country in the world in which visual and aural embroidery of such delicacy is tacked on to calico so coarse. But the English like it like that, and are right to like it so.

> Ah! who has seen the mailèd lobster rise,
> Clap her broad wings, and soaring claim the skies?
> Or the young heifer plunge, with pliant limb,
> In the salt wave and, fish-like, strive to swim?

Answer and implication are obvious. Musical comedy must keep to its medium; and if it soars it must only be into the illimitable inane. The stuff of its plot must always be sackcloth, let the critics bestrew themselves with what ashes they may. Mr. Hammerstein is no Shakespeare, and that is why he reigns in our national theatre.

April 9, 1934

SUNNY RIVER

BY OSCAR HAMMERSTEIN 2ND. MUSIC BY
SIGMUND ROMBERG

(Piccadilly)

Does this play hold water? No. But is water-tightness the criterion? The scene is New Orleans, and the date the beginning of the last century. The heroine is Marie Sauvinet, a young lady with a Voice and a passion for Renunciation. There is nothing she will not renounce. She will give up her career as an opera singer for a little husband and a little house, and is even prepared to do a little cooking. And many are the arias in which she breathes forth the renunciatory spirit. But the hero, Jean Gervais, being in the clutches of a fiancée, one Cécilie Marshall, about to become a mother, Marie gives him up and re-embraces her profession with all the roulades and grace-notes appertaining thereto. Years elapse. And now Marie, a famous coloratura singer, learns that Cécilie's impending maternity was all a tarra-diddle — shade of Hardy's Arabella! Whereby she asserts, *strepitoso e con fuoco*, her right to happiness. In other words, to take Cécilie's husband from her.

They repair to the little house only to find that Cécilie has got there first, vowing her willingness to live in as small a cot and do as much cooking and even scrubbing as any opera singer. Where-

59

upon Marie renounces for the last time, and in less than two minutes has boarded a packet for Europe. Cloakless and luggageless if you like, but furnished with a halo. And we remember Hilary Jesson in *His House in Order*: 'Nina, there are some people walking the earth who are wearing a halo. It's invisible to you and me; *we* can't see it; but it's there, round their brows, none the less. They are the·people who have made sacrifices, who have *renounced*. Nina, be among those who wear the halo.' No, reader, that is not the end. Once more Marie returns to New Orleans, to learn that Jean has been killed in the war. And there is a final scene in which the widow and the diva discuss the merits of eating your cake when you have it and dreaming about the cake you have never had. This is of an affectingness to melt the hearts of the blackest of market-gardeners.

Early in life the Hungarian Mr. Sigmund Romberg seems to have realized that a man who is going to compose some fifty musical pieces must be sparing of original inspiration. In *The Desert Song* he tipped us the wink that he knew all about Liszt's 'Liebestraum', Mascagni's 'Siciliana' and even Rimsky-Korsakov's 'Coq d'Or'. Now he reminds us of *Tristan, Meistersinger*, 'Till Eulenspiegel' and even 'The Londonderry Air'! Is it then difficult to distinguish Mr. Romberg's quotations from his original matter? I venture to think so. Since few people recognized in *The Desert Song*'s march of Arabs, Dervishes, or whatever they were, an echo of the chorus 'Fling Wide the Gates' from Stainer's 'Crucifixion', one is doubtful whether something new-sounding in the present score may not owe a debt to Orlando Lasso or Palestrina! Be all this as it may, the score is extraordinarily tuneful throughout.

The reason, then, that I rate this piece as the best since *Bitter-Sweet*? First, the plot is not more nonsensical than any other. Second, there is a complete absence of jazz or swing, the songs are sung, not crooned, and the singers have the voices to sing them. Third, there is no tap-dancing. Fourth, the piece keeps to its period and there is no low comedian to make gags about 'utility' trousers. Fifth, the stage pictures and the enchanting Empire costumes of Miss Doris Zinkeisen are a continual delight. Sixth, perceptibly if in a way hard to define, the production captures some of the spirit of Cable's exquisite *Old Creole Days*. Seventh, the piece is brilliantly acted. Miss Evelyn Laye, whether simple in turquoise or sophisticated in green, has never looked lovelier, or sung and acted so well. Mr. Dennis Noble, in fine voice, gives an admirable simulation of passion. Then there is the new discovery, Mr. Don Avory, a young American who looks seventeen, is probably ten years older, and has all the makings of a Master Betty *de nos jours*. Miss Ena Burrill copes miraculously with the impossible part of the wife, Mr. Bertram Wallis sets the piece in its right place and time, and Mr. Bernard Ansell is really funny. The management should at once cable Mr. Oscar Hammerstein 2nd for five hundred witty lines and Mr. Romberg for three more songs — he might have a look at Pepusch, Flotow, and even Galuppi — and hand the lot to Miss Edith Day, who after her first ditty is left entirely in the lurch.

August 22, 1943

GOOD NEWS

BY LAURENCE SCHWAB AND B. G. DE SYLVA
MUSIC BY RAY HENDERSON

(Carlton)

'COME, dear', said one of the characters in this busy piece, 'this is no place for the intelligentsia!' An unfortunate remark for a musical comedy. Unfortunate, because untrue. There flows through all this form of entertainment a stream of mindlessness entirely satisfying to two classes of people — those who have no mind at all and those who have too much. Both resist mental exertion, but for opposite reasons. One type has a mind to play but no mind to play with; the other, seeking change of vent, will play with anything which is not mind. Those of us who are

61

disgruntled with musical comedy are unlucky in-betweens who demand even in the lightest musical entertainment singers who can sing, dancers acquainted with grace, comedians who assault the wits. 'But wherefore should these good news make me sick?' asked Shakespeare's weary king. 'Will Fortune never come with both hands full, but write her fair words still in foulest letters?' The point about *Good News* is that the letters and the gracious creatures who represent them are fair enough, only they have nothing whatever to say.

The piece is destitute of grace, sung or spoken, and barren of wit. What, then, remains to make it the success which it undeniably is? The answer is noise. Noise and again noise. For some time past the American fun-maker has been making a god of mere sound. On the screen you cannot see the racing of chariots or the passing of troops without roof-splitting clangour proceeding from an orchestra reinforced by tons of metal. The din on the Carlton stage was ear-splitting throughout, and as insistent as the road-mender's drill. But it is to the classics that one must fly for any fit comparison.

Let it be said, then, that the sound and fury of this American study of College manners is Miltonic without being significant. No sooner has the curtain risen on Tait College than:

> open fly
> With impetuous recoil and jarring sound
> Th' infernal doors, and on their hinges grate
> Harsh thunder.

The establishment being what is known over there as 'co-educational', we were at once presented with a picture of manly prowess which not only confronted female charm but:

> Hung over her enamour'd, and beheld
> Beauty, which, whether waking or asleep,
> Shot forth peculiar graces.

It was these Peculiar Graces who made all the row. How they danced, luxurious through unrestraint, unrespited, unpitied, unreprieved! How the orchestra, preponderantly brass, aided and abetted them! Here indeed was:

> Sonorous metal blowing martial sounds:
> At which the universal host up sent
> A shout that tore hell's conclave, and beyond
> Frighted the reign of Chaos and old Night.

It was admirable. At least there were those who, looking upon 'The 'Varsity Drag', found that exercise admirable. Entirely merciless our tormentors were not. Occasionally they relented and slowed down

> In perfect phalanx, to the Dorian mood
> Of flutes and soft recorders.

It was in this subdued vein that we were enchanted with the contrasting monotony of the dirge entitled: 'Lucky in Love'.

Really, it almost seems as though in this piece the theatre had determined to turn the tables on the screen. Producers of films about love and football have been content to depict little of the tender and a great deal of the rougher passion. This play relies almost entirely upon that which was omitted from Mr. Harold Lloyd's film on the same subject. The screen showed us the arena with its thousands of spectators and the actual battle; the play gives us the outer wall of a stadium as obviously tenantless as the arena in the last act of *Carmen*. The plot? Well, it is not in the least like that of *Tom Brown's Schooldays*. It has nothing of the atmosphere which we associate with Lord's in July. But, again, why should it have? The English undergraduate is a simple fellow who, taking part in his Varsity match, desires but to win it. The American student is much more complex. It appears that if his side wins the game he must marry the wrong young woman. He could kick a goal an he would, but the face of his real inamorata appearing between the goalposts, he declines to kick that goal. Or so I gathered, though really in the din it was difficult to gather anything in particular.

But perhaps we were happier than we knew. There is a school

of philosophers which holds that you can cure pain by absorbing and enjoying it, that toothache vanishes if you dote upon toothache to the exclusion of all other sense. And if toothache, why not earache? Miss Zelma O'Neal is certainly possessed of genius for that which Mr. Polly would doubtless have described as 'Terpsichoracious angulosity'. Her motions are those of one extricating herself from quicksand and immediately plunging in again up to the waist. As for the accompanying bevy, foot-stamping and arm-flinging, one can only lay down the general principle that it is curmudgeonly to refuse applause to anything which is being accomplished with the maximum intensity of heart and soul.

August 19, 1928

FUNNY FACE

BY FRED THOMPSON AND PAUL GERARD SMITH
MUSIC BY GEORGE GERSHWIN

(Princes)

THE price even of the most recondite seat in the stalls and dress-circle for the first night of this musical comedy was twenty-four shillings. But surely everybody, except the churlish, must deem it worth more than that to see that superb droll, Mr. Leslie Henson. Mr. Henson is capable of magnoperating *in vacuo*, of emptying the world until there is nothing left remarkable except his lunatic conceptions. Like the true poet, he is not possessed by his subject but has dominion over it. To alter Lamb a little, he ascends the empyrean of pure fooling, and it is we who are intoxicated. Talking of Lamb, and presuming ourselves to be in the mood for fine writing, which ocasionally we are, how could we resist asking who like Henson can throw a preternatural interest over such common daily-life objects? Did not that first act's dumb-waiter and bowl of punch rise in his conception, aided, be it

justly said, by the owlish gusto and befuddled gravity of Mr.
Sydney Howard, into a dignity equivalent to Cassiopeia's Chair?
Did not, on Thursday night, the genius of Henson rise level with
what we are told of Munden's in *antiquating* what it touched? Did
not that punchbowl and that ladle become as grand and primal
as the seething pots and hooks of old prophetic vision?

I think this is the wittiest musical comedy I have ever listened
to. Or so these two really admirable comedians persuaded me.
Attend with me closely to them both when they have mastered
that large and lambent lucidity which connotes the sublimer
reaches of intoxication. Mr. Howard slowly imparts the information that he is a safe-cracker. Mr. Henson turns this over in empty
amplitude of mind. 'A safe cracker of what?' he asks. 'Of safes,'
replies his friend. 'Ah!' says Mr. Henson. Aeons pass. Then
presently a comment occurs to Mr. Henson. 'That must be interesting work!' It may be that this reads dull. I cannot help it.
I know only that, uttered with the portentous gravity which might
have characterized a chat between Ralph Waldo and our Matthew,
it set the huge audience holding its sides. Art is now discussed,
with momentary descent to lower levels in the confounding of
etching with itching. Next patriotism, whereupon toasts are
exchanged. 'King George for England!' proposes Mr. Howard.
This is honoured. 'King's Cross for Scotland!' insists Mr. Henson.
Then with some recollection of old training days he clicks uncertain heels, sketches a salute, and breaks into what he believes to
be our National Anthem. That which he hums is, in fact, the
Marseillaise! What, I ask, are twenty-four miserable shillings?
Away with them!

This show has a capital little actress called Rita Page, who presents a first-class skit on the young woman *à la mode*. If she dislikes
anything she is 'consumed with disgust', and her jewellery she
describes as 'revoltingly valuable'. If it should ever occur to Mr.
A. P. Herbert to dramatize his *Trials of Topsy*, here is the actress
for his heroine. I can assure him that she is quite *chaotically* unique!
Whenever we are denied the spectacle of Mr. Henson darting
about the stage like an infuriated goldfish, or Mr. Howard, his

mate, waiting with rosy, patient gills to be fed — during these lapses there is the dancing of Mr. Fred Astaire and Miss Adèle Astaire. This is very good, of course. But bless me, while the little nippers of Lancashire did much the same thing in the provincial pantomimes of thirty years ago we did not make so much fuss about it! Whereas the audience at the Princes Theatre received this American couple with applause adequate to a Massine and a Nemtchinova. Let me not be deemed grudging to the Astaires. To the delight of the assembled Joblillies and Garyulies they played their game of eurhythmical catch-as-catch-can till the gunpowder ran out of the heels of their boots. They are the Great Panjandra of their art. Let me conclude by applying to this musical comedy what the old essayist, prompted I like to believe by the Lord Mayor's Show, said of true genius: 'Its transitions are every whit as violent as in the most extravagant dream, and yet the waking judgment ratifies them.'

November 10, 1928

MR. CINDERS

BY CLIFFORD GREY AND GREATREX NEWMAN
MUSIC BY VIVIAN ELLIS AND RICHARD MYERS

(Adelphi)

SOME of my colleagues have complained that this musical comedy starts a little slowly. Well, why shouldn't it? We remember that Stevenson said of Dumas's *Le Vicomte de Bragelonne*: 'A proportion of readers stumble at the threshold. In so vast a mansion there were sure to be back stairs and kitchen offices where no one would delight to linger.' Might one not find the same excuse for the Baron's mansion as for Bragelonne's? Perhaps the better excuse would be that these go-as-you-please shows are really come-as-you-please entertainments. A musical comedy is surely a thing

66

to drop into if, *and when,* you feel 'so dispoged'. There comes a moment when the diner-out seeks for entertainment which shall not disturb his digestive processes. He has heard extravagant praise and blame of *The Mock Emperor.* But may not that play have a disturbing effect on the mock-turtle? He seeks something which shall neither fatigue the mind nor engage the senses. He thinks *Mr. Cinders* is the very ticket. I can assure him that it is.

If I hesitate to speak well of this unpretentious little show it is because praise of any musical comedy in these columns has invariably been its death-knell. *Merely Molly* received a whole column of unstinted adulation and ran no time at all. *Peggy Ann* vanished while the dew of commendation was still thick upon it. I will only say this, that following my own suggestion I dropped in on this play about nine o'clock and found that the next two hours passed more than pleasantly. The plot, instead of pretending to be grown-up, which is absurd, insists upon being childish, which besides being eupeptic is of an incontrovertible rightness. Properly-minded people, when they visit a musical comedy, put on the cap not of the thinker but of the fool, and if it be prudent to answer a fool according to his folly it is surely a part of discretion to entertain him likewise. *Mr. Cinders* is, of course, *Cinderella* all over again. Excellent! The Ugly Sisters are as much a part of the furniture of every playgoer's mind as the Witches in *Macbeth,* and their dramatic propriety suffers no harm when their sex is changed. They become brothers, it is true, of an exceeding loveliness sartorially considered, but, we are given to understand, otherwise the personifications of moral turpitude. Again excellent! He is no playgoer who is not moved at least once a year by the trying-on of Cinderella's slipper, and it can hardly be doubted that if an earlier dramatist had used the theme for a comedy he would, *à propos* of the Ugly Sisters, have made Dandini turn to the Baroness with the line:

Filthy hag, why do you show me these?

The scene is just as good when the slipper becomes a bowler hat, tried on unavailingly by all the Baron's establishment and fitting only the poor page. At the risk of blasting this musical comedy out of existence I shall say that it possesses the least imbecile plot I have ever met with in connection with these cerebrations.

Mr. Bobby Howes plays Mr. Cinders, and it must be said firmly that here is an actor of remarkable promise. I do not set this down in the familiar, damning sense suggesting a performance so bad that the next one must be an improvement. Mr. Howes plays the buffoon so well, and decorates his buffoonery with so much of comedy and something which is so nearly pathos, that hopes beyond clowning are raised. This actor has a heart in the sense that Sir Willoughby had a leg. In short, Mr. Howes may well be our next James Welch, and if a revival of *The New Clown* should ever be contemplated he would certainly have my vote. Miss Binnie Hale spikes the guns of criticism by making it perfectly obvious that she is as alive as anybody to the weak points in her playing. Her beauty is not of the statuesque order, and knowing this she does not, as some Junos affect, pose lumpishly at the feet of staircases; she prefers to flit hither and thither like a sunbeam or a will-o'-the-wisp. Her darts and dives put one in mind of the swallow, and her dancing has the quality of the lightning which Juliet predicated so acutely. It has ceased almost before you have gathered that it has begun. The chorus in this piece, apart from wearing some very beautiful dresses, has an extraordinary amount of nothing to do. On other occasions we have had something too much of American robotizing; one would now suggest that there are alternatives to perpetual motion other than marking-time. I have mislaid my programme, but a shimmering drop-curtain in black and silver either bespeaks the producing and mounting of Mr. Julian Wylie or it is as flat burglary as ever was committed.

February 11, 1929

BITTER-SWEET

BY NOEL COWARD

(His Majesty's)

THE programme bears the notification, 'The Entire Production by Noel Coward', and perhaps a good way of attacking, in the friendly sense, the stupendous opus which is this 'opérette' would be to consider how much Mr. Coward has really put into it. I suggest that to arrive at this estimate we must subtract from 'the entire production' the delightful scenes and dresses designed by Mrs. Calthrop, the equally delightful scene and dresses designed by Professor Ernst Stern, the dance arranged by Miss Tilly Losch, and, of course, the brilliant orchestration of the play's tunes by Mr. d'Orellama. This leaves the plot, the dialogue, the lyrics, the melodies as originally executed on a baby-grand, the stagecraft, the evening's sparkle, irresponsibility, wit, and fun, the power to conceive its visual delight, and the general notion of what makes a thoroughly good light entertainment. Not even Mr. Coward's warmest admirers can claim for him that he created the 'seventies and the 'nineties; but they are surely entitled to credit him with re-creating them. Night-life in Vienna was never the outcome of Mr. Coward's genius; on the other hand, its reproduction is one of his happiest inspirations.

On the whole, I suggest that readers who have done the sum with me will agree that what is left after subtracting other people's efforts is a thundering lot. If anybody can do the same sum and make more of it, let him come forward! He won't have any difficulty in getting a theatre; all the theatres will be tumbling over each other to get him. Of course, the country may be teeming with people who are capable of doing what Mr. Coward has done. Only nobody else has done it yet. Nobody else has ever done it, except Wagner. And *Meistersinger* is not strictly an opérette.

Consider what Mr. Coward's achievement means. Mozart had

need of Beaumarchais, Richard Strauss of Hoffmansthal, Johann Strauss of lots of people, and ditto Oscar Straus. Offenbach, Lecocq, Planquette, Hervé, Audran, Messager, all the Frenchmen had their librettists, and it might be conveniently remembered here that in the days when Meilhac and Halévy were writing for the French vaudeville and comic-opera stage, the librettist was a more important person than the provider of the music. Gilbert and Sullivan were the perfect marriage, after which comic opera rapidly degenerated into musical comedy and the licentious state whereby the composer took at least sixteen lyric-writers to his bosom. I have no doubt that somebody will write to tell me that at some obscure theatre, near the Oval, some gentleman did in the 'seventies, for one performance only, produce an opera which was the fruit of single cogitation. I shall not deny it. Doubtless somebody else discovered America before Columbus. But Columbus did achieve something. Let the same be said of Mr. Coward.

It is unnecessary to recapitulate the plot. Besides, it would not be a fair description of the entertainment any more than to enumerate her bones would be a fair description of the Venus of Milo. This plot is only the skeleton to enchantment. Sufficient to say that in order to persuade a modern young woman to run away with her jazz-band lover, a great lady recounts how, as a girl, she ran away with a pianoforte teacher, became a dancing partner in a Viennese café, was duly insulted, was present at the death in a duel of her avenging but inexpert husband, became a prima donna, and sang Tosti in over-heated drawing-rooms for the edification of Lady Midas, Mrs. Ponsonby de Tomkyns and others of George du Maurier's delicious circle, and finally married the Marquis of Shayne. I think we believed all this, except possibly the bit about the prima donna; voices, unlike piano-scores, cannot be orchestrated.

Is the libretto of this opera as good as its author's plays? No. For if it were we should not need the music. On the other hand, how good is the music? Let me say that, to uninstructed ears, it is what you might call travelled music. It is stuff which musicians all the world over, before the era of saxophones muted with bowler-hats, would have recognized as light music. It is cultivated, deft, witty, and, above all, tuneful. To argue that a sextet of good-night-bidding young ladies would have been done better by Sullivan is about as helpful as to say that no new essay on old china can be as good as Charles Lamb's. Much better to suggest that the quartet entitled 'Ladies of the Town' could go into any comic opera that was ever written and not be shamed. Because of *Rosenkavalier* must there be no more Viennese waltzes? Go to! Mr. Coward's gingerbread is pleasantly hot in the mouth though we may know where the gilt comes from. Some exception has been taken to the 'Green Carnations' quartet. But one would retain it, if only to prove once more that in this country, while your serious writer may not look over the hedge, your stage-jester may steal every horse in the field. Finally, the piece would be worth while if only for the second act, in which Mr. Coward shows himself to be possessed of the triple gift of your true man of the theatre — the faculty for entertaining both the eye, the ear, and the mind. The Viennese rout is delicious, and the episode of the faithful cocotte is moving.

Let it be said without hesitation that Miss Ivy St. Helier ran off with all the acting in the play, and that if this were the 'nineties and she were to wear long black gloves, all the highbrow essayists would be dithyrambing about her. It would be a moderate statement to say that on Thursday night one deemed this artist to be as good as Yvette Guilbert and Louie Freear put together. Miss St. Helier succeeded in resembling both perfectly and at the same moment. Except for Mr. Austin Trevor, who contributed a good little sketch, and Mr. Metaxa, who looked convincingly un-English, the rest of the acting did not seem to me to be worthy of the piece or of the occasion. Miss Peggy Wood invited one to believe that mid-Victorian staidness is the quality looked for by Viennese officers in Viennese cafés at two o'clock in the morning, and though Miss Wood sang agreeably enough I am not convinced that she was well cast. The dancing was excellent, though too many members of the company suggested by their accents that recruitment for this production had taken place in and about

Blackpool. There were scenes of great excitement at the finish, and Mr. Coward put the coping-stone on his triumph by steadfastly declining to appear.

July 18, 1929

CONVERSATION PIECE

BY NOEL COWARD

(His Majesty's)

THIS piece ought to suit one who, like myself, adores Brighton, admits to being of the Horse Age, and is often accused of knowing what French is about. Yet being a dramatic critic one is necessarily a mugwump, defined by your low comedian as a person who sits on a fence with his mug on one side and his wump on the other. But that is because plays have a habit of being both good and bad, and when this happens it is one's duty to say so. Whoever first divided the sheep from the goats was the first dramatic critic.

Mr. Coward's new piece shall be divided into the good and the not so good, and we will begin with the latter. It is not so good because of his bigger achievements, and people will not understand that genius need not, nay, must not, always be at full stretch. If Wagner had interrupted *The Ring* to write *Die Fledermaus* people would have thought much less of that delicious work than they did when it was recognized as somebody else's high peak. Mr. Coward tried to forestall this criticism in his choice of title, since not even the British public would expect Mr. Gunn's picture to present Messrs. Baring, Belloc and Chesterton as Michael-Angelesque nudes. A conversation piece is essentially a small-scale picture, and by his title Mr. Coward hinted at a little play.

Then perhaps the choice of theatre was unhappy, since His Majesty's is a playhouse of great magnificence, where grand opera

72

could be indulged in if wanted. All the appurtenances of spectacle were there — all the presage of ceremony with not enough to be ceremonious about. There was some talk of a little lady becoming mistress of the Prince Regent, the period being 1811, and such a story — we thought knowingly — must lead up to a grand reception in the Dome at Brighton, or wherever the royal mistresses were flaunted. But nothing of the sort happened; instead we had the usual musical-comedy second-act climax. This found Mr. Coward's heroine in tears on the kind of sofa upon which only Mme. Récamier has ever reclined. Alas that she had indulged in a tirade wholly French which left the audience, like panting Time, toiling in vain after Mlle. Yvonne Printemps! Why French? — Miss Julia Mills might appositely have asked. Frenchification here was the greatest mistake. The end of a second act is the place to bring down a house, and an audience which is already flabbergasted cannot be brought lower than it is.

And then there was the story, a confused affair about a couple of French adventurers whose twists and turns were too much for me. The curtain dropped on the second act with the female adventurer declaring her passionate love for her partner in the presence of everybody in the cast, and rose on the third act with the young woman's lips glued to those of an English marquis. Which caused the adventurer to say: 'A trifle vulgar after the scene you made last night!' It was more than vulgar; it was not to be understood. Once more the size of the house mattered; large sentiments loudly declared need a stronger backing of logic than Mr. Coward in this play appears to have started out with. Last but one, it shall be remarked that Mr. Coward had rationed himself too severely in the matter of wit, preferring to indulge in long passages of sentiment which, between ourselves, is not his forte. Last, I am not too sure about the music. There was far too much of one cloying little tune and not nearly enough of the witty, sparkling stuff whose top-line Mr. Coward invents so happily.

And now for the jewels in the case. To begin with, Mrs. Calthrop's scenery is almost the loveliest I remember having seen on any stage; nay, I will burn a boat or two, and say that it is the

most exquisite. It is not what Joe Gargery would call 'too archi-
tectooralooral', for the designer has added her own witty observation to the natty Georgian beauty, and in her indoor sets brings
the scent and feel of the sea through the open windows. Here
again there has been the feminine eye, since no vessel passes and
Brighton has notoriously fewer ships than any desert. Mrs. Calthrop's costumes are good, but they could not be so good as the
scenery. The piece, as was to be expected in a play that obviously
started in band-box vein, is full of tiny strokes of admirable crafts-
manship. Things like the first scene, in which no word is spoken
and the intensive silence keys up the audience to a giddy expectation. Things like the party scene, which is conceived in the form
of a dance. Here, whenever anyone speaks, the dancers suspend
animation like the figures on a clock that has done striking.

The play is full of such brilliant touches. The wit, when we are
allowed any, is, as was to be expected, at once unexpected, mor-
dant and bitter-sweet, as when the ladies of the town meet the
town's great ladies. The latter take themselves off in dudgeon,
whereupon one of the little ladies says, approximately: 'It's very
awkward meeting the likes of them; you see, they're the wives of
our gentlemen!' The whole production is staged with Mr. Cochran's well-known lavish and perfect taste. In fact, almost too
much splendour has gone to a little piece, which if it were done
at all 'twere better it were done modestly.

In the nature of the thing there could not be much acting,
though there is generous opportunity for poise. Such playing as is
possible falls to Mlle. Printemps, who gives a faultless exhibition
of wayward charm. There is probably more art behind this blob
of heavenly nose than the casual spectator might imagine, and
this highly talented actress has to thank Nature for yet another
gift — that of self-caricature. She can be more like Yvonne
Printemps than Printemps has right to be, and it is then that her
art attains the most significance. As ever, she sings deliciously.

Mr. Coward, who plays the male adventurer, has the air of
stepping gallantly into some breach. He has neither the momentum nor the age for the part, and his acting must take refuge in

OPÉRETTE

a patterned severity. Miss Irene Browne contributes her sense of
style, and Miss Heather Thatcher her sense of gaiety. The young
Marquis is pleasantly played by Mr. Louis Hayward, and there
is a brilliant performance by Miss Betty Shale, who, as a black-
avised harridan calling herself Mrs. Dragon, has not a word to
say and bears staggering and alternating resemblances to Mrs.
Grundy and Miss Mae West.

And now may I suggest that the long French tirade at the end
of the second act should be put back into English? Let Mlle.
Printemps accept our assurance first that she cannot fail, second
that even if she did it could only be a failure in speed, and third
that a failure in English is better than a success in any other
language. *Moi qui parle* am quite certain on this point. In the
course of the evening Mr. Coward asks an English oaf if he speaks
French. Receiving the reply, 'Oui, un peu', he has a mocking:
'I never think that is quite enough!' Let me tell him that it is too
much for an English audience.

There was a charming scene at the end when Mlle. Printemps
was assured of the unbroken and faithful regard of her English
public. It was difficult to tell whether she or the audience
was the more moved. The evening had begun by being Mrs.
Calthrop's; it ended by being that of our distinguished visitor.
Mr. Cochran has done right to cry· with Théophile Gautier:
'Printemps, tu peux venir!'

February 16, 1934

OPÉRETTE

BY NOEL COWARD

(His Majesty's)

BETTER known should be that rebuke administered by a clever
woman to a young highbrow offering some more than usually
blatant puerility. The rebuke consisted of the two words 'Hush,
darling!' So some Egeria, when Mr. Coward wrinkled his brow and

75

said: 'Hanged if I don't do another *Bitter-Sweet*!' ought to have smoothed that temple and murmured: 'No, darling!' Does not Mr. Coward know — and it really is astonishing of how many playwrights I am impelled to ask this question! — that the better is the enemy of the good? I see nothing in *Opérette* that was not brought better off either in *Bitter-Sweet*, or *Cavalcade*, or *Words and Music*, or *Conversation Piece*, or *To-night at 8.30*. The story of the new piece is all about a musical-comedy actress who refused to marry the heir to a peerage because he would have to resign his commission. This is trite. But for Miss Peggy Wood it would have seemed still triter. Mr. Coward probably realized that it was no good asking an actress of Miss Wood's resilience and buoyancy to impersonate a chorus-girl going into a galloping consumption because she can't marry a galloping major. But I have written 'trite', and the word sticks.

The *milieu* is the lighter stage in 1906, and Mr. Coward should know without my telling him that the musical comedies of that period were nothing like so dull as *The Model Maid* pretends to be. He should know this if only because he wrote the 'Mirabelle' scene in *Cavalcade*. Does Mr. Coward really think that his present back-stage quarrelling is a patch on the same thing in *Red Peppers*? But it would be tedious to go through the whole piece item by item and demonstrate where the author has already done them better. I doubt even whether Mr. Coward's tunes are as good as they used to be, though I waver not in my allegiance to Miss Elsie April and Mr. Charles Prentice, who, with cor anglais, triangle, contra-fagotto, and harp — are the *glissandos* of this last paralleled save on the Cresta Run? — once more sweeten the air with patchouli'd sound.

Mrs. Calthrop's décor? What other designer could so have caught the exact Edwardian note:

The windows were draped with deep gold-coloured plush curtains, lined with pale-green silk, and edged with a fringe bathed in both these hues ... A Wilton carpet, blending in these colours, covered the highly-polished floor, as could be

seen by its glittering sides ... Two pianos, differing much in
material and design, stood in opposite corners of the room;
while two low-lying lounges graced the others. All sorts of easy
chairs, some of them odd specimens of handicraft, stools,
settees, ottomans, etc., etc., rested here and there throughout
the room ... Great bronze pots of choice flowers bloomed on
marble tables, naïvely and neatly arranged. Spreading ferns
peeped high in abundance above their decorative rests, throwing a fanciful shade over their marble pedestals. Statues
claimed a fair share of space, too, as they stood in martyrdom,
sneering at the varying criticisms that passed from the lips of
their many shocked admirers ... 'Good Queen Bess' sat in
regal dignity, dressed in a full, flowing robe, apparently horri-
fied at Nature's naked form; while Milton smiled with satisfaction because he was robbed of the pleasure or displeasure of
expressing his opinion ... A fine old drapery hung over the
lofty door, completing the meagre description of this room.

Yes, one glimpse of Liesl Haren's drawing-room in *Opérette*
convinced me that Mrs. Calthrop had been reading Mrs. Ros on
Clapham Hall! It strikes me that that same masterpiece contains
a brilliant description of Liesl herself:

Moving to one of the sweetly-toned instruments, Madam-de-
Maine struck its keys, sending from them strains, at one time
loud and long; at another, grave, low, and pathetic. Then she
would send from its ivory octaves notes of ringing bitterness,
as an introduction to magically-mastered, sweet angelic
sounds. ...

But enough of Amanda! Mme. Fritzi Massary is a bravurista of
the highest order; any one of her gestures reduces the English
notion of acting to the likeness of a milk pudding with a grating
of nutmeg. Does the reader consider this rude to Miss Wood?
The reader is wrong. Miss Wood is an American actress, and the
English parallel for her is not a pudding, milk or otherwise, but
an honest, domesticated rose. Nobody else matters very much

except Miss Irene Vanbrugh, whom I nearly forgot. To look at acting like this is like wearing a suit that fits so perfectly that you forget you have it on. Such suits have not been made yesterday; nor is acting like Miss Vanbrugh's.

March 16, 1938

EVER GREEN

BY BENN W. LEVY AND LORENTZ HART
MUSIC BY RICHARD RODGERS

(Adelphi)

To pretend that this lovely thing is a musical comedy is to evade truth, since Mr. Cochran's latest sophistication takes after its inept model about as little or as much as Man resembles his first progenitor. There is every indication that our artist-showman set to work in good faith even to the extent of asking Mr. Benn Levy to produce the most strenuously inane idea which could be conceived as emanating from the human cranium. Mr. Levy also began loyally enough. He conceived the notion of Miss Jessie Matthews failing to enchant as a revue-star of twenty-three but winning to fame by pretending to be sixty. Add a young man sempiternally enamoured of, but at cross-purposes with, the wintry lady, and the blissful farrago was complete. Heaven knows from what limbo Mr. Levy lured this lunacy! Possibly from Sir Arthur Pinero's slightly modified: 'There can be no valid objection to a girl becoming an old woman at any moment she, with the sympathetic assistance of nature, selects.' However, there the theme was in all its vacancy. The only thing left was to protract witlessness to the length of a musical-comedy book, and hire a few lyrics and as much sounding brass and tinkling cymbal as modern jazz demands. This was done. 'Calloo!' chortled the organizer of these revels. 'Callay!' chortled back his devoted henchmen.

78

Then the two devils of Mr. Cochran's artistry and Mr. Levy's wit got together to suggest that a revolving-stage would be none the worse for a few ideas to revolve along with it. I take it that it was Mr. Levy's notion to begin with a beauty competition in the Albert Hall, whereby the proceedings started with an aldermanic oration which might have been the thing itself. 'Under this roof', boomed the chairman in Paddington's choicest frock-coat and accents, 'which has seen so many contests won on fouls more glorious than any in history . . .' From that moment we knew that the imbecile game was up, and that both Mr. Cochran and Mr. Levy, adding to themselves the musicianly Mr. Rodgers, intended to give us what they liked instead of pandering to received taste which is the one royal road to failure. I shall attempt no further allotment of responsibility. Somebody had the exquisite inspiration of engaging for the star's mother, masquerading as daughter, not one of your rough-and-tumble 'ugly sister' viragoes but that impeccable artist, Miss Jean Cadell. Somebody had the entirely right notion that to keep this part 'straight' would throw other absurdity into greater relief. Miss Cadell held her course throughout the piece with the nicest sense of how much depended upon her. To a succession of incidents which might have staggered Cleopatra she presented a front of withered circumspection which knew not amazement and leaped to allowances. Asked pointblank by a devotee of Eros in a blue pea-jacket whether she had ever been in love, Miss Cadell put her head on one side and chirped: 'Yes. But quite nicely, of course!' This artist's 'opposite number' was Mr. Leon Morton, and between them the pair ran away with the piece, or would have done if the scenery and dresses had not nailed it to that steadfast if revolving stage.

Mr. Cochran, to continue the theory of undiluted responsibility, obviously saw his theme with that inward eye which is the bliss of multitude. Calling together Professor Ernst Stern and Mesdames Peacock, Calthrop, and Zinkeisen, he determined to treat Miss Matthews to a tour of music-halldom as the latest French painters might 'see' it. Thus we had in 'A Rehearsal at the Casino des Folies' a canvas of perfect enchantment, which in 'The Interior

79

of a Tent at Neuilly Fair' gave place to an illustration from *Les Frères Zemganno*. After this came 'Neuilly Fair' itself, infinite riches in obviously little room, a twirling feat of kaleidoscopic jugglery.

Next the scene entitled 'The New Master', in which a roysterer looking for the Maison Tellier found himself at a seminary for English young ladies. I object to this scene because parents may rightly object to it, because it is insufficiently funny, and because it is taken without acknowledgment from a story by Maupassant. I invite Mr. Cochran to substitute something else before the Christmas holidays. The Finale of the first part, 'La Synthèse de la Belle de Soixante Ans', perfectly reproduced the thistledown sumptuosities of the Folies-Bergère, and, indeed, the whole show brilliantly captured the note and spirit of Paris. One felt that one would sup not in the Strand, but in the Place Blanche. It would be tedious to continue in this cataloguing, and I shall prefer to recall that it was in the second half that Miss Cadell, encountering Mr. Morton who had been robbed of his trousers, placidly announced her decision to march with the times!

It must not be supposed that this show is nothing but colour. The time comes when Mr. Cochran, deeming us sated with satins tulip-green and silks angrier than heart of volcano, desists with a sigh, and for a bit there is plain sailing. This is where Mr. Albert Burdon comes in. Mr. Burdon is a young comedian who, having set Tyne, Tees and Trent on fire, now succeeds with Thames. He is nearly funnier than most of the established zanies, and he brings to his work the peculiar properties of Lancashire gusto and Yorkshire relish. Then there is Mr. Sonnie Hale, warming to the almost credible. Miss Matthews, when she is not dancing exquisitely, shows how much of variety may enliven the seeming infantile, and once, for a passionate moment, rises above curds and whey. The acrobatics of Chica, supported in every sense of the word by the three Messrs. Carlos, demonstrate the superficiality of our notions concerning gravity, and the Tiller Girls reproduce their miracle of perfect alignment. Juno, to use a vulgarism, has little on those lilies of the field yclept Mr. Cochran's Young Ladies, Miss Joyce Barbour hovers gracefully upon the fringe of

HELEN!

the programme, and Miss Jean Barry and Mr. Dave Fitzgibbon complete an entertainment so all-absorbing that I have no notion of what the new theatre looks like.

December 7, 1930

HELEN!

BASED ON 'LA BELLE HÉLÈNE' BY MEILHAC AND HALÉVY. ENGLISH ADAPTATION BY A. P. HERBERT. MUSIC BY OFFENBACH, ARRANGED BY E. W. KORNGOLD

(Adelphi)

HELEN, thy beauty has meant all sorts of things to all sorts of writers! It has inspired the full orchestra of world-poets booming and banging and sawing away in what Mr. Robey has called 'the halls of classic consonance'. It has also served as peg for two French vaudevillists and a German melodist driving an honest trade in quips and tunes. The glory that was Greece? 'Quelle blague!' we can imagine Meilhac saying to Halévy, and Halévy agreeing.

Though the second and wittier of the collaborators died less than fifteen years ago, few playgoers can have any recollection of the first night of the famous opérette. But we can be sure of this: that Helen's time and place were definitely the 'fifties and some bandbox theatre of the boulevards — was it perhaps the Bouffes Parisiens in the Passage Choiseul? — while that which drew the applause of the now soundless clapping host was all that the librettists and their confrère could pack into the piece of French wit, French verve, French bedazzlement, and music so French that it needed a German Jew to write it. We may be sure that the heels of Helen's French shoes were as high as Ilium's towers were topless.

81

Mr. Cochran's problem was how to furbish up the old sparkle and avoid substituting a new one, to stick to the opérette and to keep the thing French. Who should do it for him? In the matter of libretto Meilhac and Halévy's day was obviously over; what about Mr. A. P. Herbert, the most English of our wits? But French poetry, even when it is grave, presents the English interpreter with difficulties; France's tragic dramatists are Restoration before the Monarchy has fallen.

Those repetitioners, Racine and Corneille, indulge in terrific mouthings about lovers slain by passion when to the English mind 'smitten' would put the case high enough: French opera-bouffe is a transposition into the key of mischief of something which, for all the noise it makes, has never to the English sense been really serious. Hence a French operette about Helen and Paris, Menelaus, Agamemnon, Nestor and all the Alexandrine crowd can only be parody at two removes, and how exactly Mr. Herbert has realized this is shown in the little verse in which the contending armies agree on the pragmatical if not the moral issue:

> No wife will take
>   Young men to bed
> If when they wake
>   They find they're dead.

Mr. Herbert is reasonably witty throughout. To be honest, I ought to say that whenever the ear is not listening to the buzz and *frou-frou* of Mr. Oliver Messel's marvellous colourings, or desists from accompanying the composer on some haunting excursion, when the eye can momentarily forget Herr Reinhardt's marshallings and M. Massine's deployings, and shut out that inventory of beauty which is Miss Evelyn Laye — what I am getting at is that when the mind has a moment free for Mr. Herbert it always finds him bright. One says boldly that no other adapter could have been wittier after that event of eighty years ago.

Perhaps one could not expect Mr. Herbert to maintain throughout the level of his best lyric, which begins: 'Is *that* the face that launched a thousand ships?' and then picks Homer's brains. But this is legitimate in one whose private thunder is good enough, and I shall quote in support Mercury's warning to Paris before the Judgment: 'You will see three turtle-doves when you begin the business, and two hell-cats when you've done.' But the fate of every librettist is to take the kicks whilst composer, producer, wardrobe-mistress, electrician, call-boy and even the actors get the kudos, which I take to be the Greek for ha'pence. Let it be recorded that the new third act, which ascends the brightest heaven of Mr. Cochran's invention, is Mr. Herbert's own.

Professor Korngold is not going to be blamed by me because he has done for Offenbach what Mozart did for Handel. Thanks to musical comedy the theatre ear is grosser than it was; Professor Korngold, compelled to augment the score to the size of the theatre and scale of production, has given volume to delicacy without encroaching on it. And how fresh, in these brazen days, is Offenbach's pure lilt! This brings me to the production, and I shall not offend if I say that Herr Reinhardt is one of the best actors in the piece. It is incomprehensible that he should have restored and redecorated and re-enacted the old thing, and made a colossal show of it without losing one jot of its boudoir, jewel-case charm.

But we must remember that Herr Reinhardt has had his hench-men—kittle cattle among whom to attempt discrimination. Let the Orgy — which will be the dream of London as it must have been the nightmare of the Censor — be put to the credit of M. Massine, since this leaves one free to say that Mr. Messel's decorations are a triumph of wit, fantasy and ravishment. 'The centuries kiss and commingle', and so do these centurions wearing the costumes of old Troy as if they were the courtiers of Louis Quatorze. The battle scene is something which old Poussin might have designed for the walls of a modern night club. Those amazing white plumes splashed with red may be baroque; I prefer to say that they look as though Jupiter's nose has bled. If this show is not Mr. Messel's, whose is it?

Miss Laye's porcelain quality is known the world over, and the blue of her eyelids and trailing robe is pure Wedgwood. Now to

Naiad airs she brings competence in the hard business of acting. Her singing is the nearest possible approach to the real thing; her breathing of 'Shepherd, have done' comes o'er us like the sweet south, stealing and giving odour. Mr. Bruce Carfax will never again be so well served by a rôle as he is in the case of Paris, nor will he better fulfil any future rôle. His eyes, slanting up into his head, give him a faun-like quality happily equidistant from Russian dancer and Oxford blue, and this permits him to look like a love-god and abjure mawkishness. In addition Mr. Carfax acts and sings as well as we would have him.

As Menelaus, Mr. Robey is the cynosure of every eye off the stage though on the stage nobody marks him, whence it will be realized that his performance is a miracle of accommodation like that of a trombone-player obliging with a pianissimo. The old-time roars have taken on a sucking-dove quality, and Robeyism, here more honoured in the breach than in the observance, is now an overtone. The gorgeous rhetoric of the halls has been subdued to the poet's 'Nicean barks', and the performance is irresistibly comic throughout. As Calchas, Mr. W. H. Berry achieves a feat similar to Mr. Robey's. His part, if not very long, is very good, and I do not think a better artist could have been chosen for it. Mr. Berry is alive throughout.

The tiny part of the Messenger is perfectly played by Mr. Hay Petrie, which may suggest to our Dull Young Things that Shakespeare is still something if only as a training-ground! Mention must be made of Mr. Leslie Jones's Agamemnon, Miss Désirée Ellinger's Orestes, and the remarkable convolutions of Eve. The chorus has an enormous rôle; whether rapt and static or orgifying and corybantic it acts as one person. The casting throughout has been a feat of jugglery combined with vision, a masterpiece of, shall I say, sleight-of-mind.

Mr. Cochran's share in all this? I take it to have been that of the connoisseur in beauty as distinct from spectacle, of the onlooker who has seen most of the game. Sole arbiter among many claimants to our attention, he has been utterly purposed that none shall be heard more than the others. Determined, too, that the production shall prevail as a work of art, a whole greater than its parts and standing up to their sum. In this latest and finest example of his superb taste Mr. Cochran has recognized old tradition and discovered new glamour.

January 30, 1932

DERBY DAY

BY A. P. HERBERT. MUSIC BY ALFRED REYNOLDS

(Lyric, Hammersmith)

THE critic at Hammersmith is in the hideous case of one who is asked by his hostess what he thinks of her country-house theatricals. There are so many considerations which, strictly, have nothing to do with the play, each of them, it may be, a flower of remembrance, of gratitude, gallantry's recognition, or any one of the hundred things for which Sir Nigel Playfair and his Hammersmith venture are famed.

On Wednesday night last there was a whole bouquet of these odorifera. First there was Mr. Herbert, who, nervously fingering his tie, modestly breathed, where he should have blown, the fanfare of his prologue. Now, how can one say of an author from whose adjacent and hospitable roof half the audience applauds its annual Boat Race that their host mumbles where an actor would declaim? Is the sensitive reader jarred by the personal note? Let him be assured that to touch it equally irks the critic. But the personal *is* the note of these intimate performances.

How, again, shall one say of Mr. Reynolds, who in the past has borne the brunt of so much melodic resuscitation, that after three hours of striving he has not produced a single tune which the commonalty will recognize as such? How gracefully get round the fact that the voice of our remembered favourite, Mr. Frederick Austin, is not what it was? How, finally, may a conscientious critic preserve his integrity when the massed intelligentsia of London comes up to him even in the first interval and instructs him that such ravishment has not been before? Must he out of pusillanimity, which is better spelled funk, temper criticism to admired intention, or shall he nerve·himself to apply the standards he would use if the play were neutrally exposed, say in Poplar, and before an audience mindless of the Hammersmith legend?

The first thing to be said is that the enthusiasm of the audience was extraordinary, the people who knew about music vying with each other in praise of Mr. Herbert's wit, and the literary people being equally boisterous as to Mr. Reynolds's score. The musicians had the better end of the stick here, since of the book's satirical excellence there can be no manner of doubt, no possible doubt whatever. Mr. Herbert's libretto teems with witty lines, though we may wonder whether his Muse has the one quality by which a master-librettist declares himself, that *jingle* which awakes and compels a corresponding lilt in the music.

But there is more to it than this. Gilbert wrote his lyrics *for music* and put his point where his colleague could see it, whereas Mr. Herbert's wit is diffuse and things are happening in the words before the accompanying strain has time to get going. In *Derby Day* the collaborators are constantly pulling away from each other. Thus when Mr. Herbert mentions closing time at the pub Mr. Reynolds responds with a phrase worthy of *The Immortal Hour*. The heroine, looking forward to the day when a merry maiden marries, finds her anticipations clothed in the rarefied atmosphere of that arabesque by Debussy whose line the music follows. 'Come with me to church', says some gay spark, and the music is as plaintive as though it were the dirge for Bredon's young woman who went to church alone.

Mr. Reynolds has been praised for not getting into Mr. Herbert's way, which is like attributing to the leader of a tandem no other office than that of not obstructing his wheeler. Whereas, as all good whips know, both animals should be of equal mettle, and the madcappery divided. Mr. Reynolds has his fling here and there, and it is then that we become most conscious of that synthetic music-making which is the worst kind of tunefulness, the near-melody which is never quite a tune. Mr. Reynolds gives his bar-maid a love-song, and there ain't no barmaid living in the land who could cope with what to her must be musical double-Dutch.

Our composer is a most accomplished musician, and his score is admirable, and we keep telling ourselves how admirable and musicianly it is. When, for example, Mr. Herbert baits the Licensing Justices we note how Mr. Reynolds's score takes on the colour used by Strauss in 'Heldenleben' to poke fun at his enemies. But Sullivan didn't require to be so scholarly, and neither did Leslie Stuart, nor Lionel Monckton, nor Sidney Jones, nor Gustav Kerker writing those tunes in *The Belle of New York* which to-day's butcher-boy, never having heard the opera, still whistles. Or you might say that while 'Brigg Fair' is a masterpiece, for the pur-poses of comic opera about a fairground the composer of 'Oh dear, what can the matter be?' is to be preferred to the greater master.

But there is another reason why the music should lead — the fact that it has always led. A tuneful and witty score has saved a dull plot and a witless book time and time again; there is no instance of the opera that has not caught the ear being kept alive through wit in the libretto. That the Hammersmith management grievously misunderstands all this is proved by the programme, which prints Mr. Herbert's name in big letters and that of Mr. Reynolds in small. These things being so, the judgment of the music must also come first, theoretically and also for a highly practical reason. It is a common thing for intellectuals to be tone-deaf, and since to them any tune is no tune, all are equally good. Hence one would expect to find *Derby Day* acclaimed as a dual masterpiece by literati, Senior Wranglers, metaphysicians and anybody else who cannot tell 'Yankee Doodle' from 'Land of Hope and Glory'. It was so acclaimed. But the public being more music-minded than grey-mattered, the test of this as of every comic opera must be not cerebration, but ear-tickling. In my view *Derby Day* does not pass this test.

But it comes with flying colours through all the other tests. Mr. Herbert has been praised, and I shall only say that if there is a flaw in his wit, it is that he allows Haddock to monopolize too much of it and to tie him at the end into a knot which there is no untying.

> It wasn't beer that made me do it —
> It was your blasted horses!

sings Rose, forced to give some reason for petty thieving. Then Bert the tipster must sing:

> Every time your 'orses start
> 'Arf the country breaks its 'eart:
> The other 'arf they comes in 'ere
> And stands the other 'arf a beer.

But we understood the opera to be *in praise* of the horse, since did not the Prologue say:

> For the brave beast would whisper if he could:
> 'We may be going, but, by God, we're good!'

No, 'blasted horses' is a mistake, for which Haddock is responsible. Mr. Herbert is much better when he attunes himself to pure fun and makes delicate ladies aver that 'the favourite is sweating', or the bold, too-good Baronet apostrophize his entry: 'Beloved horse, attend, I pray; the Derby will be run to-day!'

Was it not Stevenson who complained of his heroine's trick of growing ugly, and his inability to prevent it? Despite one's best endeavour, this notice, which was intended to be almost wholly laudatory, has insisted upon running in the opposite direction. Let me now strongly, if belatedly, insist that there is an immense amount in this show to be mightily enjoyed. There is Mr. Sheringham's scene-setting — at the Old Black Horse, on the road to Epsom, in the stables, on the rails, and back again at the pub — which never vies with *Cavalcade* and keeps to the medium of the intimate theatre. There are the immensely high spirits of a very hard-working company, all of whom act reasonably well and some better. Miss Tessa Deane, who plays the heroine, has a charming voice which she has learned to use, and quite a notion of acting. That great wireless favourite, Miss Mabel Constanduros, as a tipster's mother, gains by being seen as well as heard. Is it possible that as the tempestuously teetotal Lady Waters, Miss Mabel Sealby is nearer to satiric than to dramatic truth? In comic opera all the parts which are not heroic must be comic to the eye, and therefore Lady Waters should, like the Lady Jane, belong to the outsize, in Nature as well as in opinion. Now since Miss Sealby is the nattiest actress the stage affords the part cannot be hers, though she provides miniature delight in plenty. The audience acclaimed, and rightly, Mr. Scott Russell's innkeeper.

But the best acting, *qua* acting, comes from Mr. Leslie French. It is hard lines that your versatile player cannot proclaim versatility, since the spectator who is unaware of this quality in its possessor values him no more than he does the one-part actor or mere self-exponent. Mr. French got as near a declaration as he could when he shyly, and I hope slyly, thanked Providence and Sir Nigel for presenting him this side of the water also, whereby some of us took to remembering him as Puck and Poins and Verges and Feste and the Fool in *Lear*. It cannot be thought that these are all one part or that a player who has brilliantly embodied them in any way resembles a tipster on the Downs. Let me admit that Mr. French's Bert Bones, being something too genteel, is not so photographic a performance as might have been given by some non-Shakespearean, musical-comedy buffoon. It is not so authentic an impersonation as that of, say, the costermonger's little donkey by the little donkey himself. In fact, Bert is the least convincing performance in the show. But it is easily the best piece of calculated art, and as such must be declared the winner by many lengths. Unidentifiable pearlies and their donahs act with incredible zest, and the whole show is a great deal better than, I fear, this notice implies.

February 24, 1932

MUSICAL PLAYS

THE DU BARRY

BY PAUL KNEPLER AND J. M. WILLEMINSKI.
ADAPTED BY ROWLAND LEIGH AND DESMOND
CARTER. MUSIC BY CARL MILLÖCKER

(His Majesty's)

I AGREE that it is a sound rule which forbids the critic to blame a
piece for not being something else of the same name. But rules
exist to be broken, and I cannot help pointing out what a play
about the du Barry might be. You would, I suggest, make a
loose-knitted affair of it in the chronicle manner, beginning with
Jeanne Bécu's life in the hat-shop of Madame Labille. This is the
place in which to introduce the early lover, and so demonstrate
to playgoers who care about such things that Jeanne, to begin
with, had the heart of a song-bird as well as the voice. It might
be objected that song-birds are less concerned with early lovers
than with early worms, that their brushing from upland lawn the
dews away is merely for the satisfaction of their insides, and that
to consider otherwise is to argue anthropocentrically, and therefore tommyrotically. But let that pass.

Act Two would show the dying, witty, still Skewtonizing Pompa-
dour, rouging her cheeks and begging her confessor to stay a little
so that they may depart together. Then would come Jeanne's
cohabitation with the Comte du Barry, that scoundrel's quick perception of the vacancy at Court, and the intolerable nuisance of an
existing Comtesse making marriage with Jeanne impossible, the
diabolical plan to marry her to his half-witted brother, the palm-
ing off of his sister-in-law and mistress on to the ageing, debilitated
King, and, if the chronicler be a man of skill, something about the
way Jeanne spent her time on half-holidays and Saturdays. And
if the chronicle must be musical, why not the *lever* of the King's
mistress with a ballet of jewellers, mercers, hairdressers, perfumers,
and anything else which the Cochran-Reinhardt-Messel-Massine

90

ménage might devise? Act Three, which ends this gay, eventful history, would show the King dying miserably and alone in tapered state on his high bed, with the ante-rooms full of a crowd whose excited chattering he can hear. Last we should be shown the du Barry at fifty, clothed in a coarse white shift, and her hair cut off, being taken screaming in a tumbril to the Place de la Révolution and passing on the way the Maison Labille, whose *gentil babil*, to use Verlaine's phrase, is now the Terror's tongue.

That, I suggest, would be a story worth telling, worth putting music, dresses, and scenery to, worth acting, worth seeing, and worth remembering, and as no modern theatre or opera house has use for the idea, I make a present of it to the screen, with the title 'Versailles Dances'. Again, the double catastrophe would comfort the Puritans, since it would show the vicious coming to a bad if long-deferred end, and thus be 'of a nice morality, split my windpipe!' But the British public preferring to split its windpipe in unmitigated guffaws, Mr. Stanley Scott, who presents this entertainment, has doubtless done wisely to eschew modern notions as to what historical play or even pageant might be and give us the operetta-stuff of fifty years ago, with a mannerless hoyden for a du Barry, a Louis Quinze lacking the rudiments of characterization, and not enough story to engross a child of twelve, but with plenty of comic relief and rhymes galore about dreaming and gleaming. But I do not think that rhyming need be quite so bad as:

> I will win applause
> From the spec-ta-tors.

Still harping on what passes for plot, could not something be done about the fourth scene, in which the Comte and his friends indulge in a protracted orgy of witlessness while behind them is being set the reception-room in Madame Sauterelle's *maison tolérée*? The dresses in this latter scene look as though their wearers are about to paddle, and the resulting display will remind some of us how twenty years ago we were not allowed to see a piece about these establishments, distantly alluded to in the text, which resolved itself into a discussion as to whether for waitresses at our great railway stations a weekly wage of fourteen shillings was adequate. When, however, there *are* dresses, they are both voluminous and exquisite.

Mr. Aubrey Hammond, who is responsible for the scenery, has taken his responsibility with admirable seriousness, and I attribute to my too great proximity to the stage the notion that the garret of the poet René had been 'done out' in ordinary ink, while for the uncrowned queens' parlour the decorators had run to the more expensive or fountain-pen variety. I think, too, that Mr. Hammond has not yet 'tumbled' to the limitations imposed upon modern scene-designers by the revolving stage, whereby everything at Versailles appears to be happening in the corner of a room, with the result that Mr. Hammond's vigorous and beautiful scenery comes to resemble a large over-dressed woman sitting on too exiguous a chair. The music is tuneful and lively, though it is a pity that Jeanne's song, so conscientiously plugged, should be one of the plainest melodies that can ever have occurred to the human mind. The ballet-dancing, which to me is the art of not tumbling over oneself, resolves itself on the diminished stage into that of not tumbling over the furniture, and here a troupe of young ladies headed by Miss Mimi Crawford extricates itself featly while wearing the fixed smile of maximum apprehension.

This brings me to the acting, which means Fräulein Anny Ahlers, by whom the piece must either stand or fall. Which? The answer is neither, since it towers! Of a performance of Cleopatra by Janet Achurch twenty-five years ago Mr. Shaw wrote that it could be but faintly accounted for by the passions of that heroine complicated by seventy-times-sevenfold demoniacal possession, that he could bear it only by holding on tightly to the elbows of his stall, that he would not unsee it if he could, but that ever since he had been a broken man. This exactly describes how Fräulein Ahlers affects me.

In my boobyish way I imagined the du Barry to be a typically French milliner's apprentice with a knowledge of how many beans made five even in royal parterres, the rapacious little figure some-

thing suffused with the tenderness of the colour which was to bear
her name. But with the Fräulein such anaemic stuff won't wash.
At her first entrance she presents the complete Amazon, militant
Valkyrie, and Germanic Fury, all three at maximum pressure.
Early on in the play, and while living in a state of single iniquity
with a poet, she has refused the advances and purse of the Comte
who, finding her later in the establishment of Madame Sauterelle,
naturally offers her marriage, a proposition so insulting that
Jeanne has no option but to 'throw a Dietrich', if I may so express
myself. This she does with the energy of a railway-engine compelled to let off five million foot-pounds of steam in thirty seconds,
and so that her lightest trumpeting resembles that brassy Prelude
to the third act of *Lohengrin*.

There is no question of liking or disliking Fräulein Ahlers: the
liking is compulsory, and complete when you get used to it, like
a morning plunge into the German Ocean. This actress can do
nothing on a small scale, and I implore her never to wink, since
with her that operation attains the magnitude of drawing the
blinds at a royal palace! More seriously, it should be said that such
vitality is altogether unknown among our lighter English actresses;
her appearance over here will obviously do a world of good. Her
singing voice is magnificent, and again I think that on this
occasion not the fourth row of stalls but some other part of the
Haymarket would have been more convenient.

Mr. Heddle Nash, as the du Barry's lover-in-waiting, has to do
too much waiting, since he must spend limitless periods dropping
furtive lagrime off-stage. Mr. Nash sings beautifully, and acts as
tenors act. A fine performance comes from Mr. Lawrence Ander-
son, who is every inch a King and a good many inches of this one.
Miss Margaret Yarde is superb as the bonnet-shop's Miss Knag,
though her blossoming forth as the *patronne* in that other establishment with the same young ladies must in any realist excite
surprise. Mr. Edmund Willard acts the Comte very much as he
would act Oliver Cromwell, and as various eighteenth-century
political somebodies various actors convince themselves, though
such pronunciations as 'dooshess' and 'Goosestarve' for 'duchesse'

MUSICAL PLAYS

and 'Gustave' hardly convince us. Miss Helen Haye, with a groat's
worth of part, contributes a guinea's worth of acting, and Miss
Clarice Hardwicke and Mr. Charles Heslop easily get the better
of the comic relief. Mr. Ernest Irving, conducting with much skill
and spirit, demonstrates the idiocy of sending abroad for artists
no better than those we have at home.

April 14, 1932

CLANCARTY

ADAPTED BY PERCY NASH FROM THE DRAMA BY TOM
TAYLOR. MUSIC BY H. WOLSELEY CHARLES

(Winter Garden)

ABSENCE makes the stage grow fonder; or so my return to duty
teaches. Only extreme simplicity could have suggested dis-
interring these old bones and bedecking them with new music.
The operatic Sullivan was mute till he found Gilbert; Mr. Wolseley
Charles should have wedded his pleasant tunes to some living wit.
Tom Taylor to-day is as dead as a door-nail, and to the modern
way of thinking must have been just as dead when he drew breath
and wrote *Lady Clancarty*. In describing itself as 'a musical dramatic romance' this new version of an always absurd but in its day
conceivable melodrama tries to make the best of three worlds and
succeeds in respect of one of them. As stage success goes, this is not
a bad proportion. It shall be firmly said that Mr. Charles's music
is tuneful; one could without nausea anticipate the inevitable
reprises. But there unqualified commendation ceases, since the rest
of the entertainment is devised along lines which Beaumarchais
did not live to see, or he would have written: 'Ce qui ne vaut pas
la peine d'être chanté, on le dit!'
The reason is plain. Things other than hope spring eternal in
the human breast. Bosh, and the love of it, for example, though
not, I hasten to say, in the minds of playwrights but in those for
whom playwrights cater. Tom Taylor, though a Victorian, was

94

no fool, and having read his Macaulay realized that while truth may be stranger than the novel-reader supposes, historic fact is hardly ever dramatic enough to satisfy your theatre-goer. In saying, then, that 'this play has the advantage of being founded on fact' the programme is a trifle disingenuous. This play isn't founded on anything of the sort; it is based on Taylor's titivation of Macaulay's facts. Mind you, Macaulay, in vulgar parlance, asked for it, for the last volume of that readable but now unread History contains a categorical invitation to some dramatist to come forward and dramatize Clancarty.

His Irish Lordship was married at the age of fifteen to the eleven-year-old daughter of the Earl of Sunderland. The pair were parted immediately after the ceremony and did not meet again for many years, during which the Earl attached himself to the unfortunate James II, suffered imprisonment in the Tower, escaped to the Continent, and returned to make peace with the new King. He found an ally in his wife, but enemies in her father and brother. Sent again to the Tower, he was rescued, not by the wit of Lady Clancarty, but by Lady Russell, who obtained from King William pardon for the rebel on condition that he should leave the country and never return. Actually Clancarty did leave the country and never did return, and what happened to him history neither knows nor cares enough to invent.

Not so Tom Taylor, who knew what leading men and, *a fortiori*, leading ladies demand of history. Tom had by heart the kind of laws the drama's patrons give, one of them being that Jacobite plotters must conspire only in smugglers' dens, and another that husband and wife long separated must, as the result of a broken-down coach, meet as strangers and fall in love guiltily as they suppose. To render this mutual non-knowledge possible the couple must be supposed to have gone to church direct from their cradles, and, indeed, at the Winter Garden Lady Clancarty vouchsafes the equivalent of Gilbert's:

Ah, how we loved, that child and I!
How pure our baby joy!

MUSICAL PLAYS

Then what is the use, Tom Taylor probably asked himself, of having a plot to assassinate a King if you don't mix your hero up in it, so that entering his unbeknownst wife's bedroom he may be suspected of being an extraordinary seducer, when actually he is merely an ordinary fugitive?

So much for the duties of commission. How about those of omission? Lady Russell, of course, has to go. Clancarty's wife has enough to put up with by being a wife in name only, to adopt the phrase honoured by time and the gallery; no leading lady with any spirit in her is going to stand by while another woman saves her husband's neck. Wherefore on Thursday night last there was no Lady Russell. How her Ladyship escaped widow-hood and her husband the block I cannot depose, since my watch showed nineteen minutes past eleven, and irrelevant coryphées were still giving their version of 'Les Sylphides' on the margin of a duck-pond in Birdcage Walk.

The play was well shouted, the players taking their note from the team of coach-horses which in the first act provided a greater clattering than the Four Horsemen of the Apocalypse. Clancarty was sung but not acted by Mr. Dale Smith. But, then, I gather that Mr. Smith, who is immensely tall, is a newcomer to the stage, and I shall assume that a big man takes more teaching than a little one. In any case the part calls for all the charm, address, and skill of a Fred Terry, and even he must have failed in it with a modern audience.

Miss Enid Cruikshank did extremely well as long as she was allowed to clasp her hands and deal with arias entitled respectively 'Dreams' and 'Wonderful Dreams' in that operatic manner which contrives to be at once hell-for-leather and spell-bound. Miss Cruikshank is obviously an experienced artist well up in the Verdi country and a good Wagnerian fencer. But as your heavy-weight hunter does not 'come about' as easily as a polo-pony, so an artist accustomed to top-weight tragedy must always find it difficult to diminish herself to the petty astonishments of a Lady Clancarty. Miss Cruikshank has the physique for a Colonel of Valkyries, and could with one hand have brushed off the smuggler who en-

96

deavoured to snatch a kiss. Being rescued from a situation of no
difficulty, Lady Clancarty must archly invite the gallery to name
that fate from which intervention has saved her! It takes a Siddons
to do this successfully, and on Thursday night the Siddons herself
would have failed. But when Lady Clancarty, who could obviously have controlled a Hyde Park mob by the sheer power of
her eye, was not pleading the physical frailty of her sex and its
dependence for moral and spiritual guidance on the manlier
other — when, to put it bluntly, she was not compelled to behave
like an utter and abject fool, Miss Cruikshank was very good
indeed. Alas, that folly would keep creeping in! For example,
Lady Clancarty would ask what somebody meant by tapping at
her window 'at this hour', having just chosen it as a suitable one
to prance about her bedroom in Delilah-cum-Ortrud trappings
and deliver to her four-poster Mr. Charles's version of Elizabeth's
Greeting. Miss Cruikshank managed this aria militantly and well,
after which she must at the stranger's approach change colour and
assume maidenly alarm. This cannot and could not be done.

Mr. Franklin Dyall, an actor whose wits are always about him,
could not fail to realize the advantage of speaking in a natural
voice when everybody else was shouting. The result could only be
cataclysmically effective. I think, however, that in 1695 William
of Orange had been King long enough to know where his pocket
was and replace his handkerchief without fumbling. And why
did that King always go out of the room last? In order to avoid
getting knifed? If so, we applaud an example of Dutch sagacity
if not courage.

September 3, 1933

MUSICAL PLAYS

GAY DIVORCE

BY DWIGHT TAYLOR.   MUSIC BY COLE PORTER

(Palace)

WHEN early on in the piece so good an actor as Mr. Clifford
Heatherley faded out, one prepared for the best or the worst
according as the show was discarding from strength or weakness.
Was the acting talent so strong that Mr. Heatherley could be
safely dispensed with, or so poor that to avoid the danger of comparison Mr. Heatherley had better be got out of the way? It
turned out to be the latter. Mr. Heatherley was the one Court
card which prevented the hand from being a Yarborough, though
as will be revealed later one espied a good-looking ten and a
couple of useful nines. These could doubtless have acted but for
a natural law which I now discover and lay down. The name I
give this is the Law of Deepening Imbecility, and it insists that in
the matter of shameless idiocy Art must always go one better than
Nature. In other words, even if the acting profession were to set
itself to breed players of utter mindlessness the provider of musical-
comedy plots must spin one even more mindless. More plainly,
musical comedy will always be so unactable that actors are best
out of the way.

The present plot is about a young married woman anxious for
divorce who mistakes the man she really loves for the professional
co-respondent hired for her by her lawyers. This is not to be
played, and no attempt was made to play it, though the players
adhered rigidly, as to diet, to the words set down for them, while
a concourse of peers and peeresses, nobles and ignobles, and the
leading lights of bench, bar, medicine, art, letters, fashion and
the beauty parlour waited Micawberishly for something to
turn up. Presently Mr. Fred Astaire obliged, and there is really
no more to be said.

A very distinguished colleague began his criticism of this show
by asking what is Mr. Astaire's secret, but like somebody else on

another occasion did not wait to give us the answer. May I suggest to my pudic contemporary that the solution hangs on a little word of three letters whose appeal is as constant as that of the hospitals? Mr. Astaire's secret is that of the late Rudolf Valentino and of Mr. Maurice Chevalier, happily still with us — sex. But sex so bejewelled and beglamoured and be-pixied that the weaker vessels who fall for it can pretend that it isn't sex at all but a sublimated, Barriesque projection of the Little Fellow with the Knuckles in his Eyes. You would have thought by the look of the first-night foyer that it was Mothering Thursday, since every woman in the place was urgent to take to her chinchilla'd bosom this waif with the sad eyes and twinkling feet. It was a great night, for on it Mr. Astaire was born again to the London stage, a star danced, and the mother which is in every woman cried. But what about those of us who are not mothers? To the dull, doltish, impercipient male eye it would appear that Mr. Astaire is neither a stage-shaking dancer nor a world-shaking actor. As a dancer he is not in the Nijinsky class, nor in the Lifar class, nor yet the Lichine nor the Dolin. When he mounts into the air it is by means of a chair and a table, and his descents are similarly accomplished. Nor, I think, has he the gloom and majesty for Brahmsian ecstasy.

You say that he does not attempt these things, which is what I want you to say. But in my poor judgment neither is Mr. Astaire one of The Three Eddies, to whom he stands in the relation of quaver to demi-semiquavers. But perhaps Mr. Astaire does not attempt this either. Then what in heaven's name does he attempt? I take it to be that hybrid known as ballroom dancing, an art which is compounded equally of the lithe, sinuous panther, the lissom, supple gigolo, and the light-shod, look-slippy waiter who can steer a tray and twenty-four glasses through a crowd without a spill. Even so, there were ballroom dancers before Astaire. And now, for a change, let us say a few nice things. This charming actor wears the ineffably sad expression that was Jimmy Wilde's up to the moment the gong sounded, and James Welch's in a score of plays, that Tiny Tim and Poor Jo had their share of, and that choirboys put on with their surplices and leave off in the vestry. 'Chaplin in the flesh!' said some swooning soul as her eyes closed over the smelling salts tendered by her husband with the gift of prevision.

The remarkable thing about this great little artist is that he *is* a great little artist. Whereas Valentino and other oily dagoes have been wholly repugnant to male sense, Mr. Astaire does nothing to offend, whence it must be argued that his charm has some of Ariel's quality. He is, then, as companionable to the mind as his body is marriageable to that of his dancing-partner. The least knowing judge of dancing can perceive that it is only when Mr. Astaire's art is, so to speak, wedded that it arrives at its full perfection. It was said of Kean that he acted 'all round' people; Mr. Astaire dances all round Miss Claire Luce, now shepherding her, now buttressing, here giving her the floor, and there taking it with her in mutual rapture. It is legerdemain accomplished with the whole body, with the result that the eye endlessly follows that which in second-rate artists is second nature, but in first-rate talent is Nature itself.

Miss Luce is a highly accomplished dancer, and given something humanly possible to act might be a considerable actress. Miss Olive Blakeney once more sits around rattling off wisecracks with machine-gun persistence, and with her rapier-like intelligence puncturing the gas-bags of that false romanticism with which musical comedy's lungs are filled. It shows the wilful waste of our stage that the most Shavian of our actresses should not be acting in Shaw. Mr. Erik Rhodes gives a superb *buffa* performance as a spoof Italian, and provides the one moment in which, incredible to relate, irony is allowed to put in an appearance. The business in life of this Wop is that of a professional co-respondent, whose first thought on taking up his nocturnal quarters is to telephone messages of reassurance to the wife of his bosom. This actor must be heard of again, and it is pleasant to renew acquaintance with Mr. Eric Blore in the well-written and highly diverting part of a waiter who is also curiously Shavian.

November 5, 1933

THE GOLDEN TOY

BY CARL ZÜCKMAYER. MUSIC BY SCHUMANN

(Coliseum)

WHAT shall we say of Sir Oswald Stoll's long-heralded production at the Coliseum? Schumann's music? Utterly charming, and the cognoscenti were able to nod their heads in recognition of 'The Merry Peasant', 'Dreaming', 'Why?' and to their fair partners skilfully differentiate nightpiece from album-leaf. More seriously there was some entrancing stuff out of the symphonies, which sounded less muddy than usual perhaps because seven people have had a hand in the orchestration, and it would appear that too many cooks cannot do other than clarify Schumann's broth. Mr. René Hubert's costumes? Utterly delightful, and in their own sense, by which I mean that Mrs. Calthrop was not plagiarized, Miss Zinkeisen plundered, or Mr. Messel pillaged. The dancing? Also very nice, and Miss Ninette de Valois knows so well how to deal with exiguity of space that she must be our first authority on how many angels can dance on the point of a needle.

This brings me to the scenery, which clutters up the peripatetic stage with chunks of papier-mâché splendour to make constructors of White Cities and the like green with envy. I have never been on an Underground River or a Montagne Russe to compare with Dr. Ludwig Berger's gaieties, in comparison with which even the rock garden on Southend front pales its ineffectual fire. But surely at some time or other in the evening it must have struck somebody that the more this scenery changes, the more it remains the same thing? The ringing grooves of change are two, each of which can presumably accommodate four sets, and not even the genius of Dr. Berger can make twice four into more than eight. So we solemnly attend while seven familiar scenes revolving in darkness bring round the illuminated eighth, which on reacquaintance does not become any more novel. In fact, I could not help being reminded of a famous passage in Peacock. Mr. Gall, you will remember, after distinguishing the picturesque from the beautiful, said: 'I add to them, in the laying out of grounds, a third and distinct character, which I call *unexpectedness*.' 'Pray, sir', retorted Mr. Milestone, 'by what name do you distinguish this character, when a person walks round the grounds for the second time?' Is it lawful to ask by what name Dr. Berger would like us to call the unexpectedness of his eight scenes recurring as punctually as any decimal?

The play? Divorced from orgy, the old Indian legend on which this spectacle is based is a delicious affair about a little lady who asks whether it is possible for a girl to keep her heart virgin for some lover if fate has previously condemned her to belong to men she has not cared for. The question is an old one and has probably been asked in all the countries of the world. The Japanese geisha has doubtless received her answer in the form of a No play, and only last week I was reading a novel in which a young lady who had preferred life in a house of ill fame to the humdrum ignominy of a millinery establishment emerged from her blameworthy haunt whiter than the driven snow. When Mr. Arthur Symons made a version of this play he eked out its plot with his own wit and wisdom. Dr. Berger, being under the necessity of piling lots of Pelion on multiple Ossas to suit the revolutions of the Coliseum stage, has swollen the legend much beyond its proper size. But then what else can a man do at whose forehead is levelled a revolving stage?

This producer has realized, too, that English predilection for buffoonery whereby hang most of Shakespeare's tales. The result at the Coliseum is that the play turns out to be nearly all Porter and very little Macbeth. There is a great deal too much of clowning put in with the obvious intention of giving the groundlings something to go on with. Now it is notorious that the business of the low comedian in an English musical show is to bring his own straw with him if he wants to make any bricks, and Mr. Lupino Lane has unfortunately bought his at what must be the cheapest straw-factor's in the country. Threatened with being boiled in oil, he says: 'Don't boil me for more than three minutes or I shall be hard!' and this miserable jape is perhaps his wittiest sally. Miss Nellie Wallace also is forced in virtue of her part to be completely under the weather, and one had not thought that an Indian summer could be so glum.

The more serious portions of the play are in the hands of a shining cast, whose brilliance is snuffed out by the mere tonnage of the scenery and the necessity of skipping out of the way before the next avalanche is due. Miss Peggy Ashcroft is condemned to be plaintive on spurs and eminences more suited to a chamois than an actress. Mr. Ion Swinley declaims apostrophes to passion which he would probably be ashamed to whisper. As a mysterious priest, Mr. Ernest Thesiger looks like a Hindoo idol that has strayed into Caledonian Market and does not know what to make of his surroundings; this clever actor takes refuge in an air which contrives to be at once contemplative and wry. Mr. George Hayes as a burglar and elephant-keeper brings off miracles of appositeness to completely no purpose. But why is he not allowed to keep the elephant when he or she appears?

Mr. Wilfrid Lawson is excellent as the villain of the piece, though it is a pity he cannot invent another voice and must continually impress one like some throaty tenor essaying: 'If With All Your Hearts' at some provincial and choral whoopee. Miss Wendy Toye dances with zest and grace. But the whole show boils down to the chorus, which is all a-simmer and a-shimmer, its loveliness being like the lids of Juno's eyes. Only dimmer.

March 4, 1934

GLAMOROUS NIGHT

WORDS AND MUSIC BY IVOR NOVELLO

(Drury Lane)

MR. IVOR NOVELLO has devised an entertainment so excellent in its fripperies that it is a pity he bothered about a story which is both steep and flat. It begins well. We first meet the hero, young

Anthony Allen, emerging from his suburban home on a wet morning and at the hour when typists set chatteringly forth. This is a clever little scene of unspoken wit. Anthony is an inventor, and for his new television apparatus seeks the help of Lord Radio, who turns to it a deaf ear and rumbling stomach.

But Anthony is a trier and does not give up his idea of a machine which shall show us things happening exactly as they happen and while they are actually taking place. Point the nozzle of Anthony's contraption at, say, Krasnia, and it will show on our dining-room walls the way Krasnians behave in fact, as opposed to the fancy of the romantic novelist. This means that people who, when a hare is started under their feet and noses, like to follow its doublings, will try to pin this plot down to the terms in which it is stated. Obviously Mr. Novello must now take us to Krasnia and show, beneath ostensible resemblance to the tarradiddles of lying romantics, the stern, stark realities of existence plain and prosaic in Krasnia as everywhere else. I confess to being a little perplexed here. Will the pictures to be flashed on Anthony's screen give us a direct view of these realities, or will they show us something looking on the surface like life as lived in the pages of *The Prisoner of Zenda*, and leave to the intelligent minds the job of detecting the difference? In any case the programme has told us that the invention doesn't happen till the last scene, and there are three hours to fill in.

The first glimpse of Krasnia consists, quite rightly, in twenty-four Hussars lined up in front of a curtain and singing a rousing song entitled 'Her Majesty Militza'. This is strange, since Militza is King Stefan's mistress and not his Queen, and irony in Hussars is misplaced. We are at the fifth scene before we are introduced to the lady, an imperious Miss whose talent for tantrums is only equalled by her knack for sacrificing herself to such desperate things as alfresco weddings and hot-house renunciations. Militza is a light-opera singer, and as this is Drury Lane and Mr. Coward in *Cavalcade* had a fragment of a musical comedy, Mr. Novello presumably feels impelled to give us a slab of operetta. Now if, to put it vulgarly, the object was to wipe a predecessor's eye, the attempt signally fails and is bound to, because Mr. Coward has a remarkable flair for parody and Mr. Novello a less bountiful gift for serious operetta. Quite between ourselves, and in the general matter of building up Drury Lane spectacle on the airiest of foundations, it seems to me that obvious rivalry should have been shunned rather than courted. In other words, I hold that particular eye to be unwipeable!

In the seventh scene, outside the Opera House, Mr. Oliver Messel first finds his form in a sombre yet exciting setting for a Petroushka-like ballet, in the middle of which Militza appears in a carriage drawn by prancing horses. Somebody now fires a pistol at Militza either in her capacity as opera-singer, for we note that the crowd has not taken the horses out of the carriage, or in her rôle as royal mistress and in consequence of a political plot vaguely started in the previous scene.

Next we find ourselves on board the *Silver Star*, where Militza is pleasure-cruising. The skating waltz contributed by the other pleasure-cruisers is the second best thing in the show, being really well devised and executed. Presumably the dancers are too busy to notice an iceberg gravely looming, and one perceives no officer except the ship's purser, a functionary who, one understands, need not be nautically minded. There should, however, be time to notice this floating promontory during 'Shanty Town', a tedious 'blue' contributed by a stowaway negress. This ended, somebody throws a knife at Militza, whereupon the ship proceeds to founder! Actually it sinks about a couple of feet, and the genius of even a Waygood-Otis must regret that no ship can be made to sink lower than the ocean-floor capacity of the theatre. Much effect, how-ever, is produced by twopenn'orth of escaping steam; obviously the frenzied passengers only refrain from taking to the water because if they do they will land in the well of the orchestra; the curtain comes down, and the audience comes up for a breather well needed after two exhausting hours.

The second act, like that in any other well-conducted panto-mime, shows us shipwrecked hero and heroine patrolling desert beach in seemly rags but without the fashionable pyjamas. Now

follows a gipsy wedding, the principal figures of which are Anthony
and Militza. The local colour here is borrowed from *Carmen* and
the music from Brahms, while the abandoned peasants indulge in
something between a Polonaise and a Bolero, ending in exhaustion
like the orgy in *Helen!* Mr. Novello, making the best of lots of
worlds, here gives us the best thing in the show, and the fact that
the atmosphere is a little derivative should be put down to the
Euclidean rule that composers truthfully setting the same thing
must resemble one another. There is no reason why this rule
should not apply to the gipsies of Borovnik, or why Mr. Novello
for his Borovnikian dances should not borrow din from *Prince Igor*.
However this may be, we leave the lovers *enfin seuls*. Or rather it
is they who leave us, since they must retire to a nuptial couch
situated apparently on highest peak of ultimate Dolomite.

It is now a quarter to eleven, and one thinks that if Mr. Novello
proposes to show us the difference between the Krasnia of fiction
and the Krasnia of fact he should be setting about it. So from
Dolomite to dungeon, where somebody has captured the king and
the chief villain is forcing him to abdicate at the point of the
revolver. And would succeed had not Anthony rallied his bride's
gipsy folk and surrounded the dungeon, through whose window
he shoots the chief villain. It is now eleven o'clock, and some will
think it too late to spring upon Militza the question of whether
she shall accompany her husband to England or remain in
Krasnia to be divorced and ascend the Krasnian throne. But
Militza is a good girl who has read her *Prisoner of Zenda* and all
the rest of it, and quickly realizes that while her heart will be
ever with Anthony in his inventor's Studio not a thousand miles
from Portland Place, her person must remain in Krasnia. So in
what is known as the Palace Scene — a very handsome set by
Mr. Messel — she announces her decision to a glittering crowd. We
are now ready to return to England and the Studio, but as there
is yet another big set to be prepared the stowaway negress has to
be sent on to sing a lugubrious cabaret number. Finally, the
nozzle of Anthony's device is pointed at a dark screen, which gives
us a televized view of the wedding of King Stefan and Militza

apparently taking place, like Hermit's Derby, in a snowstorm. In what way this shows the victory of Krasnian fact over Ruritanian fancy I really don't know.

May 5, 1935

CREST OF THE WAVE

BY IVOR NOVELLO

(Drury Lane)

DOWAGER DUCHESS OF CHEVIOT: This doesn't mean a thing.
DUKE OF CHEVIOT: Not a thing.

OUTSIDE our National Theatre cordons of police held back hundreds of autograph-seekers. Inside, hundreds of autograph-givers had congregated. The audience largely consisted of Privy Councillors, Elder Brethren, Hereditary Legislators, Film Stars, Mannequins and Lovelies. As the conductor advanced to his rostrum a Parsifalian hush reigned, broken only by the crackle of a too-stout shirtfront and the rustle of an ill-mannered ruby. A Mongolian would have realized that this was the drama nearest to the British heart, the white elephant for which stables of porphyry and rose-pink marble are presently to be erected.

Crusaders chorused. These were the ancestors of the House of Cheviot, or perhaps I mean Gantry, since heraldic minutiæ always elude me. Anyway, Gantry Castle was the seat of the Dukes of Cheviot, on one or other side of Tweed. The present owner of the title was broke, and the family apparently subsisted on the sixpences paid by visitors desirous of viewing this malachite table or that onyx mantelpiece, presented by the Sultan of Turkey to the sixth Duke. One by one we were introduced to the family: first the butler; next a pyjama'd figure causing maidens to cling rapturously together and whisper audibly: 'He's thinner.' The maidens were wrong, just as they were wrong in the early years of this century when they applauded the actor who played Meynard in *The Corsican Brothers*, in the belief that he was Mr. Martin Harvey, and just as they had been wrong in 1880 when they acclaimed Mr. A. W. Pinero playing the same part, and under the impression that he was Irving. This slim young man was not the Duke of Cheviot, but the negligible Lord William Gantry (Mr. Peter Graves). Next came Virginia, widow of the former Duke (Miss Marie Löhr) and a lady of some fun. At least she speared a breakfast kidney, and, holding it to her bosom, said: 'If you don't want to eat it you can use it as a brooch.' Which flashing sally was held for wit by the assembled Privy Councillors, Elder Brethren, Hereditary Legislators, Film Stars, Mannequins and Lovelies.

But anticipation was not long in fulfilment, for now a figure in riding-breeches haughtily descended the stairs, and by the breeches and the haughtiness one realized that this must be His Grace himself. It was. It was also more than a mere theatrical Duke. It was Mr. Ivor Novello, and, as they say at film receptions, in person. Very little older, not a whit more rotund, with chin aloof as of yore and the aristocratic gaze of Mr. Beerbohm's Lord Byron about to spurn honest English dust in favour of some greasy foreign soil.

To this family in distress entered a lady snake (Miss Ena Burrill) poised on her tail and garbed with that sheathlike simplicity which betokens the villainess ready to strike. At the moment her intention was the comparatively innocuous one of buying Gantry Castle on behalf of English Quota Films. His Grace indignantly refused to sell, and would have continued in his indignation if he had not confused the snake's principal — for in the film world snakes have principals — with an underbred, generous-hearted little chorus girl of the same initials (Miss Dorothy Dickson). Dropping reptilian analogy, let me say that the villainess had no principals of any kind, was acting in her proper person, had fallen in love with His Grace, that her name was Helen Winter, and that His Grace mistook her for Honey Wortle. We next saw a production number 'featuring' Versailles, in which Mr. Ivor Novello doubled the part of Otto Fresch, an ageing film star. The Duchess was now hired by a steamship company to give tone to a pleasure cruise, and presently Her Grace, His Grace, Miss Winter, Miss Wortle, and Miss Wortle's Mamma all embarked. Then came a magnificent scene in which the pleasure cruiser was transformed into a battleship with guns emerging from their turrets and trained to annihilate the audience of Privy Councillors, Elder Brethren, Hereditary Legislators, Film Stars, Mannequins and Lovelies.

But Mr. Novello had not yet arrived at the apex of either his spectacle or his drama. We were therefore treated to a version of the second act of *Carmen*, the décor of Lillas Pastia, and all requisite appurtenances. 'Je vais danser en votre honneur,' trilled Honey Wortle. In return for which Helen Winter emptied a revolver into the small of Honey Wortle's ducal lover's back. After which the curtain descended and the grand staircase was filled with Privy Councillors, Elder Brethren, and Hereditary Legislators giving their arms to Film Stars, Mannequins and Lovelies fainting with emotion.

When we returned to these revels His Grace, whose perforations had healed, was now an impoverished film extra supporting Honey Wortle, who had become a film star of the first magnitude. It now appeared that all unknown to himself His Grace possessed a genius exceeding even that of Mr. Robert Taylor, which so annoyed Helen Winter that she arranged with Otto Fresch to wreck the train in which Honey was travelling to attend a film première. The penultimate scene was outside Gantry Castle on Christmas night in deep snow. Outside the ducal lodge and with a full view of the ducal drive leading to the ducal mansion, His Grace, in faultless evening dress, was holding colloquy with the Dowager Duchess, for by this time the Duke and Honey had been made one. 'This doesn't mean a thing,' said the Dowager Duchess. 'Not a thing,' said the Duke. 'But, oh, how wrong,' inwardly chorused the Privy Councillors, Elder Brethren, Hereditary Legislators, Film Stars, Mannequins and Lovelies. 'It means the Entire British Drama!' Last scene of all was the great hall of Gantry Castle filled with tenantry and vassalage. 'I cannot tell

you how deeply I regret that Her Grace cannot be with you,'
said the Duke. 'Perhaps next year. The doctors are afraid she
may never walk again.' Whereupon Her Grace walked in without
crutches, and brought this stilted drama to a conclusion. And
Privy Councillors, Elder Brethren, Hereditary Legislators, Film
Stars, Mannequins, and Lovelies, all deeply disturbed, left the
playhouse, resolving to support that National Theatre which is to
give us more and more waves with bigger and bigger crests. I
myself am still under too deep a stress of emotion to do more than
thank Mr. Novello for his latest contribution to a drama which has
supplanted Shakespeare in the breasts of Privy Councillors, Elder
Brethren, Hereditary Legislators, Film Stars, Mannequins and
Lovelies.

Mastering that emotion, however, I declare the music, dancing
(by Mr. Walter Crisham), and all the acting to have sparkle —
altogether a very jolly show if only one could look on it in any old
clothes, with leave to smoke, and without the silly pretence that
Here We Have an Artistic Event of National Importance. Not
that Mr. Novello pretends. He knows better. *The Happy Hypocrite*
taught him not to trust the British public with anything except
sheer, unadulterated bosh. Then who does pretend? Why, the
Privy Councillors, Elder Brethren, Hereditary Legislators, Film
Stars, Mannequins and Lovelies!

September 2, 1937

FRITZI

BY SYDNEY BLOW AND EDWARD ROYCE. MUSIC BY CARL TUCKER

(Adelphi)

'LET us have no meandering!' said the old lady in *David Copperfield*,
and on the whole I agree. But there are times when meandering is expedient and even unavoidable. Suppose, for example,
that by some freak of fate you were bidden to cross a field and

charged to take an hour over it. You would, I think, meander, and I shall not argue with the pernickety who desire to know how big was the field. There is the case of the journalist between whom and the foot of his column yawns an illimitable void, and I scorn the objection that the foot of the column limits it. Now let me narrow this down to the dramatic critic with nothing to say and the whole week to say it in. Nothing? Well, hardly anything! Let us, therefore, meander.

Few things are more tragic, or more comic, than those works of art which are born with the dust of oblivion in thick descent upon them. The still-born masterpiece has its peculiar pathos: the author has failed, and there's an end of it. The works I mean, and whose fate seems to me to be so ludicrously tragic, are those in which the author has aimed at posterity and missed it in his own day. Fishing recently in the second-hand boxes of the Charing Cross Road I hooked three out of the four volumes of the *Mémoires* of Ernest Legouvé, member of the French Academy. When this worthy died I know not; it is difficult enough to discover when, if ever, he was alive. Little is known of him except that he was the collaborator of Scribe in *Adrienne Lecouvreur*, that first-class second-rate play which is still so much better than anything that anybody, except possibly Mr. Emlyn Williams, is writing for the theatre to-day. (A perambulator meandering in a field would relieve his boredom by taking a pot-shot at a rabbit if he saw one; this must be my excuse for casually pinking the entire British dramaturgy!) At one moment in Scribe and Legouvé's play Adrienne recites La Fontaine's fable of 'Les Deux Pigeons', the piece chosen by Sarah Bernhardt for her entrance examination for the Conservatoire. Hardly had she got to the end of the second line when Auber, at the head of the jury, stopped her and told her she was admitted. Mr. Maurice Baring has said of this recitation: 'When Sarah Bernhardt played Adrienne Lecouvreur she used to recite the opening of that fable, and one felt as one heard it that for the perfect utterance of beautiful words this was the Pillars of Hercules of mortal achievement, that it was impossible to speak verse more beautifully.' Dame Madge Kendal once said to me: 'I heard Sarah recite "Les Deux Pigeons" in a drawing-room. I did not watch Sarah but the audience, and whatever it was she made the pigeons say and do, the effect on the audience was improper!' The answer to that is that the effect of anything and everything on Dame Madge was improper! Now, what were we talking about? Perhaps the next paragraph will tell us.

Of Scribe and his quality sufficient is known to realize why Heine, dying, said he had not enough breath left to hiss one of M. Scribe's comedies. Legouvé talks a great deal about Halévy who, with Hector Crémieux, wrote the words of *Orphée aux Enfers* and with Henri Meilhac that famous *succès de larmes*, *Frou-Frou*, and the opérettes *La Belle Hélène*, *La Grande Duchesse de Gerolstein*, *Toto chez Tata* and scores more, all in the genre of which our little piece so patiently waiting for notice is the legitimate successor. Returning, however, to that poor mutton, Legouvé, it is a strange irony that in the first of the volumes, discovered as I say in the Charing Cross Road, I should find him lamenting the faded glory of a personage with the altogether frightening name of Népomucène Lemercier. This individual was the friend of Napoleon, and, according to Talleyrand, the most brilliant chatterbox in Paris. Remembering what *Le Cid* had done for Corneille and *Andromaque* for Racine, the good Népomucène thought fit to burst upon the public with a drama which could only have been called *Agamemnon*. Lemercier wrote tragedies for thirty years. He tried a fall with Dante in a poem with the remarkable name of *La Panhypocrisiade* and with André Chénier in an astronomical, geological, natural-historical affair entitled *L'Atlantiade*. Where are these prodigious pieces now? Yet their author wrote nothing, according to his own confession, without asking himself what Corneille, Sophocles, and Shakespeare would have thought of it. He prefaces his struggle with the mighty spirit of Dante with the following remarkable address:

Imperishable poet, where will you receive my letter? I address it to you in those unknown regions which immortality makes free to the sublime soul of genius. Imagination, that winged messenger, will bear my letter to you in the realms where my spirit soars. Show this poem, when you have read it down to its last line, to Michael Angelo, to Shakespeare, and even to Rabelais, and if its originality appears to them to consort with your gigantic invention, then ask what sort of a future they see for it. Perhaps they will behold twenty editions before a hundred years have rolled away.

Yet we must not be led by this fanfaronade entirely to despise the good Népomucène. He was paralysed down one side, and when he walked must hold himself together with his one good hand. In this condition he fought a sword duel. Like Byron, he must swim, box, and ride better than the physically perfect; his acts of courage and of passion were protests against Nature. It was Lemercier who persuaded Joséphine to marry Buonaparte. It was he who, at Malmaison, taught Napoleon the history of France. Later on the two quarrelled; one of the first Crosses of the Legion of Honour was sent by Napoleon to Lemercier, who refused it. In revenge the Emperor forbade the performance of his friend's plays; the friend said nothing. Driven from his house, he took silent refuge in a garret. And then one day, at the Tuileries, the Emperor perceived his old crony in a corner with the other members of the Institute. Napoleon, waving the crowd aside, went straight up to him and said: 'Eh bien, Lemercier, when are you going to write a new tragedy?' 'I am waiting, Sire!' replied the poet. Surely a magnificent remark to make in 1812 on the eve of the Russian campaign!

And now the dust of oblivion covers Lemercier, and Legouvé, and Scribe, and Meilhac, and Halévy, and even that little piece which, still marking time at the head of this essay, is — and here I drive home the peg of this article — the French opérette's so well-intentioned successor. For I cannot think that *Fritzi* is immortal, and perhaps a six months' run is better than no run at all. And what about six weeks? Yet there is a great deal of negative good to be said for the little piece. At least nobody croons and nobody tap-dances, and perhaps if there were a larger store of positive qualities to be celebrated I should not have meandered. But when I see entirely charming people trying to give us something away from croon-and-tap vulgarity nothing on earth is going to induce me to blast it. Miss Rosalinde Fuller is to be remembered chiefly for her clever work in *The Unknown Warrior* and *Martine*, in the second of which she was particularly good. But it will not be claimed that either piece is a suitable training-ground for display of that saccharine termagancy which consists in lowering rebellious curls to the level of some interlocutor's middle waistcoat button and shaking them at it. Miss Fuller does her bright vivacious best, however, and the audience like her very much. But I protest against an assumed accent which says: 'Forgeeve you? Ach, no! Thees cannot bee!' That the character is French is no excuse for making her talk Viennese. And in any case why divagate from the pure Cockney of everybody else?

One last saw Mr. Leslie French in *Comus*, in which high and poetic sphere one takes leave to think he should remain, except that there is hardly a living for an actor in Milton's Attendant Spirits. This well-graced player is to be excused, therefore, for flitting to another shore on whose

> . . . Tawny Sands and Shelves
> Trip the pert Fairies and the dapper Elves.

But there are dangers in such a transfer:

> By the rushy-fringèd bank,
> Where grows the Willow and the Osier dank,
> My sliding Chariot stayes,
> Thick set with Agat, and the azurn sheen
> Of Turkis blew, and Emrauld green. . . .

At the risk of thickly setting upon Mr. French, let me say that from the spirit of *Comus* to the high spirits of a musical-comedy buffoon is too vast a leap. Too vast, anyhow, for me, who would sooner cope with the Strid in Wharfedale. However, the audience likes him very much, and no more shall be said. The last time one saw Mr. Bruce Winston was in *The Alchemist,* and there is justification for turning the representation of Sir Epicure Mammon into a sugar-daddy.

What is the piece about? There can be no harm in saying that it concerns a kind of Wendy who keeps a kind of thieves' kitchen, and is a kind of French baroness, and ultimately falls in love with and presumably marries a kind of impresario about whom it would not be kind to say more. There is no harm in declaring the music to be pretty in a familiar way. Nor in alluding to the chorus, if one grants that Mr. Cochran's Young Ladies cannot be everywhere. Neither can Mr. Cochran. Other producers must obviously be found, though I cannot think that one would ineluctably seek out Mr. John Wyse, the brilliant young intellectual whose production of *Frolic Wind* has probably been the year's best thing in the theatre. However, this frolic choice, which would make some managements windy, has been justified by its success, considering the material Mr. Wyse has had to work upon. That new brooms sweep clean does not mean that they will be allowed the clean sweep, and a dust-pan and brush were badly wanted for all the jokes in this play. But again the audience is fooled to the top of its delighted bent, and perhaps this is all that matters. On the first night it cheered as though the piece were a new Gilbert and Sullivan. Exactly. Music by Gilbert, words by Sullivan. Except that Sullivan would have been wittier!

December 22, 1935

THE STUDENT PRINCE

BY DOROTHY DONNELLY. MUSIC BY SIGMUND ROMBERG

(His Majesty's)

SEVERAL matters having nothing to do with a strictly critical analysis of this Americanized version of the German comedy called *Old Heidelberg* obtruded themselves on one's attention on Wednesday evening last. There was the peaceful invasion of this country, as witnessed by the babel of romantic noises heard in the *foyer*; there was the plutocratic pit; there was the picketing of the entrance to the gallery by a couple of mild and gentle police officers; there was the discovery that through temerity or inadvertence on the part of the American *entrepreneurs* the list of principal artists included one English name. It may be that what one might call the politics of this production are not matter for discussion here; in any case I shall not attempt it. But as a critic is bound to over-severity in the case of a friend and over-leniency in the case of a foe, so I should like to say that, disliking some things which were not of the actual performance, I tried even harder than usual to find objects of delight in the show itself.

First, then, let it be said that the chorus exhibited such perfection of drilling as to recall the time-expired soldier who, in Mr. Kipling's ballad, pleaded:

'Tisn't my fault if I dress when I 'alt.

American producers appear to have a monopoly of the virtues of the parade ground, but that is probably because we on this side have not hitherto given the subject so much attention. What Mr. John Tiller's genius for discipline did so famously for little ladies of the ballet I have no doubt could also be accomplished in the case of little gentlemen. Anyhow the Americans have done it, and if this piece should win to a success the credit will be to the rank and file rather than the officers. Sometimes one thought that the reiterative students were rather like the small boy who, as the tea party was coming to an end, said hopefully: 'Mother told me I might stay to supper if I was pressed.' They certainly took their encores with remarkable precipitance. Or perhaps one might say that the understanding between players and audience in this matter was a remarkable piece of team work.

What was the next thing to be praised? Well, one would suggest that the costumes were extraordinarily handsome, from the uniforms of the Palace flunkeys to the magnificent affair in ermine and blue velvet in which the Prince made the railway journey from Karlsberg to Heidelberg, and in which it was hinted that he had been for a row on the river. There was furniture to make Bayswater householders gape, a parquet flooring at a hundred pounds a foot laid down by Messrs. Shubert's own men, a riot of candelabra, and a sunset of such brilliance that it illuminated not only the sentimental old Doctor but the occupants of the boxes on the O.P. side. A very remarkable sunset altogether, since it appeared to take place in the bar parlour of the inn.

Perhaps the plot of the piece might be considered next, though to attempt this in connection with a light opera is not wiser, I submit, than to judge the song about the Ukulele Lady by its words. Frankly, these romances of court life are done better in France than in Germany, and I suggest certain novels of Abel Hermant dealing with the lives of minor royalties as a useful corrective to the revolting sentimentality of Herr Meyer Forster, to whom, by the way, no acknowledgment is made on the programme. The play, however, will do very well, though one still cottons with difficulty to those University students who in massed formation wave mugs of beer and sing sentimental songs in honour of their flaxen ninny. One could imagine some Lady Bracknell in the audience saying, 'My nephew would not dream of toasting a barmaid at the Pig and Whistle. He is an Oxonian.' Nor can we imagine an English royalty revisiting his 'erstwhile college chums' in full coronation robes. But though the intrepid travellers who have penetrated the bush, veldt or jungle of the smaller German States tell us that those things which the author of *Old Heidelberg* reports are substantially true, we ask rather whether the tunes are jolly and the comedians clever. One would say that the melodies in *The Student Prince* are fairly good in outline. They are so thinly orchestrated, however, that the score must look like a skeleton. There are no comedians, and such comic business as there is inclines rather to aggravation than relief.

The principals were frankly 'not very charming', as M. Sacha Guitry said of an English artist whom he did not want to dispraise. Mr. Allan Prior presented the Prince as a chubby, confident personage in whom there was no possible wistfulness, melancholy, or

117

any kind of nostalgia. One would gather that Mr. Prior is not an experienced actor, and indeed his principal claim to attention must be based upon his having one of the loudest singing voices which it has ever been our fortune to hear. 'Opposite him', as they say, was Miss Ilise Marvenga, who should have represented the *Ewig Weibliche*, but made Kathie into a semblance of one of those expensive mechanical dolls with a staccato utterance. Miss Marvenga has also a voice of exceeding stridency, and her top notes were the most piercing it has been my privilege to endure. The Princess was played by a beautiful French actress, whose English I personally was unable to follow. Good performances were given by Mr. Herbert Waterous, and by Mr. John Coast, the actor whom one took to be of these shores; and there were some moments of pleasant fooling by little Miss Violet Carlson which hinted at the talent of a Louie Freear.

The performance as a whole suggested several reflections. First, that noise can be too loud, and that light-opera singers should not resemble rival railway engines letting off steam. Second, that a piece based upon a German story, largely acted by American, French, and German artists, dressed in Paris and presented from New York, disquiets British complacency. Third, that if alien impresarios want to endear themselves to the British public they might do worse than commission an English composer to write a light opera, and say or sing it with English actors to a good, old-fashioned, reasonably priced pit. Fourth and last, that though Art has no frontiers there are some frontiers behind which there is apparently precious little Art.

February 7, 1926

YOUR NUMBER'S UP

YOUR NUMBER'S UP

BY DIANA MORGAN AND ROBERT MACDERMOT
MUSIC BY GEOFFREY WRIGHT

(Gate)

EVERYBODY remembers how the hero of *The Dolly Dialogues* shocked Mrs. Hilary by translating the sun-dial's motto: 'Horas non numero nisi serenas' as: 'It's no good when your husband's at home.' One is tempted to think that some other Latin proverbs might usefully receive the same broad treatment. Thus 'Dulce est desipere in loco' might be rendered: 'Wit in the theatre may not be wit when you get it home.' Or even: 'Wit must not be divorced from its context.'

Of course there is some wit of such blazing excellence that you can divorce it from anything and everything, and it will still remain wit. Some of Wilde's epigrams would be dazzling if you met them carved on trees in the African jungle. Remarks of Mr. Coward's like: 'Women should be beaten regularly, like gongs', could fail to be witty only in that setting because that presumably is what happens to women in the African jungle.

And then there is always Gilbert, whose fun, in and out of *loco*, is a permanent joy to everybody who has the sense not to be jealous of it. How deeply he got under the English skin is proved by the steady refusal of otherwise intelligent people to accord him his rightful place as one of the greatest wits we have ever turned out.

It is said of one of our modern humorists that he has an unerring sense of what will tell in a theatre. Invited to furnish jokes for a dull comedy he returned the script to the management saying: 'I have put in one hundred and forty-seven laughs. Is that enough?' On the first night they counted the laughs, and behold there were one hundred and forty-seven. I saw this piece, laughed one hundred and forty-seven times, and could not believe that any one of the jokes would seem funny when reduced to cold print. But there is a brand of wit half-way between the great masters and the master-buffoons which will half-bear quotation, provided the reader bears in mind the locus in which it happens.

Wit like that in the little musical comedy at the Gate Theatre is not lasting and is not meant to be. But we shall know for a few weeks at least what actress is meant by Miss Ouida Dee. Nor have we quite forgotten what is meant when somebody, asked if he speaks Russian, replies: 'Tovarishly well.' And, of course, we are right on the spot with the sentence: 'Cuteness belongs to the good old days when Bergner was just a gleam in Sir J. M. Barrie's eye.' There is probably more of permanence in the remark of the General: 'Seems to me there's a dangerous tendency to-day for education to get into the hands of educationalists.' And presumably it will always be true that: 'An uncle on the Board of Governors is worth fifty testimonials.' It may be doubted whether many school songs mean more than the one in this piece:

A, ab, absque, coram, de,
　Floreat Mulburia!
Arma cano virumque,
　Floreat Mulburia!
Magna Charta, locum tenens,
Ubique delirium tremens,
Cantabamus, omnes screamens
　Floreat! Floreat! Floreat!

Carpe diem, Postume,
　Floreat Mulburia!
Mensa quam celerrime,
　Floreat Mulburia!
Alma Mater, tibi cano,
Mens sana in corp're sano,
Credimus cum salis grano,
　Floreat! Floreat! Floreat!

But there are things other than wit which tell in favour of this little show. It begins at nine and is over at eleven. It does not bother about scenery and dresses. There is, thank heaven, no dancing. Nor any chorus. Neither is there any singing except in the blessed sense that those who do open their mouths to caterwaul know it to be caterwauling. For, my readers, let it be laid down once and for all, that even the smallest voice of any singing kind must utterly destroy songs designed not for singing but for crooning. A Lily Pons or a Galli-Curci could sing themselves off both ends of the piano without conveying the essential atonality suited to such essential vacuity as:

> There's a Baby for Everybody Somewhere,
>> So don't be sad and blue;
> There's a Baby for Everybody Somewhere —
>> Don't weep the whole day through.
>>> Don't be lonesome,
>>> Don't be sad,
>> Dry your eyes
>> And be downright glad.
> There's a Baby for Everybody Somewhere
>> If you know just what to do!

All that is wanted for this is voiceless surrender and the appeal to pity. No man lays his cards on the table who has a hand worth playing, and the only possible way to get such blues across is for the singer to lay her vocal chords on the table, when it is at once made manifest that she hasn't any. If I have digressed, let me assure the reader that it has hurt me more than it can have hurt him.

The best thing of all about this little entertainment is that the cast is made up of entirely unknown faces. If an unknown actor appears to be unfunny, you can at least hope that he will be funny by-and-by. The case is different when you are seeing for the fiftieth time some dull fellow who has already failed with you on forty-nine previous occasions. Contrariwise, if somebody is good in a new way, how impressive that new way is when you see it for the first time!

January 3, 1937

BIG BUSINESS

BY K. R. G. BROWNE, BERT LEE AND DESMOND
CARTER. MUSIC BY JACK WALLER AND JOSEPH
TUNBRIDGE

(Hippodrome)

To go to see a comedian convinced that he will be funny is half
the battle. To go to see him persuaded that he must be wistful
is the other or losing half. Whenever I see Mr. Bobby Howes
I cannot help envisaging an actor like the Player King, tears in
his eyes, distraction in's aspect, and I have more than a half-
suspicion that the other night I was not the only one in the
audience who found a particular application about the song:

> I've got a thing about you,
> Which makes me want to put a string about you,
> And hold you tight!

The women want to mother Mr. Howes. The men want to uncle
or godfather him, to see that he has nice friends, reads good books,
goes to bed early, and does not smoke till he is old enough.

Yes, this actor affects me as I should be affected by Michael
Darling grown to boy's estate, or Mr. Al Jolson's Sonny Boy in
the flesh. He has never made me feel within conjurable distance
of a laugh. On the other hand, it is conceivable that this is an
idiosyncrasy in me, and I realize that for those who are not so
afflicted Mr. Howes may provide all the fun of the best comedians.
Anybody who is not blind must see that there is not a single trick
in the whole fun-making repertory which he has not at his finger
ends. Anybody who is not deaf must realize that nine out of every
ten in the audience deem that fun-making side-splitting. And
yet!

There is a long scene in which Mr. Howes appears disguised as
a Czecho-Slovakian Professor of Eurythmics. Is this really funny

122

in the way in which Mr. Henson would make it funny? Perhaps there is room here for another 'and yet!' Then, if so, let me say that a Scotsman has told me that he thought this scene uproariously funny! The trouble is that I see in Mr. Howes a successor to James Welch, and have the same sense of waste that I should have if I saw Mr. Henson attempt Hamlet. With this complicated proviso in mind, let me unreservedly say that Mr. Howes seems to me to be doing triumphantly exactly what his audience wants him to do, wherefore I advise him to take no notice whatever of anything I may ever write about him. But if ever he plays *The New Clown*, then let him sit up and pay infinite attention. For he will be praised to the top of my bent.

Again, in my personal view, Mr. Wylie Watson is not nearly so funny as Monsewer Gray, who performs in the same vein. And there the comedians come to an end, since Mr. David Burns is a legitimate actor, and an extraordinarily good one. His bowler hat is to my mind far funnier than anything else in this play's male line.

The ladies are another pair of shoes. There is Miss Vera Pearce, an actress magnificently abounding in her own sense. There are times in this play when as the genius of avoirdupois she is all weight, all heaviness, so that her acting is all that Pope meant by:

> When Ajax strives some rock's vast weight to throw,
> The line too labours, and the words move slow.

In the next scene she is all buoyancy, all lightness, dances like thistledown, and so becomes the perfect interpreter of the same poet's:

> Not so when swift Camilla scours the plain,
> Flies o'er the unbending corn, and skims along the main.

The way Miss Pearce skimmed along the main on Thursday evening was an eye-opener.

While this superb artist's genius is for attack, that of Miss Bertha Belmore is for defence. She stands in the centre of these musical comedies immune from assault, like one of my Uncle Toby's outworks. She is the lidless-eyed dragon of all the proprieties, and I can think of no higher praise than that Dame Madge Kendal would have approved of her. Is it conscious or subconscious imitation which makes Miss Belmore wear dresses of the exact shade of puce, and occasionally break into the same heliotrope smile? Whatever the reason, the resemblance is complete down to the Parma violets in the bun. Miss Enid Dixon-Orr as the ingénue pitches her performance, with a precision wholly remarkable, exactly half-way between the vapid and the inane.

February 18, 1937

THE LAUGHING CAVALIER

BY REGINALD ARKELL AND STAFFORD BYRNE
MUSIC BY WAINWRIGHT MORGAN

(Adelphi)

IT is said that Chinese doctors are paid only so long as their patients remain well, and that when they fall ill the payments stop. I imagine that Chinese dramatic critics only criticize the Chinese drama when it is criticizable, and that when it amounts to nothing, nothing is written. If I had my way this would be the end of my notice of *The Laughing Cavalier*, about which I find myself with less than nothing to say. But the Western world is not so ordered, and I am faced with the task of filling the usual pint-pot with not even a teaspoonful of matter.

Of what are Buddhists thinking when they contemplate their navels? What did I think of, chin-huddled in that stall, as wave after wave of nothingness swept over me? Of the lowness of the Low Countries. I remember an old Derbyshire farm-hand whose country of origin was the Isle of Wight. Asked why he migrated he said: 'It wur that low-lying, I thought it wur going to sink!' To me Holland is a country surrounded entirely by dykes, a country which the waters would overwhelm were it not for an army of little heroes waiting to plug holes with their thumbs. Yes, my view of Holland has always been that of a low country in Dick Phenyl's sense of the word 'low'. The reader remembers, of course, how Dick explains to Mrs. Gilfillian that Lavender is the daughter of a Mrs. Rolt 'who resides, to put it plainly, in the basement'. Mrs. Gilfillian says: 'A low woman?' and Dick answers: 'Geographically — not otherwise!' Of Motley's *Rise of the Dutch Republic*, that masterpiece to be read after Mommsen's *History of Rome*, for which I have not found time in forty years. Of the game of golf which, an old print tells me, was first played in Holland.

Of *Count Funnibos and Baron Stilkin*, the best of all children's books. The two had a housekeeper, named Joanna Clack, remembered from infancy as more truly alive than Catherine of Russia or St. Joan. Of E. V. Lucas's wanderings, whose account redeems the country from its flatness. Of tulips black and otherwise. Of Flying Dutchmen who never quite live up to the Overture which ushers in their story. Of Van Tromp who led the Dutch Navy in a war the reason for which no history book has ever made clear. Of the icicles which somebody in *Twelfth Night* declares to hang on a Dutchman's beard. Of the Dutch affinity with the toy-shop's Noah and Mrs. Noah. Of Hazlitt's successive declarations about Holland: that there is something lumpish and heavy in the aspect of the country, that Amsterdam is a kind of paltry rubbishy Venice, that the hotel accommodation at Rotterdam is fit only for American sea-captains, that you do not see a set of clean teeth from one end of the country to the other. Of Canning's jingle about Dutchmen giving too little and taking too much. Of the Dutchman's addiction to the game of draughts, noted by Dr. Johnson. Of Dutch courage. Of Dutch cheese. Of double Dutch. I have no doubt that I should have thought of a great many more Dutch things if the piece had permitted me to remain awake.

The Laughing Cavalier — for this, after all, is the piece we are discussing — will probably be very popular in this country, for it is the kind of thing the English always like. A great many people are employed in it. An immense amount of money, time and care has been spent on it. The plot, which tells how an errant soldier makes love to a painter's wife, is of the last banality. There is not a line of wit, and the music is as commonplace as it is abundant. Yes, this is musical playgoing in all its grandiosity.

Mr. Arthur Margetson looks credibly like the famous Hals portrait and acts as well as his wretched material permits. Mr. John Garrick as Hals himself paints as well as a man can who every ten minutes or so is turned out of his studio by cohorts of tuneful soldiery. Mr. Charles Heslop is sent on for the funny bits. My view of this actor is that while he is an admirable comedian — as everybody must admit who saw him as the Judge in *1066 and All That* — he is not cut out for the low part of the business. In other words, while he can act a droll part when that part is drolly written, he is not droll in himself. The part of the painter's wife is sung by Miss Irene Eisinger with a voice like that of a linnet on some dew-drenched Tennysonian lawn.

October 24, 1937

THE FLEET'S LIT UP

BY GUY BOLTON, FRED THOMPSON AND BERT LEE. MUSIC BY VIVIAN ELLIS

(Hippodrome)

It would, I think, be a safe bet that Professor Ernst Stern's favourite author is Gautier. As scene after scene discloses itself in this nautical-vortical-piratical-fanatical extravaganza the critical mind, in its search for pabulum, flies to that volume at which one has not looked for forty years, but whose pages are stamped on the memory as firmly as a film star's footprints are fixed in

126

Hollywood cement. What is the 'Seahorse Night Club' except 'a motive of Giorgione executed by Rubens'? The same applies to all the Professor's tableaux, whether they represent a battleship in action or a Sultan's Palace at the hour of the siesta.

In *Mademoiselle de Maupin* occurs this passage: 'Three things are dear to my heart: gold, marble, purple — sheen, solidity, colour. My dreams are made out of these elements; the palaces inhabited by my chimeras are built of these materials. In my world is neither mist nor vapour. My sky is cloudless, or if there are clouds they are solid, chips from some sculptor's statue of Jupiter.' With both artists everything is more than life-size. Gautier's women become goddesses, and whole pages are devoted to the laws regulating his mistress's attire. 'I will not abate her jewellery by so much as a ring or a bracelet. Her robe shall be of velvet or brocade; I think twice before permitting descent to satin. In my dreams my mistress is queen, empress, princess, courtesan — but never shepherdess. A beautiful woman must possess carriages, horses, lackeys, and the fortune that goes with these things. There is an essential harmony between beauty and its envelope.' Yes, I think Gautier would have approved the outsize aigrette worn by Miss Adèle Dixon, which must surely have been plucked from the tail-feathers of a Great Auk.

Our Théophile demanded that in his ideal world men should be built on classical lines, uniting the grace of Antinoüs with the frame of Hercules. 'I am a man of Homer's time.' So equipped, his heroes were to make very small beer of Tiberius and Caligula. They would out-Nero Nero. 'Thy house of gold, O Nero, is a mud hut in comparison with the palaces of my building. The beasts in my circuses, O Heliogabalus, roar louder than in yours; my arenas stream with wetter blood. My perfumes bring about more fierce contraction of the nostrils. I have superber slaves. My chariot is drawn by more resplendent odalisques. The heel I place on mankind has a greater scorn than your heel.' It is possible that Mr. Ralph Reader comes poorly off in any such comparison. Let it be said that this clever dancer and arranger of dances has probably not envisaged the parallel.

127

All this, the reader will courteously agree, brings me to Miss Frances Day, a heroine made to flit through the pages of this impossible romantic. Insisting upon an intensely material world, Gautier looked for a theatre tenuous and impalpable. In his orchestra the flautist shall be a nightingale. The 'cellos are the peel of lemons held between the ivory knees of sylphs drawing a bow of Titania's eyelashes over strings made from spiders' webs. The curtain is a butterfly's wing. Gautier would have his magic extend even to the audience. His stalls are mother-of-pearl, and in them recline the souls of poets using for opera glasses dewdrops mounted on the pistils of lilies. And though he does not say it, we lay it down for him that his actresses shall be moonbeams. Which again brings one to Miss Day, since here is an enchanting performance of chequered moonshine, turning the stage into the floor of some forest where busy tree-tops and idle moon play a game together. Descending to the gross particular I will concede that Miss Day is sometimes in danger of being crushed between Professor Stern's iron-bellied clouds and Mr. Stanley Lupino's earthy humours. When this happens, this clever little actress shrugs her shoulders and herself descends to earth.

Must I at this point pretend to go into the question of fleets lit and unlit? Does the reader wish to be told what this entertainment is about? I should be delighted to oblige, but for the fact that I have not the vaguest idea. There is nothing that any rational person could call a plot; there is nothing that even an irrational person would call wit; there is no room for anybody to move; and the cluttered-up vacuity of the whole thing makes it impossible to pay attention to the music. There is a point in exasperation at which the mind says NO.

Let me be constructive. Discard the entire 'book' and get a new one. Co-opt Mr. Douglas Furber, or other competent wit. Cart away as much décor as five pantechnicons will hold, and let that aigrette be included. Open up the stage. Give the dancers room to dance, and let Mr. Reader, when he is not dancing, beat time in the wings. Let him be content with one talent; after all, Lichine and Lifar do not find it necessary to sing. Invite Mr. Lupino to look more closely into the taste of his broader sallies. Let Miss Day have the stage to herself more often.

And the result of such constructive amelioration? Presumably that the show would be an instant flop. Having almost every conceivable fault and no merits that I can discern, it will probably run a year. For if there is one thing on which the British public dotes it is poverty of idea richly dressed.

August 21, 1938

WALTZ WITHOUT END

BY ERIC MASCHWITZ. MUSIC BY CHOPIN

(Cambridge)

MEMBERS of the Jury, the charge against the prisoner at the Bar, Eric Maschwitz, is murder, in that on the 29th day of September, 1942, at the Cambridge Theatre, in a piece entitled *Waltz Without End*, he destroyed the reputation of Frédéric Chopin. The Prosecution says that to alter a composer's rhythms, keys and tempi is to murder that composer. That to debase to blatant, mischievous and comic purpose part or parts of the B Flat Minor Scherzo and the finale of the B Minor Sonata, to divert from the piano to the voice some part or parts of the third Etude, the E Flat Nocturne and the Waltz in D Flat, and to make such voices sing words that are the acme of tawdry nonsense, is to destroy the reputation of an exquisite composer. The Defence argues, and I must ask you to consider this very seriously, that Chopin's reputation cannot be harmed by these vagaries, however extravagant and nauseating, since musical people will keep away, and what the unmusical think is of no importance and can be disregarded. You will ignore the evidence of the witness A., who said he was ashamed to belong to a country which not only tolerated but welcomed artistic vulgarity of this order; buffooneries in this kind are not intended for him.

But the Defence goes further. It maintains that the prisoner, so far from destroying the reputation of a great composer, has actually given him a fame which he did not enjoy before. (I see from my Notes that 'enjoy' was the word that learned counsel used.) That tens of thousands of ignorant and uncultured persons, who had never heard of a Scherzo in B Flat Minor or any other key, will now go about the town singing 'Fools Follow a Rainbow' to a tune of greater elegance than they normally use. That this musical comedy, for which the prisoner admits responsibility, will presently be filmed, and that hundreds of thousands of persons even more ignorant and less cultured will be stimulated by the waltzing and vocalizing of, say, Miss Jeanette Macdonald and Mr. Nelson Eddy, to the point of buying a gramophone record of a tune which must heighten their musical perceptions. And that all this creates fame in minds in which that fame did not previously exist. It is for you to weigh the validity of this argument.

I come now to that part of his speech in which Counsel for the Prosecution suggested that musical plays of this nature tempt the public away, and hold them back, from such admirable revivals as that of *Hedda Gabler* at the Mercury Theatre. You will give that argument its due weight and no more. You may think that Ibsen's play is a masterpiece of dramatic art, and as such presents no attraction to the musical-comedy public. You may hold that the force, distinction, intelligence and sheer acting capacity of Miss Sonia Dresdel, and the fact that she does not burst into song, are a further discouragement to that public.

The prisoner is not charged with failing to encourage the arts of music and drama. You may conclude from the evidence that the only charge which he is called upon to answer is that of furthering the business of public entertainment, of meeting the lawful requirements of a large section of the community in a straightforward and demonstrably successful way. You may think that in presenting an imbroglio of maximum inanity, in which history and sentiment contend which can be the falser, in eliminating wit in favour of gross and stale humours, in the complete disregard of everything we know about the principal character to the extent of presenting him as chubby and bucolic, the prisoner has done what he set out to do, and with commendable skill. The Prosecution admits that the principal performers, Mr. Ivor Sheridan and Miss Jane Carr, acquit themselves in the manner approved by custom and the kind of audience they are seeking to please, that the dresses are agreeable, and the dancing less lumpy than some more pretentious cavortings.

In conclusion, the Defence contends — and the Prosecution has put forward no counter-argument which is at all convincing — that the music of Chopin, however garbled and mutilated, is more beneficial to uneducated taste than the atrocities of jazz and swing presented in their horrid integrity. Counsel for the Defence has gone so far as to claim that Chopin himself would have preferred the destruction of his melodies — if, *before this audience*, the mutilations amount to destruction — to that degradation of the public ear through jazz and swing which, the Defence claims, is the only alternative.

Putting that aside as not being the real question can you say, taking the evidence as a whole, that you are satisfied beyond reasonable doubt that the reputation of Frédéric Chopin no longer exists, and that it was the hand of the prisoner and no other hand that destroyed it? If you are not so satisfied, whatever your feelings or prejudices may be, then it is your duty to find the prisoner not guilty. If you *are* so satisfied, equally it is your duty to find him guilty. Members of the Jury, will you now consider your verdict?

October 4, 1942

REVUES

LONDON CALLING!

BY RONALD JEANS AND NOEL COWARD

(Duke of York's)

For years the critics have complained that the people who produce revues persistently ignore the wits whilst paying attention to the wigs, fretting themselves into a fever as to the covering of the actors' heads and indifferent to the clothing of their authors' minds. Latterly, there have been signs of a change, and in his present venture Mr. André Charlot has gone to the length of impressing, in the person of Mr. Noel Coward, the youngest, and who shall say that that does not mean the brainiest, of our intellectuals. Is dullness the consequence, or is this revue rendered thereby 'screamingly funny'? The answer, I think, is to be found in the serried rows of those grave and reverend signors, the critics, who, on Tuesday afternoon, forsook their glum misanthropy, and laughed themselves, so to speak, free of their critical shackles.

In this connection three things come to mind which are not, perhaps, popularly accepted. The first is that, just as there is nothing quite so abysmally boring in the theatre as your author who has got no brow at all, so there is no wit like that of a high-brow who is really witty and is not merely a humbug giving himself airs. The second is that, nine-tenths of criticism being a smacking of the lips or a rolling of the tongue — the art of tasting and appreciating, in a word — the critic who must hold both his sides is not divesting himself of his functions but fulfilling them. The third is that there is no reason to despise revue, which springs as much out of the temper of modern minds as Greek drama from Greek thought, or the morality play from the desire to be preached to. Revue fits the times, and there is no critical sense in being sniffy about this particular form of dramatic art. *London Calling!* is one of the best revues I have seen.

To begin with it fulfils its function, which is that of slating public vanities and foibles by laughing at them. Miss Gertrude Lawrence pinks you prettily like an adroit fencer; she will play a whole scene like that entitled 'Early Morning' with a verisimilitude worthy of Maupassant or Pett Ridge or any other great realist, doubled by a mockery which makes you nervous lest, somewhere in the house, there be a real Poppy Baker covering up her face for shame. Miss Lawrence, besides being an accomplished actress, is also a graceful dancer and a charming singer.

Miss Maisie Gay employs not so much the rapier and stiletto of wit as the belabouring cudgel of broad fun. Her caricature of an ultra-modern poetess declaiming 'rhythmi-coloured' verses beginning 'Phlegmatic are my feet' roused so much laughter that many of the admirable lines were lost. Hernia Whittlebot, hung and festooned with bunches of grapes, has two brothers, Gob and Sago, who, when they list, and in a sad mingle of Harris-tweed bags and velvet jackets, grate on their scrannel pipes the leanest of accompaniments. It is, perhaps, a trifle cruel, but this is an over-squeamish age, and cruelty has its uses. The actress was good, too, as a fond mother trying to learn the fashionable slang. It is significant that the original 'This motor-car is not even moderately efficient' was received with roars, whilst the more modern 'The 'bus is a dud' was accepted as normal. Bravo, Mr. Jeans!

Miss Gay was possibly at her best in 'What Love Means', where she portrayed a battered harridan of the kind Leech loved to draw. There was a queer, inverted pathos here, a glistening of the eye and a tremble of the lip which belied the grotesque words. And only a short while before the artist was revelling in the archness of fifty and the persistence of the favourite who will not leave the stage. She reproduced with extraordinary fidelity the technique that was accepted in our father's and grandfather's day. Miss Gay is the very genius of burlesque. Of the other artists I must single out Mr. Tubby Edlin, who in his doubling of the droll with the woebegone has something of the quality of Dan Leno. He can sing of glorious Devon, and take all the glory out of it. Mr. Coward, as actor, is something of a difficulty. He is both self-conscious and self-assertive, and not, I think, a very great success.

The scenery is formal and charming, the dresses are exquisite, and I shall visit the show again as soon as the little lady in the typewriting scene shall have learned to sing in tune.

September 9, 1923

THE BLUE BIRD

FROM THE IMPERIAL THEATRE, MOSCOW

(New Scala)

LIKE the Chauve-Souris Theatre, *The Blue Bird* combines the extremes of childlikeness and sophistication, unclouded naïveté of outlook and the most intense artistic consciousness. There is a shattering poignancy in many of these scenes, which moves the heart like some page from Dostoievsky. As these marvellous pictures are discovered it is as though the heart of Russia were being laid bare; and it is a dull mind upon which, at one or other disclosure, no perception dawns as to the case for Revolution. The scene entitled 'Burlaki', depicting haulers on the Volga, is agony seized at its supreme moment, agony of body stopping short of ecstasy, since the mind is gone. These seven pulling on the rope are spiritually dead. Two of them are young. One has the features of a Christ in whom faith is as a lamp that has gone out, the other has the head of a Joan of Arc listless and benumbed. The rest, one of whom hides his face, are nameless horrors, and as they stand to the rope, careless of the sunset against which they are poised, you know existence as a world-without-end pain.

'Barrel Organ' has all the ache of the streets, the smart of rehearsed and mechanical gaiety. Here is none of that English sentimentality, which will set 'A che la Morte' 'pulsing with the sunset-glow', and lighting up the eyes of the passer-by with a 'wild Italian gleam'. The emotion is not the lively, casual one of the wayfarer, but the dead heart of the mendicant who turns the handle, of the drab who quavers and throws a lifeless somersault, of the half-wit comprehending alms and no more. 'Catherine the Great', in bronze, at whose feet are pedestalled a great statesman, a famous general, and a poet, all of her time, harks back to the St. Petersburg that was. The thing is a monument to the mind as well as to the eye. As the Empress sings of Voltaire and Sans-Souci the lights go up in the restaurant behind the statue, and down some avenue the files of soldiers pass. Catherine's General salutes the Danube; light thickens and fades. The Empress, St. Petersburg, Russia, are again one with the past, death and nothingness.

And here, perhaps, the sturdy English mind is likely to rebel. Can even the Russian, whose whole life is misery, be wretched for successive quarters of an hour? Does the hauler on the Volga know nothing of bread and cheese and beer? Is that beggarly *ménage* utterly without joy? Shall the new Petrograd know no cakes and ale? We are inclined to think that these Russians parade their melancholy a trifle too insistently. There is something a little ghoulish even about their pleasantries. 'The Cossacks' is cruel, in spite of the prancing horses and the flowery mead. 'Evening Bells' has nothing pastoral about it. In place of 'these dells', which Moore walked and sung to such innocent purpose, there is a belfried view of a sleeping city, the descent to which is sheer, like a sudden failure of the spirit. This is an exquisite picture, which again must sadden the beholder. Even 'Time is Money', the skit on American romanticism, is strangely sober of hue. To Russian eyes, America may look like three sandwich-men and half a dozen wax models. Sovereign stupidity may or may not rule over there, but if you are going to tear a country to pieces you should expose, I think, something more vital than the spleen.

Lest I should appear to be carping, let me say straight out that the show, as a whole, is one of strange, exotic, wilful and wistful beauty, and one which no lover of the theatre should miss. The first item, 'The King called for his Drummer', is the richest and most significant stage-picture which I have ever known. The King's hand, extended against the dark background, is whole dramas in folio; and the very texture of the brocades and the manner of their disposal speak to you like a scene out of a play. I do not know what is the art-jargon to be applied here; I can only suggest that this is the theatre of the eye. If I may offer a hint to the management, it is that they should do away with the blue lights at the entrance, which turn the theatre into something half-way between the Egyptian Hall and Tutankhamen's tomb. Also that they should shorten the intervals between each scene. The music is good, and Mdlle. Shuster fiddles delightfully. But there will always be talk in England during interludes, however musical. At this Russian theatre chatter is inevitable. Not all the nine symphonies of Beethoven playing together would keep me from discussing with my neighbour so challenging a thing as the Haulers' Song.

Nothing is to be said of individual actors. They play together with extraordinary delicacy, finish, humour, and understanding.

October 4, 1923

LA CHAUVE-SOURIS

(Strand)

'LA CHAUVE-SOURIS' is 'pure theatre' — a phrase which is more familiar abroad than it is at home. The special virtue of our race is that we are non-temperamental; and, indeed, the display of pure emotion is, to our notions, hardly good form. You might say that as the English theatre-goer pulls on his dress-shirt he puts on Colonel Newcome. But these Russian fellows are different. With them theatrical emotion can afford to go naked, since we who look on are unashamed. If we blush at the lack of reticence, at least we do not blush for our own. There is hardly an actor in

the troupe who has not the passion to play Othello, or the gor-
mandizing humour for Falstaff. And, of course, they are real
Russians, and not our musical comedy sort, whose steppes are
Riceyman's.

The masterpieces of Chauve-Souris are pure theatre in the sense
that when they are not in being on the stage they do not exist.
They are not the acted form of something which may be conned
in the study; they are the sudden fusion of things seen and heard
and felt.

These pictures are not illustrations, because they depend from no
text. Take, for example, 'The King Orders the Drums to be Beaten.'
You feel, as you watch the flowering of this miniature tragedy,
not that the *décor* and dresses are subsidiary to a tale, but that they
are the tale. The despotism of the tyrant is in the shape and sub-
stance of his papier-mâché crown; in the wig of the knight who
yields up wife and honour is the whole court of le Roi Soleil;
unyielding brocade bespeaks the Queen's rancour; submission lies
in the drooping gown of the knight's lady, and compassion is all
the minion's pose.

Or take the tableau called 'Les Zaporogues' after the picture by
Répine. The Sultan of Turkey has sent to these Ukrainian Cossacks a letter demanding payment of a war levy. Only one of
them can write, and the others crowd round him dictating what
he shall answer, and suggesting the gibes with which their reply
shall be decorated. I do not know a word of Russian, and must
therefore be ignorant of the insults. But I know their tenor from
watching the face of the youngest of the band, peering slyly from
under the scribe's arm. Take the malice out of the lad's face, and
the letter becomes a model of polite correspondence.

Barbarian ecstasy, gallantry under French Louis, naïve buffoonery, the porcelain sentimentality of Sèvres or Dresden — all come
alike to these superb artists. 'Love and Hierarchy' shows a lady at
the barrack gate ogling and being ogled by drummer boy, sergeant,
lieutenant, and colonel. Finally, a fat general appears, bursting
with glory at every button, and to him military discipline accords
the fair. This is pure ribaldry after every soldier's heart. 'The

Shepherdess Interlude', from Tschaikowsky's opera, *La Dame de Pique*, was supposed to be a re-creation of Watteau. That is if one understood M. Balieff aright. But just as the Tschaikowsky seemed to be pure Mozart, so the scene in its curious solidity was pure Staffordshire pottery. The painted trees were obviously glazed ware from one to two inches thick, and their place was the mantelpiece. On the other hand, 'An Ancient Cameo', to some old music by Weckerlin, was perfect Sèvres. Anything more delicious than the *coup d'œil* here cannot possibly be imagined.

But the best piece in the collection was, to my way of thinking, the last one, 'A Country Picnic in a Distant Province of Russia'. You must imagine moonlight on a sleeping river, and the hour when even revellers grow sentimental. The last of the champagne is being savoured, and presently the baskets will be packed, and packed, too, into their calèches will be these elegant ladies now disposed to a pretty lassitude. There is dancing, and, here and there, beneath the trees, a whispered conversation. A young man, seeking one who should share his melancholy, peers into the faces of the talkers, and finding not his bliss moves on. Now comes singing — sisters we guess. The others dispose themselves about the grass, or on the roots of trees. The words are Russian, but we murmur:

> Ma Douleur, donne-moi la main; viens par ici,
>   Loin d'eux. Vois se pencher les défuntes Années
> Sur les balcons du ciel, en robes surannées;
> Surgir du fond des eaux le Regret souriant;
>   Le Soleil moribond s'endormir sous une arche,
> Et, comme un long linceul, traînant à l'Orient,
> Entends, ma chère, entends la douce Nuit qui marche.

But the mind has play here, and can wander where it listeth. Whether the corroboration which it seeks be a verse of Baudelaire, a page from Turgenieff's *On the Eve*, or a canvas by Renoir, the mood is the same — that *recueillement*, or folding in upon oneself, for which our language has no single word.

December 7, 1924

RIVERSIDE NIGHTS

BY A. P. HERBERT

(Lyric, Hammersmith)

MR. NIGEL PLAYFAIR has produced a highbrow revue, nearly all of which can be very heartily enjoyed by anybody who cares to make the effort. A little of it is dull, of that peculiar shade of dullness of which only intellectuals are capable. Consider the dialogue between Bossuet and the Duchess de Fontanges, taken from the *Imaginary Conversations* of Walter Savage Landor. Let it be granted that modern taste is not bored by this author whose page, as Swinburne said, is 'dark with excess of light'. Let it be granted that Mr. Playfair's audience recollects who Bossuet was, and does not confound that gentleman with Boileau, whose memory is kept green by a public-house on the further side of Hammersmith Bridge, Heaven knows why! But all that is no reason why we should listen to a long recitation of the school-room order by a young lady whose Duchess does not suggest anything more French than a milk pudding.

Then isn't it something of a mistake to give *Thomas and Sally* after *The Policeman's Serenade*? Of the two little operas I personally infinitely prefer the modern one, of which the score by Mr. Alfred Reynolds is pure enchantment. I suppose Arne is still a delight to many people, but I confess to having had quite enough of the eighteenth century for the time being. *Rule Britannia* is all very well, but, again personally, I would give the whole of English music except Purcell, Sullivan and Elgar for five bars of *Rosenkavalier*. I realize that to say this is unfashionable, but I hate the schoolmaster in music, and *Thomas and Sally* is a prim bouquet culled and offered by a pedant. However, there is this much to be said for this insipid stuff that it will not bring the blush of passion to any listening ear, and that to like it is in itself a mark of respectability.

Dr. Arne out of the way, the entertainment loses its museum

139

aspect and becomes altogether jolly and delightful. There is an historical drama entitled *Lambert Simnel and Perkin Warbeck in the Reign of Henry VII*, written by Master Michael Cowlen, which I take to be the pen-name of Master Michael Playfair. This is obviously the work of a young dramatist in the making. 'Do you not think our followers may turn upon us after they have been sticking up for us for some time?' is a question which must have occurred to the greatest of all historical dramatists. But perhaps the most delightful sentence is Perkin Warbeck's 'Hurry up with your rebellion, Lambert, as I am getting mine ready in case yours doesn't come off'. After a rapid throw-back to the sixteenth century in the shape of an admirable soldier song, we come to what is easily the best thing in the show, a little song entitled 'It may be Life . . .' The scene shows a servant's bedroom. At the head of the abominable iron bedstead stands a screen powdered with Gloria Swansons, Ramon Navarros and other stardust. The little slavey compares her life with the heroes and heroines of the screen. Her daily, weekly, yearly round you know already; she is to enlighten you as to her night out. We gather that she spends it under a lamp-post enfolded in the arms of a stolid unimpassioned 'clurk'. In the mind's eye you see what the poet calls 'the dejected 'haviour of the visage' as he glues his cheek to hers. At the approach of some rival does his revolver bark? No. All the fellow does is to say glumly ''Op it!' And the rival 'ops it. There is sublimity in the refrain:

> Then 'e says: Friday?
> And I says: Right,
> Then 'e says: Same Time?
> And I says: Quite.

This is a little masterpiece of writing by Mr. A. P. Herbert, admirably set to music by Mr. Dennis Arundell. Miss Dorice Fordred sang it with something approaching to genius. There was desolation in the way in which she threw herself on the bed and described in the air tragi-comic circles with her black woollen-stockinged leg. Was ever drudge so bored?

After the joyless Landor we had some music-hall songs resusci-
tated by Miss Elsa Lanchester and Mr. Harold Scott. I don't
quite understand what this clever pair of artists mean by their
performance. If their intention is to give these old songs their
original vigour and point they fail badly. If they are trying to
burlesque them they fail again for the simple reason that their
renderings are too near the originals. In fact, I detected in everything that they did a horrid note of Bloomsbury superciliousness,
of pity for the lowbrows who were once amused by such a song
as 'More Work for the Undertaker'. I remember Miss Lanchester's
admirable performance as Larva in *The Insect Play*, which was
a realistic and very clever portrayal of a thing definitely intended to
be ugly. But I cannot pretend that I like her present material.
Mockery in itself is not a sufficient quality for an artist, and I do
implore Miss Lanchester to look round for something in which
she can for once be sincere. She might begin by learning the
rudiments of the harmonium, and not perform arpeggios in the
treble when somebody behind the scenes is playing chords in the
bass. There can be no doubt about the cleverness of these two
artists, who should, however, go into the fresh air for their next
material, and discard the preciousness of Sunday-night coteries.
Mr. Scott, when acting in the legitimate, is an artist of very great
talent indeed, and I have a grateful recollection of many performances of singular pathos and beauty. But I suggest to him
that he and his colleague are making a great mistake in offering
Mr. Playfair's highbrows a programme unworthy of the Victoria
Palace.

I have left too little space in which to do justice to the burlesque
of Tchehov. This is parody of the very highest order, and entitles
Mr. Herbert to sit down even in the presence of Mr. Max Beerbohm. I am not going to describe anything that happens in this
brilliant piece of fooling, and will content myself with saying that,
however wild with rapture it will make the non-Tchehovians, they
will be outdone by the disciples of the Russian master. Miss Marie
Dainton as Mrs. Patrick Campbell rhapsodizing over a bowl of
goldfish is sheer delight, and so, too, is Mr. Nigel Playfair himself,

who contrives to look like John Bright, Walt Whitman and W. G. Grace all rolled into one. Mr. Malleson contributes a newsvendor of adorable pessimism, and perhaps the only fault in an otherwise perfect cast is Mr. James Whale, the goalkeeper who shoots the wrong person. The mistake about Mr. Whale is that he is too perfect. He is, you see, a Tchehov player, which the others are not, and everything that he says and does is impregnated with a melancholy futility which is altogether too authentic. The proper thing to do, I submit, is to have Mr. Whale removed and give the part to some doorkeeper, who would play it ten thousand times worse, and for this particular purpose ten thousand times better. Altogether à very clever and thoroughly enjoyable entertainment in spite of one or two poor patches which have doubtless been cut since the first night.

April 11, 1926

THE CO-OPTIMISTS

(His Majesty's)

How many people realize the enormous prevalence in this country of the inane habit known as Musical Comedy? Turning the leaves of a recent little book about the theatre, which I incidentally wrote myself, I happened on the statement that of the fifty-four plays which have achieved a run of six months and over during the last twenty-five years, twelve only were serious pieces against forty-two light comedies and farces. Yet in that same period no fewer than eighty-five musical comedies and revues had run six months and over. Statistics, it is always said, can be made to prove anything. They can't. I defy any statistician living or dead to produce, imagine, or invent any figures whatsoever showing that the English have at any time since the Conquest, or before, taken the slightest interest in the serious drama, except possibly during the age of Elizabeth. There is another proverb which declares that facts are stubborn things. This commands my complete respect.

One evening during the war I overheard a party of lively young men discussing what to do after dinner. Piece after piece was mentioned but they could come to no decision. So I approached them and said: 'Gentlemen, I have some acquaintance with the theatre of this town. Would you like to see a play of spiritual purpose and noble intent, couched in fine nervous English, which will send you to your beds braver and better men?' The highest spirit of the party replied at once: 'Good God, no! We don't wish to see anything of the sort. *We're on leave!*' The truth about the English race is that whenever it goes to the theatre it considers itself to be on leave. Let me eat, drink, and go to *The Merry Widow*, for to-morrow I may drop down dead — runs through the mind of every Englishman as he fingers his dress tie. But what the Englishman thinks about the theatre has never been of the slightest importance, because the Englishman does not go to the theatre in any considerable numbers. It is the Englishwoman who rings up Keith Prowse, and haven't they got anything better for Thursday fortnight than the middle of the fourth row of stalls, and are they quite sure that darling Sir Gerald will be playing that night, and has dearest Gladys really got some pretty frocks, and does the young gentleman at the other end of the 'phone think they would suit the speaker, she being fair and not slim and the other side of forty? And so on and so forth. From time immemorial the British drama has been fashioned to please the flapper and the hen-witted — Shakespeare being the one honourable exception. But I do not believe that any flapper ever saw any play by Shakespeare or, seeing it, knew what it was about.

There are mornings when the sky hangs over me like a pall made of porridge, all my faculties are numb and the world seems to have lost definition. My breakfast-knife turns into india-rubber, and with a pointless fork I stuff my mouth with pieces of bacon made out of Berlin wool. I do not summon the doctor because he would be of no avail. What is the matter with me is that I must that evening at eight o'clock undergo a musical comedy. At ten o'clock the first act may possibly be over, and for two hours one will have endured the water-torture of the middle ages, the water being replaced by buckets of tepid whitewash. I will frankly say that in this matter I am not one with my kind. For all round about me I see eminent surgeons, barristers, judges, stockbrokers, drinking in the performance with eyes, ears and mouth, and applauding the wan efforts of Miss Tittlebat Twittermouse as though she were a Rachel, a Duse or a Bernhardt. I think that is the thing which annoys me most about musical comedy. I really do see red when I reflect how long and arduous must be the struggles of any player of talent. I see red when I remember Edith Evans's long fight against lack of appreciation, and when I realize the battle that is in front of so brilliant an artist as Martita Hunt. I see red when charming little noodles are hailed as terrific geniuses. And I suppose that as long as I am a dramatic critic I shall go on seeing red, and ultimately die of purple iridescence.

Is it a jaded appetite which suggests that the Co-Optimists are possibly a shade less good than they used to be, or is it that they eschew the dead level, and like the temperamental golfer prefer alternations of two and ten to an unemotional series of sixes? Mr. Gilbert Childs is horribly bunkered in a number entitled 'The Underworld of London after Dark', and no niblicity of humour could get him out of it. It is a long time before Mr. Austin Melford is allowed a glimpse of the pretty, though when once on the fairway he accomplishes the rest in par figures. Mr. Stanley Holloway is stymied by a song called 'The Old Blue Boar', which is a ballad of unimpeachable banality, fragrant with the dust of ages. This capable artist should really be given some material more closely connected with the ironic scheme; one can hear ditties about the sands of Dee or Deptford at any ballad concert. Even Mr. Melville Gideon has too often to play out of the rough. Witness that piece of tiger-country in which a young lady simpers up-stage over a balustrade and a gramophone and repeats palely to the moon that which Mr. Gideon has already given out in the glare of the footlights. For a good half of the time the ground, so to speak, is under repair. And I suggest that as golfers are allowed to drop

off ground under repair, so the Co-Optimists should not allow
themselves to be dropped on to it.

But the rest of the show is excellent. One or two numbers are
retained from the previous programme, and with very good reason.
Can anybody tire of the ghost who, on gibbet-duty at the cross-
roads, sees a motor-car go right through him? Even better, because it is legitimate comment, is the Proposed Ghost Union with
four-hour haunts, and passing through walls and carrying head
under arm considered skilled labour. Both Mr. Childs and
Mr. Melford admirably reproduce what Prosper Mérimée's belated biographer has just called his 'lunar incertitude'. But far
and away the best item is an extraordinarily good little sketch,
entitled 'Our Albert'. In this one little scene Miss Doris Bentley,
who plays the part of a Lancashire wife, has all the little chits and
ninnies and noodles of musical comedy tied up in a bunch and
beaten to a frazzle. No simpering in the moonlight here, no
virginal swooning on the shirt-front of a tenor with a voice like a
glue-pot. Mr. Gilbert Childs, as the husband wanly irate, does
some capital acting now, and the pair execute a gloomy little
dance which recalls the misadventurous side of Charlie Chaplin,
and explains why the Lancashire mill-hand has to keep whippets
or pigeons to make life bearable. In the slow ritual of these sad
steps there is all the melancholy of goalless Saturday afternoons
and the threnodic incitation of knurr and spell.

If there could be a better item than this it would be that one
entitled 'Melville Gideon on His Own'. The phrase is something
colloquial, but we know what it means. We know we are to have
this fine little artist in single radiance, unaccompanied by moon or
balustrade or bright little lady palely loitering. Mr. Gideon by
himself is immense, which, though a contradiction in terms, is
nevertheless the sanest of pronouncements. With his crumpled,
monkeyish mask, admirably assumed and hardly ever discarded,
his unaffected ease, his crooning of sentimentalities in so low a
voice that they reach what old-fashioned people still call the heart,
his voluntary jazzing and guying of the same melodies so that they
are purged of treacle, his knack of charming the tinniness out of a

piano — all these qualities might entitle this artist to declare: 'Le Co-Optimisme, c'est moi.' Two things only prevent this: one is Mr. Gideon's modesty, and the other is Mr. Davy Burnaby, who on such a subject might have one or two words to say. He has more than one or two words on general matters to utter during the performance, and is as perfect a *compère* as shall be found on this side of the Channel. His imitation of a well-known jazz-conductor will bring balm to the souls of those who deem Chopin's Funeral March Sonata unsuited for performance on the bones, triangle, and a saxophone muted by a pound of carrots and a bowler hat.

December 5, 1926

COCHRAN'S REVUE (1926)

BY RONALD JEANS

(London Pavilion)

It would be absurd not to recognize at once that the amount of taste, invention, ingenuity, and discrimination which have gone to the creation of this revue place it in the forefront of anything the lighter stage has seen for a good many years. Some of the dancing is as good as the best Russian ballet. But then it *is* Russian ballet, and it is not postulating too much to say that a thing is as good as itself. The music where it is old is adorable, and where it is new is never worse than dull; some of the staging is as good as the best Komisarjevsky; the dresses are as imaginative as they are sumptuous; there is some tolerable comedy; and there is Spinelly. The whole show bears witness to direction by a single mind. Now one knows quite well which parts of the show are to Mr. Cochran's own personal taste; they are the bits one likes best oneself. This revue is a mountain of culture cloudy of apex. But even Mont Cervin, craggy and nubbly with delights for climbers, has lower slopes for the delectation of less adventurous souls. I imagine Mr.

Cochran, 'soul-hydroptic with a sacred thirst', as Browning puts it, must from time to time have roundly snubbed his finer palate and taken an intentional pull at a recognizably commoner flagon.

There are at least four quite best things in this revue. First there is 'The Tub', a Florentine ballet to Haydn's music, which makes us feel that the Medici are living round the corner. Then there is 'Gigue', a ballet on classic themes by Bach, Handel, and Scarlatti. This is a magnificent jumble. The costumes are vaguely Louis XIV, the music is more or less Georgian, the only ornament on the stage is a Roman statue, the scenery consists of a bit of dirty yellow canvas upon which one who is obviously a modern draughts-man has hinted at something which he may some day turn into an archway or a window. Against this bit of haphazard mastery are the motionless bronze and the figure of Massine snatching from the air a pose which a sculptor would have frozen for all time. These present a piece of theatre which is entirely admirable. Let it be said here that in both these ballets, and indeed throughout the evening, Nemtchinova danced magnificently and wore clothes possessing which no Peri could have ever hankered after Paradise. Possibly the best thing of all is 'The Masks', brilliant both in con-ception and execution. And last there is 'Birdcage Walk', which takes us back quite deliciously to the age of Mr. Crockford and Mr. Nash.

On the lower slopes there are such pleasurable scrambles as 'Tahiti', which sets one wondering what the Polynesians are doing about the silk tax, 'Southend-on-Sea', jolly enough to make one realize what a happy land is England to be able to afford such an impost, 'The Roman Baths at Deauville' inviting us to share Mr. Podsnap's view of French manners, 'Aladdin' which takes the advertising bull by the horns and milks it as it were this year's dairy champion. 'Les Aromes de Coty' to the subtle perfume of Debussy's *Plus que Lente* sends my lady's nose questing after fragrances for which Cleopatra would have given whole provinces and thrown in Antony as make-weight. These things are done as well as their lesser genius permits, and in them are incorporated the healthy English charm of Miss Annie Croft, the chubby

147

virtuosity of Miss Peggy, the Spanish *fougue* of her partner, Mr. Cortez, and the altogether amazing ballroom accomplishment of Mr. Billy Bradford.

Foremost amongst the comedians is Mr. Thesiger. Now Mr. Thesiger is a very good actor indeed, whose temporary loss the legitimate stage can ill afford. He does well in the present show, yet I venture to think that it is not good for us that an actor should spend too much of his time in deploying too little of his talent. Mr. Cochran has announced his intention of abandoning revue in favour of musical comedy, which can only be to the advantage of that sad art. But let him return Mr. Thesiger to the legitimate stage with appropriate compliments — we will provide the thanks. Miss Hermione Baddeley also does well, and is the life and soul of sketches which exist solely for her justification. There are one or two numbers which might with advantage be cut. One is 'Missing Links', which is a savage skit upon late-comers. Here an unfortunate allusion is made to the managerial practice of announcing that the interest of the play begins with the rise of the curtain. May a weary critic protest that the interest of too many plays begins only with the fall of those admirable folds? Two other items which might go are the 'Head Over Heels' shop scene, which is quite wantonly dreary, and 'I'm Crazy on the Charleston', of which the music is more depressing than threnody, dirge or coronach.

Remains Spinelly, now making her first bow to a London audience. Let me say at once that the adoring Parisians are right to take no notice of the thews, bulk, and big assemblance of a *diseuse*. Spinelly is the smallest parcel of wit that ever invaded these shores, and may rightfully claim allegiance from all subjects of Queen Mab. She can hardly be said to act, or to dance in the splendiferous, opulent sense, and she does not make even a pretence at singing. It is rather that she communes fantastically with herself. Fancies are spun in that cobwebby brain which are too near gossamer for gross utterance; these she will translate by play of the hands or a flick of a nose ending abruptly like a cliff interrupted by laughing seas. Or you might say that her eyes' sparkle is like a jeweller's window in the Rue de la Paix. Perhaps her best moment is in the Deauville scene, when she discards a mantle at which hundreds of dressmakers must have stitched night and day, and reveals a *négligée* invented by a Beardsley for a Titania. It is in this rapturous costume, held together by a handful of diamonds, that the diva proposes to return to her native foam. In other words, she is going down to the sea to bathe. Was ever impertinence so pertinent? If there be such a thing as a kingdom of the *chic*, one can be perfectly certain who reigns. Is it suggested that our theatres are too big for her? Then must we build bandboxes.

May 2, 1926

THE CHARLOT SHOW OF 1926

BY RONALD JEANS

(Prince of Wales)

ONE of the difficulties of criticism is to rid oneself of personal bias. Indeed, it is doubtful whether this demon can ever be completely exorcized. My own private and particular bugbear is that I cannot put up with waste, and that vacancy delights me not. To be present while the talents of incredibly perfect revue artists like Miss Binnie Hale, Mr. Claude Hulbert and Mr. Jack Buchanan are frittered away upon perfectly incredible banalities first dispirits me and then fires me with a blaze of economic fury. Surely this is unforgivable waste? And yet may there not be another aspect? Put three such talented players on to the stage, deprive them of material, and bid them amuse an audience for three hours — may not the result be the quintessential extract of personality? Do you not in this way get the Binnieness of Hale and the Claudity of Hulbert? Are you not taking your Buchanan neat? Or you might put it that the vacuity of musical comedy is really the 'intenser day' of Shelley's wave, in which personality reaches a definition and significance unattainable in the dry, blurred light of reason. Years ago in *Punch* Du Maurier poked fun at Lady Gorgius Midas refusing a synopsis of *La Dame aux Camélias* on the grounds that she had ·come to see the acting and had no desire to understand the play. The tendency in spectacular entertainments is to go a step further, and, by eliminating interest in the acting by the simple expedient of providing nothing for the actor to act, concentrate attention singly upon the player. Well, this is no new thing. How many virtuosos in the fiddling line ever perform anything of musical interest? How many coloratura singers colour anything except imbecility? Have we not all in our time booked seats for a world-actress in the hope of a new, splurgy Sardou and in the secret fear of being fobbed off with *Phèdre*?

Let us, then, not indulge in too many shrugs of horror at the people who like a big musical affair principally for the people who play in it. Yet those of us who, even in a light entertainment, are all for the play and consider actors only as the play's interpreters, do upon occasion come into our own. *Charlot's Revue* contains several admirable actors who are interpreters first, last, and all the time. There is Mr. Herbert Mundin, who refuses to obtrude his Mundinity, and out of some invisible wardrobe dips for personalities as Lamb's old actor, whose name so closely resembled his, dipped for faces. Mr. Mundin will forgive me if I say that he was always a clever comedian who has now improved out of knowledge. His study of the old cab-driver has all the humour and pathos of Albert Chevalier without the exaggeration. Whether he is portraying comic villain, Yankee policeman (film variety), gentleman's gentleman, or liftboy, he is careful to preserve that little touch of character which differentiates the fine art of burlesque from the grosser one of mere clowning.

Then take Miss Jessie Matthews, who, I am assured, is not yet out of her teens. It was obvious as soon as this little actress came on that she possessed freshness and natural high spirits in keeping with her tip-tilted nose, wide smile, and china-blue, saucer eyes. One thought of the phrase found by Sarcey for Réjane on her first appearance — a '*petite frimousse éveillée*' and 'an air too wide-awake for the house of Molière'. But an actress can hardly be too wideawake for the house of Charlot, and of this fact Miss Matthews seemed admirably well aware. She sang a clever little song with a complete semblance of spontaneity, and danced as one delighted to be dancing. But even so, I was not prepared for her admirable French maid, whom she presented with all the *verve* and distinction and sense of fun of Spinelly at her best. It must be remembered, too, that in giving us a French *soubrette* Spinelly is pretending to be what she is, whereas Miss Matthews succeeds in being to the life what she very obviously isn't. This little sketch revealed talent of a singularly high order, and I suggest that it was a pity to bring this young player on again to sing, in a scena of complete mediocrity and a *négligée* which Mrs. Micawber might have worn, an utterly dull song.

The excellence of this revue is proved by the fact that almost its best item is one in which neither of the two artists mentioned above appears. This is a skit upon broadcasting talks entitled 'Atmospherics'. Here a lecture by a health crank gets mixed up with one by an explorer of sorts and another by a tram-driver in the employ of the Manchester Corporation. The results are not to be described in print. It has been suggested that this scene ought to be censored. If this should unfortunately happen I hope to be given the hint, so that I may attend again before the cuts are made. The whole scene is, in my opinion, an uproarious affair which is entirely healthy. There is more decency, some poet should remark, in honest doubtfulness than in half the permitted, sniggering creeds. Rabelais carries his pardon with him wherever he goes. Where everybody is so good as in this sketch it is invidious to make distinctions. Nevertheless, I shall distinguish, and point to Mr. Allan Macbeth's Major Knapsack, who is like a composite cartoon in which Bairnsfather, Low and Kapp have held the pencil in turns. From time to time Mr. Anton Dolin dances beautifully, and his skit at the expense of the Russian ballet passes triumphantly the test for true parody — that it sends you back to the original with greater pleasure.

151

But however good the acting, singing and dancing, the success of any revue depends in the last resort upon the 'book', which in this case is excellent throughout. One of the most amusing scenes is a burlesque of Italian opera where the entirely felicitous idea is hit upon of first performing the music of the sextet in *Lucia* and then speaking the words in cold blood. One thinks that the idea might be usefully expanded. How would it be to blare out the tune of that chorus in *Sunny* which begins with the word 'Who?' and then let us hear in all its simple virtue the rest of that complicated interrogatory? But the book of this revue is good even when it is spinning its own fun and not finding it where others unconsciously put it. Mr. Charlot apparently believes in Opie's recipe. One should add that the brains with which he has mixed his entertaining colours are those of Mr. Ronald Jeans.

October 17, 1926

BLACK BIRDS

(London Pavilion)

WHEN Hazlitt wrote his famous essay in praise of the Indian jugglers, he troubled his head no jot as to whether they were white or black or red or yellow. They were just supreme artists doing 'what none of us could do to save our lives, if we were to take our whole lives to do it in'. I have never seen dancing to compare with that given by these *Black Birds*. The meanest member of the chorus puts into her work the virtuosity of a Rosenthal circumventing a twelfth Hungarian rhapsody, using, in my judgment, more ease and naturalness. After all, it is comparatively easy not to perform a piano Concerto; whereas these dancers could not keep still if they would.

I am afraid to say what I think about the three male dancers lest I be accused of extravagance. Let it just be stated, then, that in this particular job we can no more find anybody to beat them than we could find somebody to knock out Jack Johnson. Whereupon, I suppose, we shall have to meet objections beginning, 'But hang it all, old chap, these black fellahs, don'cher know. . . .' And the argument continues on the lines laid down by Hamlet's Aunt at the dinner-party. 'We see (black) blood in a nose, and we know it. We meet with it in a chin, and we say, "There it is! That's (black) Blood!" ' For myself I have exceedingly little patience with arguments about the colour-line in general. Doubtless our national poet meant well when he said that 'the regimental bhisti, for all 'is dirty 'ide, was white, clear white, inside'. But what should we think if we found Mr. Rabindranath Tagore writing of some scouring of the Waterloo Road that for all his pallid hide he was black, clear black, inside? And when it comes to the question of public entertainers, be they boxers or jugglers or dancers or what-not — I cannot see that it matters whether they are gamboge, cerise, or burnt sienna. It may even be that the whole continent of Africa is but an extension of the Tottenham Court Road, and that all its dusky sons, like Calverley's victims —

> Plunge after shocking lives
> Razors and carving knives
> Into their gizzards.

After all, it is their own affair, and what any public performer does when he is not performing never has been anybody else's business. Personally, I am convinced that our visitors go home to a bowl of bread and milk and early bed. They are athletes in training.

Miss Florence Mills is a superb artist, whether she is imitating the epileptic frenzy of a witch-dance or indulging in her native melancholy. The notes she warbles are real wood notes, and you would say that her voice is untrained. Untrained because of its astonishing facility. This singer has taken her high C and come down again while more ponderous prima donnas are still debating the ascent. You may say either that hers is the 'quaintest, richest carol of all the singing throats', or that she is like a dove of the fir-wood 'crooning through the coo'. I don't suppose Mr. Cochran will mind which choice you make after paying your guinea. And if it should happen that any American *diseuse* of authentic pallor would like to learn how to sing a sentimental song with restraint . . . But I grow foolish.

September 19, 1926

ONE DAM THING·AFTER ANOTHER

BY RONALD JEANS

(London Pavilion)

Tнᴇ London Pavilion is the home of the *dernier cri*, where the time is not only after dinner, but also the end of the century. The revues produced there are the last word in modishness, and that Mr. Cochran could be behind the times is the extreme of the unthinkable. These things being so, was it not a little remarkable that almost the best thing in the new show was the singing by Little Gwen Stella of that song of Bishop's which the makers of talking-machines insist upon calling 'Lo! Here the Gentle'? This aria was sung to its delicious end, and was rightly applauded. One rubbed eyes and ears even more bemusedly when a young lady threw herself into the recitation which begins: 'The quality of mercy is not strained.' But this did not proceed to its appointed end, for upon the incitement of some hitherto unsuspected lilt in the words, the *cacoethes Charlestoni* seized not only upon plaintiff and defendant, but also upon the Doge of Venice, who, mounting upon the senate-house table, delivered herself — if I mistake not the gender — to the worship of St. Vitus. In and between there were a number of items some of which were very good and some of which were not good at all. Indeed, one might tender to Mr. Cochran advice akin to that offered by Hamlet to his mother — that he should cleave his revue in twain and throw away the worser half of it. For example, the sketches entitled 'Community Singing in the Home', 'The Lady of the Lake', and two others about a butler and a problem picture, did not hit the mark. One knows, of course, that every item in a revue is a gamble. In these four sketches the coin was tossed up and came down tails.

But against these misapprehensions one would set many delight-ful things. There is the delicious scena, 'My Heart Stood Still', beautifully played by Mr. Richard Dolman and that rogue in porcelain, Miss Jessie Matthews. There is that long sustained piece of irony entitled 'Progress', in which the modern jazz and shuffle are shown to be simplifications of aboriginal ecstasy. There is the skit upon dancing grandmothers which is biting. There is a delightful number called 'My Lucky Star', in which Mr. Sonnie Hale and Miss Mimi Crawford repeat, only in a lighter key, the burden of M. Lenormand's 'Les Ratés'. Here, too, Miss Crawford dances exquisitely. She is easily the best dancer in the show, and that which she does is a part of art. The audience rose at her, and I suggest that greater scope should be given to this talented per-former in the direction in which her talent lies. After all, you do not engage a fine fiddler for a concert and then invite him to sing.

Miss Edythe Baker at the piano contributed syncopated arabesques and fantasias, which showed that jazz only awaits its Chopin to become music. It occurs to me as rather a pity that Miss Baker, who does one thing supremely well, should give us so little of it and decline to other forms of entertainment in which she can be, and is in fact, excelled. One of the best things in the show is the dancing of Mr. Max Wall, who performs in a dinner-jacket many steps more appropriate to the coster's jersey. Why this craze for an absurd gentility? With discriminating direction Mr. Wall would probably be one of the best eccentric dancers in the country, though he should, I suggest, always dance in character and refrain from singing. Mr. Art Fowler is a large young gentle-man with a large endowment of charm and a small ukulele, from which he extracts something approximating to melody. Nothing succeeds like success, and Mr. Fowler is to be congratu-lated on getting away with a lyric which contains such couplets as:

> Why does a young baby
> Marry a man of eighty?

I had almost forgotten Mr. Morris Harvey, and the reason is

simply that this most accomplished comedian has been inadequately provided for. He looks best as Shakespeare, and is funniest in his excursion into domains hitherto explored by German professors only.

But I am conscious that I set out to praise this revue, for it contains many little touches of which Mr. Cochran alone knows the secret. It is full of the loveliest colour throughout, Miss Doris Zinkeisen's costumes are treasures, and much of Mr. Aubrey Hammond's scenery is pure joy, the gold, silver and azure curtains bring with them the sheen of the Arabian Nights, the pace throughout is admirable, and if one's praise is a trifle halting in places, it is only because Mr. Cochran has himself set a standard which is almost impossibly high. Yet, for my own part, I should be delighted to see the revue all over again to-morrow. Only I should demand a little more dancing from Miss Crawford, a little more piano-playing from Miss Baker, more and better songs from Miss Matthews, the abolition of a fearsome ditty in a bassinette, a wittier use of Mr. Wall's dancing, and a new part for Mr. Harvey. But the chorus is perfect, and should be changeless.

May 29, 1927

CLOWNS IN CLOVER

BY RONALD JEANS

(Adelphi)

It was, of course, pure coincidence that the first thing to strike one's attention on emerging from the Adelphi Theatre was an omnibus bearing a hieroglyphic inscription in the shape of two raised eyebrows and a low-crowned hat. One had just laid it down, first, that the new revue was the best since *The Bing Boys*, and second, that no revue which didn't contain George Robey could be as good as one that did. The second half of this pontification was, of course, about as sensible as to pretend that no comedy of Shakespeare can be perfect which does not contain Jack Falstaff. The fat knight cannot be in every comedy, and our imp of eyebrow fame cannot be in every revue. With this reservation, which is no reservation, I am going to say, without any beating about the bush, that *Clowns in Clover* is perfect, meaning that on its own plane it is an entertainment without fault. It contains everything which a revue should contain and nothing which it should not. The items have snap, vim, punch, and delicacy. They have variety, and are types of perfect pleasure, since they stop just when one hopes they are going on. They are conquests over dullness. They are made up of wit and humour and oddity and buffoonery and simple fun.

If three people star in a revue, one must be considered first. Let us then consider Miss Cicely Courtneidge. Miss Courtneidge will not take it amiss if one says that she hardly sings, hardly dances, and possesses none of that appealing wistfulness which so appals. She is that rare thing on the revue stage — the 'talented artist' who relies solely upon her talents. These are — to speak nicely — enormous. Those of this artist's talents which lie in the plane of burlesque exceed the normal in that plane, and those which magnoperate closer home are as good as any artist need wish to possess. Miss Courtneidge's modern blade, effulgent as to topper and breast-plated in white marcella, may not outdistance our old favourite, the Midnight Son, in the search for ultimate beauty. Perhaps we may even say that Miss Vesta Tilley was better. But the younger artist's singing of 'There's a Trick in Pickin' a Chicken' is every bit as good as can be looked for in these degenerate days. In the matter of the pure grotesque, of outrageousness marriageable with Grock's, Miss Courtneidge is exceeded, I suggest, by Miss Maisie Gay. But on the plane of reasonable burlesque, where travesty is so faint yet so sure that you fall to wondering where last week you saw the character or the thing travestied, she has no rival.

In 'The Secrets of Good Health' we are actually shown all that Miss Ruth Draper tells us about the crankful ladies who cultivate uncomfortable minds in comfortless bodies. Our parodist's eurhythmic dive lasts only a second, but that fell swoop is enough to slay whole armies of health-and-beauty fads. The middle-aged helpmeet reading to her shop-encumbered and neglectful lord his love-letters of fifteen years 'back', and finally deciding to accept the assistant's proffered escort to the pictures — Clara Pullet is as fine an illustration of 'Against the blown rose may they stop their nose that kneel'd unto the buds' as you shall see in a Sunday-night's play. Do you want to know how bluestockings looked in the early days of bicycling? Miss Courtneidge will show you. Have you been driven almost out of your mind by the mindless ineptitudes of Parisian *diseuses* leading the rout at the Folies-Bergère? Miss Courtneidge will persuade you that you have. Would you deem it possible that a modern audience, crazy for American dance-measures, would uproariously applaud 'The Calinda', in which every horror of modern motion is held up to odium? I promise you that if you visit this revue you will swear by every saint in the calinda to mend your dancing ways.

Now take Mr. Jack Hulbert. Does one like him best as a master-plumber — one would swear at least to the plumber whose mate has been sent home with both bags — recounting exorbitant adventures of unusual greyhounds? Perhaps he chooses his songs poorly. Or as a Benedick finding Beatrice married to have lost none of her disdain? Or as six-foot of Oxford casualness ingratiating itself with the pretty owner of a Baby Something-or-other, but totally unable to adjust arms and legs to the minuscule seating accommodation? Then there's our third star, June, whose singing-babble is like the poet's hidden brook that to the woods all night singeth a quiet tune. But singing is not supposed to be this artist's forte. It is in her dancing that she pours forth her profusest strains of highly premeditated art. One thinks that whoever invented the phrase about the poetry of motion might have waited a bit.

But there's a fourth artist in this show who is probably greater than any I have mentioned. That artist is Mr. Hulbert's chorus, which is an entity composed of limbs subservient to minds and of

minds obedient to one controlling intelligence. It is the personi-
fication of rhythm, and one feels that it is solely due to his artists'
sense of rhythm that Mr. Hulbert has been able to present so
successfully his interpretation of ballet in terms of line and juxtaposition of masses. Time and time again the house rose at the
really miraculous co-ordination of the manœuvres which accompanied Mr. Bobby Comber's skilful singing of 'I Can't Get the
Rhythm'. The ardour and perseverance of Mr. Hulbert's chorus
have become proverbial, and on Thursday night these little ladies
earned their full reward. The labour we delight in does not physic
pain — it prevents it; and the reason this chorus delighted us is
that it was itself delighted.

December 4, 1927

WAKE UP AND DREAM!

BY JOHN HASTINGS TURNER. MUSIC BY COLE
PORTER

(London Pavilion)

CIRCUMSTANCES over which, on this occasion, I really had no con-
trol made me miss the very early item entitled 'Split Seconds with
the Great'. I regretted this throughout the entire evening, since
it seemed likely that Mr. John Hastings Turner had that scope
here which was to be denied him later. *Non omnia*, etc. We cannot
all of us do everything. I shall presume, therefore, that wit had its
innings in this early number, for it did not put up a big score afterwards. What a chance, too, Mr. Turner had! There can be joy
in mere juxtaposition, and just think of these: Mrs. Siddons and
a modern journalist; Ruskin and Mr. Noel Coward; Sir Isaac
Newton and Professor Einstein; Dr. Johnson and Mr. Shaw. The
great Sarah and those others are beyond the reach of satire now.
But who knows how much Mr. Shaw may benefit by Mr. Turner's

'Split Second' with him? If wit is absent from the rest of the show, which perhaps it quite isn't, it is only because Mr. Cochran has other fish to fry.

Rainbow trout they are, too, handled in the spirit of Lalique. Never on any stage have I known so much lustre, or seen so many beaded bubbles winking not at the brim but in the glass itself. Or you might put it that huge though the dictionary of modern colour may be Mr. Cochran has invented new words. What is the shade in that satin which is bolder than primrose but not yet daffodil? That velvet cloak to which the satin is married — did Mr. Cochran go to the rose or the orchid for it, or perhaps steal a little from both? But colour is a mystery. I remember as a boy seeing a picture called 'The White Counterpane', going up to it, and discovering that the hypocritical coverlet was largely composed of blues and yellows, whereby I realized once and for all that colour is not so simple as it looks. 'Pas la couleur, rien que la nuance', preached Verlaine. But I doubt very much whether the decadent poets of the 'nineties, or to-day's distraught young men who with rose-madder make Chelsea still more so, have anything 'on' our impresario.

One of the most delicious scenes ever presented is that entitled ' "Coppelia" from the Wings', where we see part of the famous ballet as it would appear to anybody standing at the stage side. Whoever thought of this hit upon an invention of the utmost felicity. 'The Gold Rush: San Francisco, 1849' is another delightful ballet, and there is a capital series of skits entitled 'Bedtime Stories'. Very few items misfired on the first night, though one might suggest the removal of 'Only a Schoolgirl' and 'The Man with a Red Tie', which are largely responsible for a dull patch in the middle of the second part. It is said, as usual, that Mr. Cochran's second part is not as good as his first. The answer to this is that none of his second parts ever has been or will be — the first half does its job too well. I have no doubt that the spectators at the first performance of *Hamlet* were encouraged by the great soliloquy which ends the second act to hope for better things in the third. Which was nonsense. A cricketer can do no more than hit the ball out of the ground, and the best of billiard-players cannot score more than ten with one shot. In other words there is no bettering a bull's-eye. It is all Mr. Cochran's fault. His first part should not leave us 'blasted with ecstasy'.

In the matter of individual performances it behoves me to go carefully. I suppose I was the only person in London who did not rave over 'Gothic' in Mr. Cochran's last revue. To tell the truth, I find all stained-glass attitudinizing as unamusing as that high-brow profundity known as the 'art of mime'. My mediævalism, if I pretended to any, would be affectation. For about the alleged rhapsody of pose I cannot help echoing what Patience said about Bunthorne's poetry: 'Well, it seems to me to be nonsense!' On this occasion Mr. Cochran has been merciful, and there is a refreshing absence of the nineteen-twenties' equivalent of the 'too, too utter'. Miss Tilly Losch now moves freely in the guise of a human being instead of something plastered upon a wall in Tuscany. Perhaps I should put it that Miss Losch makes that concession to lower intelligence which permits me to understand what she is about. Her performance is lovely and entertaining instead of lovely and 'amusing', in the precious sense which makes Mr. Aldous Huxley so angry. With Miss Losch, as the lawyers say, is Mr. Toni Birkmayer, an admirable dancer. Then there is Miss Tina Meller, who is much too newly come from Spain to convince me that she is Spanish. Ten years of performing *Carmen* for the American talkies would doubtless modify Miss Meller's obviously mistaken notions about her own country. In other words, I find a strange and disturbing quality of truth in her very arresting performance, and I beg her not to do so much as tidy her hair in her search for Spanish truth as revealed in the fastnesses of Hollywood to, let me say, the Misses Mea, Thea, and Maxima Culpa.

Miss Jessie Matthews we all know, and her odd little beauty and queer little talent are as ravishing as ever. That good actor Mr. Fred Groves has little to act, and so resembles a sailor without a ship. But his fortitude is admirable. Mr. George Metaxa lets off a number of high notes with the unimpaired gusto of a steam-organ at a country fair; that excellent comedian Mr. Sonnie Hale

adds to the gaiety of at least one nation by his miraculous impersonations of Sir Thomas Beecham and a Queen of the Night
Clubs; and Messrs. Lance Lister and Douglas Byng are always
agreeably there or thereabouts. Then there are Mr. Cochran's
Young Ladies, who are uniformly young and ladylike. Last I
come to some performances of obvious difficulty and explicit merit
which do not need to be passed through any interpretative filter.
These are dancing acts. One is that of Mr. Chester Fredericks,
who makes us believe that the stage, like Time, is slipping under-
neath his feet. And slipping with maximum celerity. The other
act is done by a Russian trio, the Berkoffs, who excite us as the
Indian jugglers excited Hazlitt — that is, by doing one thing
supremely well.

March 31, 1929

THE JACK POT

BY ROWLAND LEIGH AND GREATREX NEWMAN

(Prince of Wales)

— Et c'est là cependant
Que toi, mon seul amour, toi, mes seules délices,
Tu brames tous les soirs d'infâmes ritournelles,
Et que, la bouche en cœur, l'œil clos, le bras pendant,
Tu souris aux voyous, ô la Reine des belles!

— HUYSMANS

FIRST, since this revue enshrines Miss Marion Harris, let us talk of
cabaret-singers in general. Why cabaret? — as Miss Julia Mills
might have asked. The answer is that a cabaret-singer is a vocalist
who does something other than that done by opera-singers,
concert-singers, music-hall singers, drawing-room singers, public-
banquet singers, community and street singers. To discover that
something other we will apply the old legal maxim: 'Quis, quid,

ubi, quibus auxiliis, cur, quomodo, quando', which one believes might be translated: 'Who, what, where, with what, why, how, when?' Of these seven questions the first, third, and last are already answered, since everybody knows who cabaret-singers are, where they sing, and when. The fact that they use the ordinary vocal organs and maintain the upright position like other singers disposes of the fourth and sixth questions, 'with what' and 'how'. Thus the issue is narrowed down to: What do these artists sing, and why?

It will be convenient to reverse the order here. The reason why cabaret-singers exist is to give pleasure to a number of people in evening dress bemused by food and wine, dizzied by the previous dance and the smoke in which, like the cigarette-girls in *Carmen*, they have been swaying. But this is not contested, so that our research into the quiddity of cabaret-singers is whittled down to the all-important 'what'. What, then, is the matter that they sing? To proceed by negatives, one would say that this must not be concerned with beauty or art, since the audience is in no mood for either. It must not be of the stuff of brains, since we know the audience to be befogged, though it should still have some flattering suggestion of the intelligible. This leaves only the passions, distilled to that emotion to which the whole of night-club creation moves, a perfectly realized but hardly formulated senti-mentalism, babble of embraces under the moon whereby some young man innocent of Shelley will ask his dance-partner during the drive home what were all those kisses worth if she kiss not him.

But romanticism is out of date, and the singer must echo the post-war *malaise*, the nineteen-thirties' extreme of disillusion. 'And shake the yoke of inauspicious stars from this world-wearied flesh', spouted a young man who would have gone to night clubs if Verona had had any. Cabaret stars may be inauspicious, though this will not matter so long as they realize that the gleaming shoulders unyoked by them are fashionably world-wearied. But would it not be a humiliating reflection for our Bright Young Things — presuming they ever reflected — that all this disillusion is no more than our old friend the coster's: 'Wot's the good of anyfink? Why, nuffink!'

To sum up, then, a cabaret-singer must not be able either to sing or act, or if these handicaps are present must abjure them, since to exercise either function is like letting daylight into a ballroom. Or I will put it that there is no modern cabaret which an Yvette Guilbert or a present-day Aristide Bruant would not ruin in a week. Yet the fortunes of these places are nightly made by singers of lavish voicelessness who could not hit a note correctly if they possessed one, and by amiable young men of weak wit coaxing nostalgia out of neoprimitive zithers. The art of cabaret-singing, finally, consists in having the least exacting audience at your feet while you look unutterable things and bleat about sweeties deserted by honeys, the lyric bejewelled with such rich versification as

> There was a time
> When you were mine.

Miss Marion Harris looks lovely in geranium, and when she elects for black — or is it white? — in which to indulge Mamie's heartache or Sadie's self-pity concedes nothing to the legitimate actress in her suggestion of ineffable woe. With this difference: that your actress proper, having postulated woe, will 'get on with it', whereas the law of cabaret not only grants but enforces stay of execution. Now I am not such a duffer as not to know that Miss Harris' art is something more than standing motionless by a piano. This clever artist does what one glibly calls nothing, but puts that nothing over in a manner to recall Huysmans':

> Yet on this poor stage
> You with hoarse ditty infinitely move
> Me to the memory of old love and rage,
> Whilst with red mouth and lax luxurious mien
> You tease pale cut-throats, O my Beauty's Queen.

Nevertheless, old fogeys may be forgiven for wondering whether

cabaret-singing, even with Huysmans' warranty, is an advance
upon Marie Lloyd's:

> Stand us a cab-fare, ducky.
> I'm feeling awfully queer!

In the way of honest-to-goodness fooling there is Miss Phyllis
Monkman, whose parodies have the proper quality of cruelty,
while a sedulous scanning of the ceiling reveals Barbette, whose
terra-firma imitation of Marlene Dietrich is infinitely more amusing
than those researches into the morbid psychology of the trapeze.

May 15, 1932

FANFARE

BY DION TITHERADGE. MUSIC BY HENRY SULLIVAN

(Prince Edward)

THE best of an *olla podrida* is that if you don't like the *olla* you may
like the *podrida*. Perhaps the surest way of arriving at the good in
this revue is the old business of elimination, which may take a
little time, though some good will almost certainly be discovered.
What is the first thing one looks for in a revue? *Décor?* By my,
Mr. Messel's, and anybody else's halidom I swear I have never
seen anything less distinguished than this jumble. A possible exception is the setting to the Wilde ballet, 'The Nightingale and the
Rose', a parable which exhibits that master's ignorance of at least
two worlds, the ornithological and the horticultural.

Or does one look first for melody? The music to *Fanfare* is
chiefly din, but din on the grand scale beside which a Clydeside
dockyard is a lover's whisper. The band was most spectacularly
conducted by very young Herr Franz Steininger, who in three
short hours used up as much gesticulation as a Toscanini or a
Beecham will permit himself throughout an entire opera season.

165

REVUES

However, the proof of the pudding is in the eating, always provided
we take no account of the eater's hunger, and it will be safe to
give Herr Steininger every credit for the passion, ecstasy, and pain
which every player under his bâton seemed to feel about nothing
in particular. And feel it all together and at the same time, unlike
those battleships in the naval review at Spithead, the thunder of
whose guns, said the imaginative reporter, was 'not only sublime
but simultaneous — first the *Irresistible*, and, shortly after, the
Irresponsible'. True that to the detached observer it seemed
at times that more was going on in the accompaniment than
in the thing accompanied. But let that pass. Herr Steininger,
though a foreigner, was good enough to make us wonder whether
there are any more at home like him, meaning our home!
The sketches? I had almost written that these were of an
appalling ineptitude, except that 'appalling' should be reserved
for that which appals — plagues, landslides, and that sort of thing.
As these drivelling little snippets passed before our eyes we merely
wondered how the idea that they might entertain could have
entered the human mind. I except from this moderate stricture
Mr. Beverley Nichols's 'On Dit', which is an opuscule showing how
a pebble of gossip may become an avalanche of slander.

Or is wit the first thing to be looked for in a revue? If there is
to be no wit why not a realistic scene or two? Why not a scene
at a bridge club? Readers know the kind of thing I mean.
Spinsters tottering on the verge of the grave make the passionate
declarations which they have never received, retired Colonels
throw away tricks just as they did lives, while the better-halves
of diamond merchants burst into tears at five shillings a hundred.
Twice in my life I have ventured into one of these dens of tea and
toast, malice and uncharitableness; and my recollection is of a
nest of bosom enemies or a vulturine congress flapping baleful
wings. To sit at the same table with a woman bridge-player is
one of the dread things of the earth.

But it is time to deal with the principals, and here I record
two undoubted successes. I have mentioned the conductor,
and now comes Miss Violet Loraine. This delicious actress,

who now returns to the stage, is so endeared to us by old recollection that it would be impertinent in all senses of the word to inquire whether she has the piquancy of Miss Gertrude Lawrence or the *vis comica* of Miss Maisie Gay. Perhaps she has a bit of both, and she is certainly endowed with that personal charm which, unlike executive ability, must always be proof against comparison. She sings snatches of the old war-time songs, notably 'If you were the only Girl in the World'. Now, though many philosophers have had their say about reason, few have pointed out how in any battle against sentiment it crumples up almost as precipitantly as a British heavyweight boxer in a fight for world championship. Rationally considered, the characteristic thing about love is the power to make its own isolation, the whole virtue of being the only girl and the only boy alive among the world's millions. To the logical mind there can be nothing less romantic than a pairing which admits of no choice; you either pair or you don't, in the second case lamenting, or rejoicing at, enforced chastity. But did any Officers' Mess perceive this? No, and rightly no. Nor is it proper to perceive it now. In a recent essay about battalion reunions Mr. Edmund Blunden writes feelingly of the hatred for anything like superannuation and substitutes: 'In that dizzy period of dreams, rumours, upheavals, fears, escapades, vanities, immeasurable moments, apprehensions, that which one had gained as a sheltering, steady, warm abiding-place in nature became especially precious. At one time it was actual, present, daily and hourly — and when that date was expired, among the other dreams this dream stood long. . . .' Strange that a little music-hall ditty should have become one of these places of shelter and steadying. But so it was, and while other music-hall songs abide our questioning this one and half a dozen others must for ever go free. Miss Loraine, when she sings the old song, can hardly help moving everybody almost as much now as she did then. On the first night this number held up the show.

The Condos Brothers are a pair of dancers whose extraordinary agility is necessarily matched by their lack of grace, since the execution of this kind of step-dancing demands the bowed pose of the gorilla. Mr. Joe Cook is an American comedian whose humour consists almost entirely in the 'props' that he is funny with. For example, when he desires to light a cigarette he does so by means of a candle produced from the handle of his walking-stick, and the number of his 'props' must exceed those dreamed of by Mr. W. H. Berry in his wildest nightmare. Miss Rose Perfect sings frequently and loudly, and best when she is loudest. Lastly there is June dancing imponderably as of old, though her singing still resembles 'the earliest pipe of half-awakened birds'.

June 26, 1932

CRAZY MONTH

(Palladium)

THE late A. B. Walkley, concerned to explain Grock, did so by reference to Bergson, Brunetière, and Benedetto Croce. But Walkley was a man in whom even a molehill of talent — and Grock is a genius — evoked mountains of erudition, and this presumably was why he could not content himself with saying that Grock is another Ally Sloper. One wonders what the great critic would have had to say about this week at the Palladium, and where he would have found the metaphysicians for our funny fellows to derive from. Even the simple-minded critics who are content to say who or what somebody or something is like and why, have their present difficulties, since there are not enough Ally Slopers to go round. Shall we say that Jimmy Nervo is a Walt Disney version of a masterpiece by Botticelli? His vernal caperings suggest that the comparison is as apt as anything else we are likely to stumble upon. Shall we say that Charlie Naughton of the vestigial nose and enigmatic smile is the incarnation of the Sphinx? Or that Bud Flanagan is Mr. Epstein's reduction to stone of Anatole France's 'L'Ile des Penguins'? Coming to Miss Nellie Wallace, one simply says: Shall I compare thee to a summer's day? — except of course that she looks more lovely and that her behaviour must by the terms of her art be considerably less temperate.

All these are easy triumphs which, however, do not pave the way for success in the matter of Eddie Gray. Of this artist even Walkley might perhaps have been satisfied to say that he abounds in his own quality, which, strictly between you and me, is what every artist does who is worth a penful of ink. What, then, is Gray's quality? I shall say that it is an inherent invincible seediness, a compendium of poor-relationship, a vade-mecum of down-at-heelness, an epitome of traipsing Nosey-Parkerishness like an income-tax inspector taking a busman's holiday, the whole enveloped in a Michael-Angelesque dignity. It is this dignity, this remnant of Man's lost majesty, which permits this wander-wit to don an invisible cloak and proclaim himself an Ozymandias, King of kings, who out of caprice chooses to wear frayed dickey and sagging collar, steel spectacles, and lustreless top hat. It was said of George Herbert that he wore his soul divinely loose about him. So it is with Eddie, who is 'touched', though not by human finger. In other words, this is a superb buffoon, and if he and Grock were to meet face to face I will lay a shade of odds on Grock being the first to laugh. Thus the critical wheel comes full circle — an odd statement in connection with an entertainment in which, according to the programme, 'even the Palladium clocks aren't right'.

It is always said that a play is not a play till the audience has helped to act it, though, owing to the dependability of sane audiences in a sane world, this concept does not make the act of playwriting impossible. But at the Palladium it is Crazy Month in a crazy world, a world in which cause is not bound to produce effect, and effect need not necessarily proceed from cause. And since gravity has also been abolished it follows that the Palladium has invented that space-time continuum which Sir James Jeans and Professor Einstein have declared to exist in fact. But I have neither the space nor the time to go into this, and the immediate wonder is how these clowns rehearsing before no audience know which jape will drown the next. Their intuition has been marvellous, though at times it almost seems that first the audience laughs, and that to meet this laughter some jest of mind and more often of body is hastily improvised. If I have a criticism it is that Miss Wallace is thrown away just as a prima donna would be lost whose Mad Song should be eked out by a chorus of maniacs ululating each according to his whim and fancy.

It would be wrong to assume that mind is absent from this entertainment; it isn't. Its whole object is to lead the under-standing of the audience up the garden paths of misplaced sentiment. Or you might say that the whole show is a long lane whose turnings belong somewhere else, which is well exemplified in the rambling approximations of Bud Flanagan. Say that in some Egyptian scene there is a question of slaves. 'The fellows in bandages?' queries Mr. Flanagan hopefully. 'You mean bondage!' says somebody. 'No, I don't,' retorts Mr. Flanagan. 'That's whisky!' This crazy world, we begin to perceive, has its logic — a poor logic but its own.

March 12, 1933

STREAMLINE

BY A. P. HERBERT AND RONALD JEANS. MUSIC BY VIVIAN ELLIS

(Palace)

'DANCING', says Ernest Dowson, 'to put thy pale, lost lilies out of mind.' But the dancing in this, Mr. Cochran's twenty-first revue, is intended to have the precisely opposite effect, at least in the case of Miss Tilly Losch. This very fine artist has three lovely dances, of which I am able to understand two. The first is a delicious period piece showing a Parisian Miss of the Meilhac and Halévy period (music by Offenbach) in the perturbations attendant upon posting a letter. The second, to an air by Rameau, is a pictorial

Hymn to Music, in which the dancer, at rest relative to earth, dances from the ankles upwards; these noble curves and sweeps, recalling the bowing first of Neruda and then of Suggia, have the breadth and majesty of a theme by Brahms. The third and less intelligible dance is like a page torn out of a book on baroque architecture by Mr. Sacheverell Sitwell, and one is tremendously impressed without knowing why! Miss Losch is a wonderful little artist, and if one has a criticism, it is that she is always threatening to go Gothic and does not let cheerfulness break in as often as it might.

The dancing of Miss June Hart is beyond criticism in the vulgar sense. One is tremendously impressed, and one knows exactly why; this is the most of grace, agility, and poise that ballroom-dancing has yet achieved. Miss Hart's first dance was of such flame-like beauty that it brought tears to the eyes, after which there was nothing to do except shout oneself hoarse, which everybody did. Her second dance was like the fluttering of some golden moth, and again the audience went into ecstasies. The difference between Miss Losch and Miss Hart is that the first is dancing of the mind, to which mind must be brought as to the reading of a missal, whereas the second is dancing of the body, which may be appreciated in terms of simple wonder. Beauty is a large house in which these two artists occupy separate flats, one on the top floor of fancy and the other on the ground floor of fact.

Spendthrift of loveliness that he is, Mr. Cochran has given us a third dancer, La Jana, whose flat is about half-way up the stairs. Her dance, entitled 'La Femme et le Pantin' (music by Granados), takes place on a kind of drum between a Spanish toreador and Whistler's mother. The idea being grasped, it only remains to admire some lovely convolutions. On the male side there is Sherkot, very good at acrobatics and a master of caricature. The first-night audience took intense joy in his professional goal-keeper, whose mind is a vacant space, but whose feet are alive with cerebration. Seldom before has class of both kinds been so distinctly portrayed; the fellow is lout at one end and genius at the other.

171

It is good that there should be so much dancing, with the resulting opportunities for Mr. Cochran's dazzling sense of *décor*;
Mesdames Doris Zinkeisen, Cathleen Mann, and Messrs. Rex
Whistler, Cecil Beaton, and Tom Webster have served him wittily,
wisely and well. It is good because the spoken wit is a trifle un-
even, meaning that when it is sought it is not always found, but
that when it is found it is a bobby-dazzler. In the early part of
the revue both Mr. A. P. Herbert and Mr. Ronald Jeans are a
little off colour, and the sketches entitled 'Fashions for Men,' 'Pink
Knickers', and 'The Private Life of Napoleon Bonaparte' should be
struck out, because they are nothing. In the sketch showing news-
paper readers at breakfast as much moved as the spreaders of
news suppose, Mr. Jeans is at the top of his form.

Then comes a really brilliant pastiche of Gilbert and Sullivan.
Here Mr. Herbert has perfectly reproduced Gilbert's knack of
being pseudo-portentous in sentences two words long. The ducal
father of twin heirs declining to say which is the elder, Perseverance looks up from under her sun-bonnet and says: 'Extravagant
predicament!' Mr. Herbert has turned Gilbert's mind inside out
and given us some of the old silver lining. The same thing has
been done for Sullivan by Mr. Vivian Ellis, whose re-creation
might not be re-creation at all but a newly discovered fragment
from the *Patience* period. It has all the well-known mannerisms,
together with Sullivan's way of leading up to a particular kind of
air, and then giving you the air that you expected. This takes
doing, and Mr. Ellis has done it. Miss Zinkeisen's scenery here
is a delightful jumble of all the operas.

Mr. Herbert is very good, too, in 'Speech Day', and the two
humorists join brains in a dressing-room skit on evolution, which
proves, if it proves anything, that the nuder the body, the nicer
the mind. But I am not sure that all these wonders and marvels
do not pale before the acting of Miss Florence Desmond, who not
only has a white-hot sense of the ridiculous but can present it in
a dozen different disguises. She has suburban enormity perfectly
taped, as they say, and this culminates in the appearance at the
microphone of a lady who has taken the accent of Muswell Hill

to the North Pole and scattered it over those wan wastes. Just as Wordsworth's nun was breathless with adoration, so this air-minded heroine is so vowel-bound as to be almost speechless. This is satire at its best, in which kind the crueller the better. A dozen times in the evening Miss Desmond nails the grotesque truth to the board; she is a whole show in herself.

September 30, 1934

FOLLOW THE SUN

BY RONALD JEANS AND JOHN HASTINGS TURNER. MUSIC BY ARTHUR SCHWARTZ

(Adelphi)

THIS sunny revue, like George, second Duke of Buckingham, is everything by starts and nothing long. Which is as it should be, given that the function of revue is to mirror the taste of the day. *Follow the Sun* is as breathless as Dickens's Flora: 'Venice preserved too I think you have been there is it well or ill preserved for people differ so and Maccaroni if they really eat it like the conjurers why not cut it shorter.' But you could not cut Mr. Cochran's scenes shorter. Dawn is hardly up on any of his prospects, and in the twinkling of an eye the glimmering landscape has not only faded but merged into the next. The result is mental indigestion, like that occasioned by an author who should serve up Dryden, Dickens, Corinthians, and Gray in his first paragraph!

There is a moment in every one of his revues in which our impresario goes Gothic. This time the moving spirit is Heine's *The Three Holy Kings.* It is in my mind that Richard Strauss has composed a song on this subject which Mme. Elisabeth Schumann sings, and I have no doubt that Mr. Cochran would have engaged that great artist but for the necessity of inviting her later on to rub shoulders with his rumba dancers, which can hardly

be the concern of lieder-singers. He has done very well to engage
Miss Irene Eisinger, a beautiful little lady whose small but charming voice is perhaps more suited to Glyndebourne's flowery
meads than to Covent Garden's. Miss Eisinger still flutes loudly
enough, however, to get the better of Herr Hannes Ruch's Handel-
and-water. Professor Stern's composition is an arresting one,
and strikes the note to which he adheres throughout — that of a
modern Albrecht Dürer working in gold and silver paper and the
gayer shades of claret, olive and pimento. In this instance it
cannot be said of Mr. Cochran that, like Bunthorne's, his mediævalism's affectation. May I suggest that it springs from a quarter-
century's admiration of the greatest stage-designer of our time?

Are the Professor's scenes a little too cloying in their rich
succession? Possibly, but he can be simple as well. His 'Polonaise', in which the dancers are mere silhouettes, is a good
example. And then there is 'Sleigh Bells', the last scene of all. This
begins with the most uncompromising elaboration, merry-go-
rounds, prancing horses, and the general impression that the
cardboard industry has been working overtime. But presently
the scene melts to nothing, leaving us in an empty world, alone
with the falling snow. After all, the function of scenery is sometimes to leave the stage free for the cast, and this revue's delightful
close suggests that either the Professor has realized this or does not
want to give us what Lady Macbeth calls the stern'st good-night.

And now perhaps we are ready to follow the sun. We begin
with 'Strolling Actresses Dressing in a Barn'. This, thanks to
Mr. Hogarth, is one of the most satisfying things in a show which
seems to conduct its peripatetics on the principle of the snipe.
Or rather, Mr. Cochran appears to be following two hares — the
sun, and the playing conditions for actors in all climes and times.
And why not? With the playing conditions of 1750 are contrasted
those of 1936, a scene so good that it might well be longer. Now
Mr. Paul Meeres and Miss Barbara Meade execute a dance which,
like atonal music and ultra-modern poetry, is so ugly that it must
be beautiful. I shall hazard the guess that these are the best
dancers in a show full of dancers. Next, 'The Lady with the Tap'

wherein Miss Claire Luce in an exotic skirt breaks into a barracks of adorably simpering infantrymen, none other than Mr. Cochran's Young Ladies. Why, if as we suppose Miss Luce is a spy, she should tap on the floor to call attention to her theft of documents, escapes me. The programme tells us that the idea has been conceived by Mr. Vincente Mennelli; he should either have conceived a different idea or called the present one 'Claire Lucas a non Lucendo'.

And then at long last we arrive at Cuba, where the condition of tickling one sense would appear to be the annoyance of another. Never in all my life have I heard cacophony so blaring, so vulgar, so inane, as the row presented here. It offends me to the very soul to see a stringed instrument slapped instead of played, and I would rather tolerate the vilest cornet blown than see it muted, when, of course, it brays just as loudly. One cannot walk out or cover one's ears, because to do so would be rude; I can only say that so far as I am concerned all the pleasure derived from Professor Stern's remarkable scene and the antics of these simple coloured folk was negatived by the vile noise they made. Here an important point occurs. Are we watching the natural exuberance of a primitive people? Or are they the sophisticated entertainers, and we the gaping simpletons? Is it our reason, or theirs, which, as Hamlet says, 'pandars will'? Either way there is no denying that our visitors are the life of the show, and that against their enormous physical energy everything else pales. In so far as these are conscious artists I imagine that they must be perfectly calm and collected inside, that what looks like epilepsy and paranoia is the merest simulation, and that it is the onlooker who is 'apoplex'd'. Choose how, as Lancashire people say, I do not think that:

> Nor sense to ecstasy was ne'er so thrall'd
> But it reserved some quantity of choice

will ever be our visitors' motto. They are just about as reserved as a third-class railway carriage bound for Epsom on Derby Day.

The best thing in the second part is the delicious Edwardian ballet. In this Mr. Osbert Sitwell, Mr. Cecil Beaton aiding and abetting, has imagined pheasants capering about a wood which, judging from a telephone and an easel-portrait, is also a drawing-room! The plot concerns a shooting party given by a nobleman who has married into the chorus, there is a shooting accident, and presently the guests dance off to Mr. William Walton's entrancing strains and luncheon-baskets from Belshazzar's, Ltd.

February 9, 1936

SPREAD IT ABROAD

BY HERBERT FARJEON. MUSIC BY WILLIAM WALKER

(Saville)

THE week under notice begins and ends Sparkenbrokishly. In his new novel Mr. Charles Morgan has explained how, if there is no life beyond death, then poetry, music, and even the multiplication table are not only meaningless but fraudulent, since they announce a transcendence, a something-to-comeness which does not exist. Now here in this revue is Miss Ivy St. Helier sitting in a café over a glass of absinthe and explaining at much less length than Mr. Morgan how the almond blossom and the birds and the human lovers walking beneath the trees are their own transcendence:

> Paris in spring, spring in the air,
> Birds on the wing — everywhere.
> They all find out one day
> There's nothing to find out!

Mr. Farjeon might have rhymed, as Horatio says, but the sentiment is pure Sparkenbroke for all that. And how well Miss St. Helier does it, looking the perfect Degas just as in *Bitter-Sweet* she

176

looked the perfect Manet. Her dressmaker sketch is a song of the shirt in the modern astringent key, with all the pathos wrung out of it, and the town will be divided between her musical-comedy diva of 1966 composing wholly unreliable memoirs and her Italian prima donna returning to one of her many first loves.

Miss St. Helier is grandly partnered by Mr. Nelson Keys, who is so good throughout that he can probably bear to hear that his Charles Laughton is only middling. But see him as two school-masters — St. Winifred's *circa* 1862 and Groundsel present day. Or as a hairdresser and an operatic tenor, intoxicated by their Italian temperaments. Or as an English Major bibulous in the bulldog, monosyllabic way.

Miss Dorothy Dickson brings a breath from another world — the world of soap-bubbles and sea-foam. Her dances are the complete refutation of Mr. Morgan's theories as to ecstasy to come. The summer's flower is to the summer sweet, and that probably is all there is, or ever was, to be said! Yet this clever little artist, whose skill seems to be less of art than of nature, can, when she wants, swoop to the humdrum like some ethereal, feathered warbler with a surprisingly good eye for a worm. Her holiday photographer is devastating enough to make us resolve to tear up our snapshot albums, or at least never again exhibit them. By the way, I noticed that throughout the revue Mr. Keys never meets Miss Dickson. If the reason is that they do not know each other, I shall be delighted to introduce them!

Of the many other items quite the best is Mr. Lyle Evans's rebuke to cabaret. This is called 'Dirty Songs', and in it the whip is used with scarifying effect. Many galled jades did in fact wince. This is perhaps the place to say that wit, satire, and the lampoon must always be the pillars of revue, the dresses and the *décor* being no more than the capitals, pleasant affairs to the eye but doing little to support the building. That revue which is all spectacle always sends its audience away grumbling about the absence of wit, whereas nobody has ever been heard to say after a really witty revue that they could have done with more dress-making and scene-painting. What is here of these two arts

177

satisfies any reasonable appetite. The *décor* by Coombe and the dresses by Mr. Norman Edwards are remarkably good in their kind, and in the ballets called 'Aubade' and 'Plaid Interlude', the music to the latter being by Lord Berners, there has been some expense of imagination. With a trifle of good will one need not hear the rest of the music, which is dullish.

April 5, 1936

BLACKBIRDS OF 1936

BY LEW LESLIE. MUSIC BY RUBE BLOOM

(Gaiety)

THE first item in the programme is a 'Negro Cavalcade'. This has the sub-title: 'From when the Negro Dance-Rhythm of songs in Folk-Lore, Jubilees, Plantation Ballads, Levee Pastimes, Rag-time, Syncopation, Jazz, and the Blues began.' This, again, is prefaced in the programme by a quotation from a writer unknown to me, Mr. James Weldon Johnson. Mr. Johnson writes about the early days of the African slave trade with the American colonies: 'These people came from various localities in Africa. They did not all speak the same language. Here they were, suddenly cut off from the moorings of their native culture, scattered without regard of their old tribal relations, having to adjust themselves to a completely alien civilization, having to learn a strange language, and, moreover, held under an increasingly harsh system of slavery; yet it was from these people this mass of noble music sprang; this music which is America's only folk music, and, up to this time, the finest distinctive contribution she has to offer the world.'

Obviously this links up with the warning which Walt Whitman towards the end of his days gave out to Americans and the world in general — the warning that the American people was not ready and could not be expected to produce any national art: 'At present the States are absorb'd in business, money-making, politics, agriculture, the development of mines, inter-communications, and other material attents — which all shove forward and appear at their height — as, consistently with modern civilization, they must be and should be . . . A national literature is a great mirror or reflector. There must, however, be something before — something to reflect . . . Certainly the United States do not so far utter poetry, first-rate literature, or any of the so-called arts, to any lofty admiration or advantage — are not dominated or penetrated from actual inherence or plain bent to the said poetry and arts. Other work, other needs, current inventions, productions, have occupied and to-day mainly occupy them.' At the same time, adds Walt, who had a keen eye for his compatriots' weaknesses, Americans 'are very "cute and imitative and proud" — can't bear being left too glaringly away far behind the other high-class nations — and so we set up home "poets", "artists", painters, musicians, *literati*, and so forth, all our own (thus claim'd)'. All that was uttered some fifty years ago, and there would seem to be evidence that in that short space America is getting nearer a national contribution to the art of the world. Not very much nearer, perhaps, but something. And I would instance her theatre — so far as I who have never been to America am able to judge — her fiction, and her comic draughtsmanship in which she leads the world. In Hollywood she leads the world's vulgarity, but then films constitute not art but excellent business, and that is not quite what we are talking about.

It is certain that the items based upon folk-music are the best things in this revue. The whole of the 'Cavalcade' is excellent alike in its pictorial quality and in its race fulfilment. Is it a trifle noisy? Yes, but these are the children of noise. Now consider the spiritual entitled 'Great Gittin' Up Mornin'', to the singing and enacting of which goes as much fervour, though of a different kind, as Blake or any other painter has put into his Last Judgment. Beside such leapings, boundings, and body-convulsions the European method of conveying emotion through facial expression only is inexpressive indeed. But then all these Africans are like the froward man in the Book of Proverbs: 'He winketh with his eyes, he speaketh with his feet, he teacheth with his fingers.' Or you might put it that the sons of Ham are not ham actors. Or are only so-called by people who cannot act. For jealousy besides being 'the rage of a man' is the mark of your indifferent actor.

The moment these unsophisticated players cease to follow their own bent and bend it in a sophisticated direction, they, not to put too fine a point upon it, fail. The item entitled 'The Opera Barber's Shop', in which barbers, customers, manicurists, and bootblacks guy 'gems of opera', meaning *Rigoletto* and the others, is a grotesque and prolonged mishap. And though there is some good singing in 'She Done Me Wrong' there doesn't seem to be much point in reproducing the well-known 'Frankie and Johnnie' ballad as though it were the last act of *The Bells*.

Matters are restored when our visitors again return to themselves and replace their early simplicity with their own sophistication, not ours. This means dancing, and it is all nonsense to pretend that the white races have ever produced anything comparable to the performance of the Four Bobs. It is absurd to argue that these are not Nijinskys; grace is not their aim, and they do not attempt it. But neither did Nijinsky attempt this particular kind of pedal virtuosity; the two things are totally different in kind. An afternoon with the Faun made one faint with pleasure; an evening with these Blackbirds makes one faint with exhaustion. Here is dancing as the plain man can understand it. Mr. Shaw once remarked that whether *King Lear* is a good or bad play must always be a matter of opinion, whereas a boxer lying insensible on the floor and unable to get up is a matter of fact. In the ballet called 'Jardin Public' the tatterdemalions drooping like fuchsias in the rain ask me for an opinion which I am not competent to give; these black dancers do not need to assure me that their feats are incredibly difficult, for I can see that for myself. Almost they seem to take to it as ducks to water. At least I incline to believe that Master Harold Nicholas must have danced in those swaddling clothes from which he has so recently emerged. He is unique among infant phenomena in that he is both a tot and an artist; his turns were the smash hits of the evening, the audience not knowing which to admire most, twinkling feet or slow, baby smile. But all the dancers are superb, and it would be wrong to omit to mention by name Danny and Edith, Gordon and Rogers, and Anise and Aland.

Possibly the show is a little weak on the distaff side, though this must ever be so long as the memory of Florence Mills persists. Mr. Tim Moore and Mr. Gallie de Gaston are two grand comedians. In his slowness of appreciation Mr. Moore shows himself to be an actor of the school of Dodd: 'You could see the first dawn of an idea stealing over his countenance, climbing up by little and little, with a painful process, till it cleared up at last to the fullness of a twilight conception—its highest meridian. . . . A glimmer of understanding would appear in a corner of his eye, and for lack of fuel go out again.' Mr. Moore's partner is an actor of no school at all, because he is too little to have any. He is the tiniest of creatures. Of him it might be said, with the old philosopher: 'A point hath no dimensions, but only a whereness, and is next to nothing.' But what an amusing whereness! Mr. de Gaston is the perfect partner for Mr. Moore — a happy coupling of Ubiety and Dubiety!

July 12, 1936

O - K A Y   F O R   S O U N D

BY R. P. WESTON AND BERT LEE

(Palladium)

THE management at the Palladium has apparently been struck with the notion that crazy nights, like crazy pavements, should have some *raison d'être*. Why not? One leads you up an empty garden, the other to a full house. Our genial management has put a frame round the new production by suggesting that what we are watching is the making of that extraordinary thing which the film trade calls a musical. The show is neither the better nor the worse for this, just as boiled mutton remains the same whether you eat it off gold, silver, or tin; it all depends on the caper sauce. Let it be said that the Palladium's great bunch of comedians is as saucy and as full of capers as ever.

The studio is called The Goldray, its boss being Mr. Goldmine. Mr. Joe Hayman portrays the type wonderfully well, with a nose fuller of acumen than egg ever was of meat. One wonders where Mr. George Black found Mr. Hayman, and perhaps Mr. Hayman wonders where he found himself. Anyhow, it is an astonishing find, affording equal pleasure to Jew and Gentile. Were it necessary to find a meeting ground for the two races, that Cyrano-esque nose would serve. Unlike the old-fashioned dramatist who gave his plays one *scène-à-faire* and one only, Mr. Goldmine insists that his productions shall have at least six. The first is entitled 'An Episode of Don Juan', with *décor*, if you please, by Professor Ernst Stern. This *décor* is not the same thing as the old-fashioned music-hall setting, since that used to be exciting and vulgar, whereas this is exciting and handsome. The orchestra does admirable justice to Mozart's music, for here are ten full minutes of magic flutes and equally enchanted bassoons, clarinets, and fiddles, all blowing and scraping away in the best Glyndebourne manner. Mr. Lino Carenzio looks like Beardsley's drawing of Valmont in *Les Liaisons Dangereuses*, and even like what operatic singers imagine they look like as Don Giovanni. This is immediately followed by the same episode as Messrs. Nervo and Knox have imagined it with the sympathetic assistance of Messrs. Naughton and Gold, and the burlesque immediately banishes the notion one has just formed of seeing the Palladium company invited next May to run the operatic gamut in a byre in Suffolk.

Now Mr. Goldmine begins to get into his stride, for from the sublime to the ridiculous is exactly the same size of step as that which separates art from patriotism. This last may or may not be, as Dr. Johnson thought, the last refuge of the scoundrel; it is certainly the first virtue of a producer of popular entertainments. The first of 'Three Epics of the Sea' is 'Plymouth Hoe, 1580', and shows

Sir Francis Drake interrupted at his game of bowls by Queen Elizabeth on a day when, according to the Aldershot Tattoo and other authorities, she was elsewhere and otherwise engaged, to wit in reviewing her troops at Tilbury. The episode is enlivened by period dialogue as when one young lady says to another: 'Marry come up! I trow these mariners think too much of their outdoor games to have much time for a farthingale!' The second episode is entitled 'On Board H.M.S. *Victory*, 1805', and reveals Lord Nelson setting out for Trafalgar and seizing the occasion to thank Romney for painting Lady Hamilton! Nelson also takes occasion to remark to Captain Hardy, apropos of the press-gang, that Britain has won all her naval victories on scum. Which is a hard saying for an admiral who was the darling of his crews. At the same time the remark brought back to one spectator the opening sentence of one of the best mock-diaries ever written. This is the book of an old salt which begins: 'Some Scumb has stole my boots.'

The third 'epic' is called 'Navy Week, 1936'. Here Messrs. Flanagan and Allen join the comedians already named in a delightful song entitled 'Say Ta-Ta', after which Lucienne and Ashour execute an apache dance, which is equally appropriate to Plymouth Hoe, the deck of the *Victory*, and Portsmouth Harbour. But this turn is just too good to be left out, and Pompey may as well have it as anywhere else. The first half of the dance is perfectly normal, with the girl left for dead every five seconds or so. But it would seem that the whirligig of apachery has its revenges, and presently it is the man who is being laid out for good and plenty. An admirable item. 'Navy Week' is brought to a conclusion with the *Queen Mary* gliding into Portsmouth Sound dwarfing the assembled fleet of Britain and diminishing her naval might to the size of the little boats lying off Burnham. I must not close this sketchy account of the first part without mention of Mr. Bobby May and Mr. Bob Busby's Sea Scout Band. The former does juggling feats of astonishing virtuosity with a nonchalance which is more than taking; this is the best juggling I have seen for a very long time. As for the Sea Scouts, it is obvious that they have the making either of good sailors or of good musicians.

The second half of the revue begins in a manner reminiscent of the sentence in a romance written by a native Indian: 'Saying this, the poor gentleman turned his face to the wall and died *sotto voce*.' That joyous fellow, Mr. Bud Flanagan, croons a ditty entitled 'There's a New World', and I do not think the microphone exists which can make his *voce* other than *sotto*. The scene is now a nigger plantation, and for a time three little nigger boys in magenta shirts and apricot trousers bring off dances which would exhaust wonder if we did not have to produce a new stock of that commodity to welcome the Four Robenis, who are very remarkable acrobats. 'A Running Commentary' demonstrates the different way in which American and English wireless commentators function. The American has all the breezes of the Atlantic in his manner, and you feel that his handshake hurts. The Englishman has the limp, well-bred way with him, and you know that his hands are like slices of cold turbot. Mr. Teddy Knox is brilliant in both impersonations, and indeed this is largely his show.

September 6, 1936

ALL CLEAR

(Queen's)

WERE the pearls belonging to Lord Bitchette's mother bogus? It would seem so since Marion Day, the overworked, under-dressed night-club singer, while eagerly snaffling the rubies of a second admirer and the diamonds of a third, left the heirloom for her maid to pocket. Such indifference has not been seen since, at the Baron Hulot's dinner-table, the greatest of Balzac's cocottes swept an armful of pearl bracelets on to a plate and offered them to her rival as a last, avengeless insult. But you would wrong Miss Beatrice Lillie if you confined her mordancies to the lower ranks of the human comedy. What other character is evoked by that *mélange* of impudence and black velvet? Here for me is the answer:

> La marquise d'Espard était une des personnes les plus imper-
> tinentes de son temps; elle avait un caractère aigre et malveillant
> sous les dehors les plus élégants. Froide, égoïste et coquette,
> elle n'avait ni haine ni amour; son indifférence était profonde
> pour tout ce qui n'était pas elle-même. Elle n'écrivait jamais,
> mais parlaiṭ, sachant que deux mots d'une femme peuvent faire
> tuer trois hommes.

Tut tut, says somebody, but that's French! The tut-tutter is right.

What seems to me more important is that in this brilliant sketch,
'Weary Of It All', Mr. Coward declined to think in the sentimental
way laid down for our guidance in a kindred matter by Mr.
Priestley in his *Music at Night*. A sable coat being promised for the
morrow, Miss Lillie's dazzling drab first drops an inadvertent
'What time?' and then pleads for an old sun-bonnet instead.
Upon the offer of a country house complete with car and footmen,
she inquires if there is a tumble-down shed at the bottom of the
garden. For it seems she would recapture the joys of innocence.
All of which is pure Sybil Linchester in Mr. Priestley's play.
Miss Lillie's view of the matter begins at the top right-hand corner
of the forehead and an eyebrowish pucker which, gathering
momentum, sweeps across the whole countenance and disappears
at the left-hand corner of the chin. The avalanche has lasted only
a second. But a second is enough to floodlight that mentality
which sturdily maintains that if a thing is not 'nice' nobody can
possibly like it.

Yes, Miss Lillie is certainly 'our first authority on the second-
rate', as Wilde said of Kipling. First-rate on anything from
amateur philosophizing to professional gate-crashing. Hear her
account of a 'marvellous party' where, while the guests are top-
drawer, the chest is that of the Riviera's modish riff-raff. What,
again, is Miss Lillie's choir-boy but Kipling's Lew or Jakin, whose
cherubic appearance was but the lid to a well of depravity pure
and undefiled. Yes, our lighter stage's first authority on the
second-rate.

Much of this artist's success is due to her multi-radiance. It would be foolish to say that she is always Beatrice Lillie when, in the course of the evening, she will exhibit six or eight different Lillies all growing out of the same stem. There is the young woman of taste who, undertaking to rearrange a friend's flat, puts bulls in china-shops to shame. There is the slightly *passée* actress, everybody's favourite, industriously beglamouring the troops with coynesses which even the remoter provinces would hesitate to describe as arch. And last to be mentioned here, there is that spy drama which comports a railway waiting-room somewhere between Omsk and Tomsk, and a countess — Miss Lillie, of course — in a dress which, while impervious in front to blizzards, rejoices in a backlessness so chaste that even the snow does not melt on it. To say that these waiting-room walls have ears would be an understatement; the very legs of the chairs are vocal with whatever it is spies are vocal about.

Is it supposed that Miss Lillie, dashing from one *tour de force* to another, becomes something heated? But no! At the end of the evening she is the same icicle as at her first appearance. And in truth she has done nothing beyond a *moue* here and a pat there. And why should she do more, since unwritten pages may be more eloquent than written ones? Why wrinkle that brow when, unwrinkled, it is a sufficient comment upon a perturbed and foolish world? Why further tilt a nose whose exquisite contour already speaks satirical volumes? Why do anything at all where merely *being* is delicious enough? And why, harping on this conjunction, should I be at so much trouble to explain this great little artist when Mr. George Jean Nathan has done it so much better: 'This girl, with her genius for healthy low comedy, is pretty hot stuff.'

Is it thought, then, that Miss Lillie runs off with the revue? The answer is that I should like to see the entertainment which could be stolen from Mr. Fred Emney, who is gloriously funny in the rather limited opportunities afforded him. Did my eyes deceive me, or does one here and there spy that clever Miss Adèle Dixon? Mr. Bobby Howes is always on the point of being good only to see his material snatched from him, and Mr. Robert

Eddison contrives to be good without any material for snatching. Where, we ask with reasonable annoyance, has the latter actor's Hon. Maud vanished to? Entertaining though that frigate is, she carries no guns that need frighten that major battleship, Miss Lillie.

December 24, 1939

LIGHTS UP!

BY RONALD JEANS. MUSIC BY NOEL GAY

(Savoy)

'LADIES and gentlemen', says the chairman of an Old Dance Hall, 'I have the honour to announce Miss Cora Pearl!' And I have the honour to suggest to Mr. Cochran that he ought to put a slip in his programme telling young highbrows, who know 100 per cent. of nothing about anything that happened yesterday, who Cora Pearl was. Her real name was Emma Elizabeth Crouch, and she was the sixteenth child of the composer of 'Kathleen Mavourneen', and much envied by the other fifteen when, going to France, she became the greatest courtesan of the Second Empire and mistress of Napoleon III. Knowing herself to possess neither elegance nor grace, she played up her loudness and vulgarity for all they were worth, and created a new school of gallantry — *le genre d'écurie*. On being sentenced to banishment, Cora said: 'Nonsense! I am a public monument!' She ran through several fortunes and died in the gutter, after having been a thoroughly amusing sort all her life.

Anything less like Cora than Miss Evelyn Laye it would be difficult to imagine. On the other hand it is impossible to believe that Miss Laye can ever have been more like Miss Laye at her best than she is in this brilliant traduction. There is the old exquisite prettiness, the endearing self-confidence, and the aplomb with

187

which the difficulties of the singer's art are skirted. Next to Miss Laye one would place Miss Phyllis Stanley, 'divinely tall and most divinely fair' — a quotation whose triteness is relieved when one remembers that C. E. Montague applied it to the Pentland Edition of R.L.S. And next, Miss Doris Hare who is the show's best comedian. For in my view a comedian is exactly what Mr. Clifford Mollison is not. I have said for years that he is one of the best young actors on the English stage; he is certainly responsible for the most pathetic death-scene (male) I ever saw. This disalignment of talent is not unusual. Sarah Bernhardt once revealed that the young man who won the first prize for Comedy in her year at the Conservatoire afterwards made a fortune as an undertaker! I congratulate Mr. Mollison on his reappearance in this show as an actor.

Then there were many other extremely clever persons bobbing up and down as this, that, and the other — so many that I began to doubt whether the resources of Mr. Cochran, or indeed of the English stage, could afford them all. I finally decided that they were Mr. Martyn Green. Another comedian, Mr. James Hayter, was, I felt, insufficiently built up, though this, I now realize, was probably part of Mr. Cochran's policy of building up, not individuals, but the show as a whole. He has certainly succeeded in producing a gay and sophisticated *mélange*. Remembering a previous experience, when his taste proved too good for the general palate, he has, I think deliberately, seen to it that the same mistake should not occur again. But there are places where the old Cochran will out, and these, in their Zinkeisen settings, are lovely. Every country gets the revues it deserves, and frankly I do not think that we deserve anything better than this one.

I am persuaded that the public will hum Mr. Noel Gay's numbers if it can remember them. For myself, the thing I propose to remember is the train of Cora Pearl's dress after Miss Laye has disappeared. That famous train of La Tosca's, wriggling like a green snake long after Sarah had gone, has been too lonely. Here is another to bear it company.

February 9, 1940

DIVERSIONS

DIVERSIONS

BY HERBERT FARJEON. MUSIC BY WALTER
LEIGH

(Wyndham's)

WERE we, the Victorians, as absurd as the Aspidistras would have us suppose? I trow not. Looking through the music-holder of a well-known bass singer the other day, I discovered among the rubbish about Devon, Drake and Dead Men, that forgotten little masterpiece 'Hybreas the Cretan', by a composer named Elliot or Elliott, and sung by Signor Foli. Now I knew Foli, who was no signor but an ex-Irish policeman called Foley who, in the early 'seventies, whenever he sang in Manchester used to visit my grandmother in company with Malibran's nephew. I was not born then, and my meeting with the great bass did not happen until 1896, when, with Albani, he made a concert tour of the Lancashire manufacturing towns. My point is that he was not a ridiculous creature but an imposing and rather terrifying one.

The Aspidistras will hold, I imagine, that this burlesque is directed not at the great ones of the Victorian age but at the parlour mediocrity. Well, their burlesque irks me; I do not recognize even the germ of truth in it. In my view the male singer in this trio is as remote from the vocalists of my mother's drawing-room as Mr. Billy Bennett's obstreperous baritone is from the crooner of the pre-war 'party'. You see, I have an affection for the writer of piano pieces who was called Claribel, and I doubt whether anything in to-day's 'sweet' music will last as long as the unremembered composer's 'Silver Threads Among the Gold'. There is the faithful reproduction, there is pastiche, there is burlesque and there is guying. Is it suggested that the Victorians did not know how to turn over, and that when a piano duet was playing all four hands had to stop while Treble turned the page? No, this is pure guying, and as a Victorian I will have none of it.

I hasten to say that Miss Elsie French and Messrs. John Mott and Cornelius Fisher do a mistaken thing very well indeed. In my view what they do should not be attempted and could not be bettered.

Contrariwise in Mr. Peter Ustinov's 'Madame Liselotte Beethoven-Finck' I see no burlesque at all, but a portrait of complete authenticity. Here the matter is comic but the manner wholly tragic. This is a forgotten opera-singer whose present ugliness, as Pater might have said, is a ravaged beauty wrought out from within upon the flesh, the deposit, cell by cell, of strange thoughts and fantastic reveries. Here is one who has been a diver in deep seas, and keeps their fallen day about her. Creaking, bedizened, grotesque, the Mrs. Skewton of the old Viennese stage, this scarecrow is pathetic because she too has not passed away, but is still of this world if indeed there is any life at all under that powder, paint, false hair, and all the other cloaks to decay. She is like an Empire in ruins, and there is one of those great seventeenth-century sermons in the libidinous cackle which falls from these senile lips.

Equally true and just as biting are Miss Joyce Grenfell's studies of modern manners in both canteen and drawing-room. This country has waited long for its revenge for Miss Ruth Draper's 'Showing the Garden'. Miss Grenfell supplies it in that lesson in which an American mother would have her daughter learn by heart Shelley's *Ode to a Skylark*. There can be no more delicious moment in modern light entertainment than that in which this exponent of American culture says: 'No dear, I don't know what it was if bird it never wert.' Miss Vida Hope has a robustious talent for burlesquing Red-hot Mommas, fan-dancers, and other modish and quasi-modish phenomena. And Mr. Walter Crisham would wring many withers in his study of an elderly and more than *passé* chorus-boy, except that likeness will not strike home but be taken to apply to all the other antediluvian Erics and Reggies.

Respectfully I suggest that Miss Edith Evans hardly fits into this welter of parody. She has an enchanting prologue and epilogue, and reads poetry as it ought to be read. But her hop-picker? No. I just do not believe that the most golden-hearted of these ladies ever spoke with the silver tongue of Millamant. 'Stick to your dancing, girl', is the traditional advice tendered to the dancer who trespasses into the singer's domain. And I shall venture to say to Miss Evans, 'Stick to your poetry, august and revered lady'.

Miss Irene Eisinger sings some teeney-weeney trifles from Mozart and Rossini, neither of whom were teeney-weeney composers, and I suggest that this brilliant little singer should be given her head a little more. Miss Joan Sterndale Bennett and Mr. George Benson contribute each according to his riot and fancy. There remains Miss Dorothy Dickson, about whose dancing shall be said what Florizel said to Perdita — something about wishing she were a wave o' the sea who might ever do nothing but that. I have forgotten the exact words, but that's the gist of it, just as exquisite dancing is the essence of an artist whom Time itself is powerless to burlesque.

November 10, 1940

SILHOUETTES

___

PÉLISSIER

THE height, weight, and girth, the habit of the player and the tricks of his body are as much the property of the public and the concern of criticism as the configuration of temperament and intelligence. Irving recognized this when he bent and subdued his genius, and twisted brain and mind to accordance with a personality which, as the 'humble servant' of the public, he knew it was his business to lay at their feet. Actually he did very little twisting and torturing of his own mentality. It was the mentality of other people that had to do the submitting — the Sardous and the Shakespeares; it was the actor's rôles, the absurd Robespierres and Dantes, and even the Hamlets and the Lears, that had to accommodate themselves. There are many definitions of acting, and all of them include the exploitation of the personality of the actor. Old Irving knew perfectly well the salient features of his personality. The simple and popular impression of him, and the first answer a foreigner would get to his question as to what our great actor was like, was to the effect that his legs were preposterous and that you could not hear what he said. There is no doubt that Irving did his best to accentuate the popular impression, that he maintained a studied oddity of gait — he could walk about a room naturally enough — and that he wilfully elaborated an individual and eccentric code of articulation.

Now one supposes that the first impression of Pélissier was one of an exceeding fatness, an impression carefully fostered by a comedian alive to the values of the flesh. The critics did not waste time in euphemisms as to 'amplitude' or circumlocutions about 'fullness of habit'. Appreciation of Pélissier's quality as an actor began, as it did with Irving, in a distinct and explicit recognition

192

of a grotesque personality on which the comedian had as much right to insist as the tragedian, and perhaps even more need. And here one comes upon a curious contradiction. If the actor's personality is to be considered an integral part of his art — and we remember that it was so in the tragedian's case and in the cases of the late George Weir and Henry Kemble, whole merchant's ventures of the comic spirit, both of them, and mountains of pure flesh — how was it that Pélissier's unctuous revellings in portliness were amongst the least of his successes, that his studies in the colossal could be quite unamusing, that he so often contrived to shear adiposity of its natural quaintness? The explanation was to be found in the curious divergence between his intellectual temper and his 'exteriors'. Weir and Kemble were all for the *œillades* of the audience. They relished the 'appetite of our eyes'. They would echo Falstaff's 'Sometimes the beam of her view gilded my foot, sometimes my portly belly' in a perfect *crescendo* of justifiable pride. Their temper was a simple affair of generosity, somnolence, rumination. Pélissier's spirit was quite other; it was critical, judicious, and faintly acid. He would have resented Pistol's 'Then did the sun on dunghill shine' and Nym's zestful applause. Pélissier could not write a ditty about the amours of a toothbrush and a sponge without conveying a whole criticism of sentimental ballad-singing and the people who indulge in it. The study of 'Réjanehardt' was a merciless exposition of the technique of French acting, a scathing exposure of the ridiculous basis the sublimities have, on occasion, to put up with. His 'Voice Trial' was a surgical joy, and if ridicule could kill, the lighter stage must long ago have bled to death. It was only when the actor descended to frank fooling that he got the most out of his personality and the least out of his wit. The Comic Spirit must have laughed up her sleeve when she fitted so steely a soul to so generous a body. In a word, if he was not always elementally funny, he was always an indictment. In simulating a series of preposterous deals between an enraged amateur and a broker in 'objets d'art et de vertu', he would give a complete representation in buffoonery of the whole commercial life of a city. In burlesques like *The Whip*, gorgeous in fidelity to Drury Lane, Pélissier's clowning rose to great heights. He had a Gargantuan inebriety of bewilderment. Sometimes he would stand in the middle of the stage, utterly unable to compass another word, a mass of quaking stolidity, not, like the old actor in Lamb, primarily astonished by the elemental sun, moon, and stars about him, but the victim of his own improvisation and exuberance.

FRED EMNEY

ALL the world is the poorer for the loss of Fred Emney. It was at Arles in the south of France that I heard of his death, and I needed no help from the indistinguishable smudges in the halfpenny journals to recall the broad countenance of fun, the roving, bibulous eye, the high-pitched yet masculine voice, the rolling gait which would lurch rather than steer to the chair and table, composing with bed and box the entire *mobilier* of this astonishing Mrs. May. I can see him now in the habiliments of the monthly nurse as she lived — for live she did upon the stage in absolute verisimilitude. I can see the door in the exact mathematical centre of the garret's infamous back wall. I can see it opening to disclose the equivocal figure monstrously bedecked, grotesquely turban'd, the neck swathed in a 'boa' of fabulous cockatoo. I see again the elastic-sided boots covering traditional bunions, the chamois leather gloves protective against the devastating effects of the grate's black-lead. I hear the dissimulatory cough of the dissembling midwife as she fumbles for the intonations of gentility. 'Is Mrs. May h'in, my good woman?' The preamble is a trifle uncertain — mere nerves, however. With the success of the plot the voice steadies to the superciliousness proper to Mayfair. Again in recollection do I hear the colloguing at the door, the mind's eye and ear gladdening afresh at the dignified entry, the infinite affability of this visitor of distinction.

The imbroglio is adequately preposterous-history, as the French

say, of a monthly nurse in debt to her landlady. 'Pay up, or you go!'
is the harped announcement of that virago. The midwife receives
a call to an urgent case in the country. 'Pay up, or you don't go!'
is now the tune. And so Mrs. May — the very name is redolent of
brass plates in back streets, significant only to the worldly-wise —
Mrs. May has recourse to stratagem and to the finery of an actress
on the next floor. In monumental disguise she assumes the personality of a wholly fictitious sister, whose air of affluence is to renew
the credit of her temporarily embarrassed relative. With what
glee do we follow the unequal combat, the visitor gaining in the
grand manner as she loses in strict sobriety, the landlady going
under to her sense of snobbishness, her common 'cuteness an easy
victim to her sense of social distinction. She attempts a faded
rivalry; she would have it understood that she, too, knows what
horses are: 'My pa kept *a quantity* of 'em, but nothing would induce
me to go near 'em ——' She agrees that gin is 'common stuff',
professing to have it in the house 'in case of measles'. But it is
essential for the reader's comprehension that he should have a taste
of this absurd dialogue, and I append a slice of it as nearly as my
memory serves me. The reader must imagine the exaggerated
drawl of Emney's 'Mrs. Le Browning' and the common patness of
the lodging-house keeper:

MRS. LE BROWNING Is Mrs. May h'in, my good woman?

LANDLADY (*doubtful*) Well, no, Mum, she ain't, Mum.

MRS. LE B. Well, I won't come h'in. Will you please to tell
'er that 'er sister, Mrs. Le Browning, 'as called?

LANDLADY (*impressed*) 'Er sister! Oh! I might 'ave known it,
Mum, from the strong family likeness. Do come an' sit down,
Mum. Mrs. May won't be long.

MRS. LE B. Well, I'll come in for a few minutes, but I daresn't
wait longer, or the 'orses might get cold.

LANDLADY Why not try a motor, Mum? I've an 'orror of
'orses. My pa kept a quantity of 'em, but nothing would induce
me to go near 'em.

MRS. LE B. (*with indifference*) Oh, h'indeed. The h'only thing

I object to in 'em, they make such a fearful dust. Do you know, my mouth is full of it?

LANDLADY Could I presume to offer you a cup of tea, Mum?

MRS. LE B. (*politely*) There's nothing I should like better, but I daresn't. You know, tea h'acts like poison on my system. It does, I assure you.

LANDLADY I can quite believe it, Mum, you being accustomed to the best of everything. But is there nothink I could offer you? Your dear sister'd be dreadful worrited if she knew you was dry and wouldn't take nothink.

MRS. LE B. Well, if you should 'appen to have a little *barley-water* ready, Madam.

LANDLADY There now, I 'ad some in the 'ouse only a month or two back. If you could wait for an hour or two . . .

MRS. LE B. I wouldn't trouble you for the world (*with social ease*). I suppose you 'aven't a little drop of Madeira sherry wine?

LANDLADY No.

MRS. LE B. No, then, don't worrit. You know the doctors order me gin, but it's such common stuff I suppose you don't keep it in the 'ouse?

LANDLADY Well, Mum, to tell you the honest truth, I have a little. What I keeps in the 'ouse in case of measles. If you'll excuse me for a minute . . .

MRS. LE B. Oh, serpintly, serpintly.

LANDLADY If I'd known I was going to 'ave the pleasure of seeing you, I'd have 'ad the h'other. I shan't be a minute. (*Exit Landlady.*)

MRS. LE B. (*in a crescendo of violence*) Ah, you wicked old cat, you! You wicked old . . . Done 'er! done 'er! (*Subsiding.*) She don't know me! She don't know me! (*Mimicking.*) I shan't be a minute. (*Voice rising to a scream.*) Bah! you old faggot, you! you wicked 'ussy! you BRAZEN 'ussy, you! (*Subsiding again.*) I knew she kep' it. And when I asked 'er to lend me 'arf a quartern or so only the other day she swore she never 'ad none. But she ain't recognized me yet. Now I'll lead 'er on. (*Enter Landlady.*)

LANDLADY Your dear sister said to me only this morning —

Daisy, dear, she said, if my sister was to call 'ere, she says, you'd
know 'er by 'er likeness to me, she says. Well, love, I says, all
I can say is, she must be a very good-looking lidy. Any water,
Mum?

MRS. LE B. (*in the actor's own deep voice*) No water, thank you.

Surely this absurd dialogue, compact of the low-conditioned
humours which are the common property of the music-hall, is as
true to Dickens as Dickens was true to life. Now there is a point
at which all art in its portrayal of humanity must fall short of
actual flesh and blood, though any such statement is the flattest
critical heresy. In sheer despair will Dickens describe and re-
describe the attributes of Micawber, the walk, the air, the genteel
roll in the voice, always using the same words over and over again
in an attempt to force them to a higher degree of expressiveness by
sheer reiteration. Lamb finds himself in similar plight when he
would reduce an actor to the printed page. In conscious effort
to force words to a higher power he will expend on a description
of a work-a-day player the Pactolean treasures of inexhaustible
imagery. And that is why you find him investing the acting of
Munden with talk of Cassiopeia's chair, Platonic ideas, constellatory magnifications. He would make us wonder as he himself
wondered, at the fertility, the richness, the variety of the actor.
He would, one thinks, have used similar means to make us wonder
at poor Emney's great creation. Expressiveness was in every
inflection of Mrs. May's voice, every cock of the actor's eye, every
readjustment of the tumbling spectacles, in the veerings to the
floor, in the way he would come to anchor by the chair. The
scissor-like propulsion from door to table had all the nice calcula-
tion of the drunkard; the denunciations of the mean-spirited landlady were so many delirious trumpetings. 'Brazen hussy' could
have come only from a throat of brass. And then there were the
shrugs and leers and winks, a complete outfit and armoury of hints,
of euphemisms, of wrappings-up, of calling things by polite
misnomers. In Mrs. May the whole ritual of the profession
stood revealed. Here, you felt, was a riotous old hag, whose mind

was a jumble of 'interesting conditions', of 'being worse before being better', of grotesque sympathies and jocose encouragements. She trailed baby-linen; she was implicit with the mystery of cauls. The illustrations to Dickens contain one picture which may give some faint idea of the physical presentment of Mrs. May — the drawing by Phiz, 'Mr. F.'s Aunt is conducted into Retirement'. In both countenances we find the same stony implacability, the same riotous bewilderment, the 'yonderly' expression of a stern and much-tried nature *aux prises* with Destiny.

Yes, the world is indeed the poorer for this actor's passing. One would bestow on him an old-style farewell. May his voyage to the Shades be less ignobly harassed than his earthly travellings! Deal leniently with him, Pluto! Charon, thou 'murky rogue', as Lamb called thee, be not too insistent on payment of thy fare! 'Pay up, or you don't go!' was the earthly menace. A like threat, O Ferryman, and thou doom'st thy fare, stripped of whatever securities a tin box may afford, to wander everlastingly on the hither shore. At the coming of the Egyptian lovers Dido and her Æneas were to want troops. It is in my mind that by now Egyptian banterings may have grown stale and that the house waits for our homely comedian. Is it too daring a speculation that, with bonnet awry, the familiar figure is now fumbling at the latch? 'Your door *does* open, doesn't it?' Is it unlawful to suppose that the lips framed to old habit are waking the ghostly haunt with their familiar and pertinacious 'Is Mrs. May h'in?'

THE BROTHERS GRIFFITHS AND SIR HARRY LAUDER

WHEN I arrived at the Princes Theatre it was to find the house in delighted uproar over a comedy of manners enacted by the Brothers Griffiths. It was a question of a sleight-of-hand performance to which the more robust of the brothers, in the genteel get-up of a theatrical manager, was making conscientious objec-

198

tion. Perched upon that round, bullet-like head, and significant
of 'the front of the house', was the authentic topper, a shade too
small. But only a shade. The discrepancy, less than that connoted
by caricaturists of Mr. Churchill and Lloyd George, was of an
extraordinary *vraisemblance*. Cylinder became coping-stone of
the man of small successes, of one who has a snug sum put by.
Finis coronat opus. The tile crowned a life-work. Yet was all not
well. The least spark of argumentative heat and the hat would
take a tilt over the nose to the extinction of rebuke. A gesture
imperfectly restrained, and it would slither rearwards to discover
a witless cranium. This dressy fellow and enforced equilibrist
must walk delicately, with haviour protestant yet static. Now
adjustment is slight, now it gives place to magnopérative retrieval.
Reiterant, the disputant picks up the thread of his discourse. He
gets a sentence well under weigh and his countenance relaxes into
security. He rounds his period and starts with confidence on the
next. But his certainty is ill-founded; he had done better to heed
the famous advice of Heine to his countrymen: Above all, no
emphasis! For now must he run the gamut of fearful apprehension — from the first shade of anxiety to the complete agony.
Slowly the hat begins to decline over one ear ... O polish'd
perturbation! silken care! Never once does the Mr. Griffiths
whom I take to be Senior descend to gross fooling; the quandary
is from real life. So a civic worthy who has picked up the covering
of a lesser brain. Coquelin's burgess was not more amusing, nor
was the key of presentation greatly different. When, later, the
Brothers became a corporate horse of pantomime variety, they
still kept in touch with the world of intellect. And here, surely, is
the essence of supreme clowning, that it shall derive, originally,
from the brain.

The interval was filled with an orchestral rehearsal of Sir Harry
Lauder's familiar choruses. All around me was a tremor of anticipation. And then the curtain drew up to disclose, not Sir Harry,
but an American-Indian Princess, defined on the programme as
a prima donna. This lady's native wood-notes wild were, one felt,
inopportune. She should have sung herebefore. When, finally,

her top F had trailed away, there was a gladsome rustle. The backcloth now drew up to show a vacant stage, and the house settled down for the little man.

Let it be said at once that there is nothing cringing about Lauder. He has the great artist's overweening conceit of himself. He emerges from the wings like the sun from base clouds. He irradiates his world, flattering stalls and gallery with sovereign eye. That a creature like ourselves should glow with such intensity of self-appreciation warms the cockles of the most sceptical heart. Here is one who tastes life to the full, and insists upon our tasting it too. He gives of his superfluity munificently, like a cup that runneth over. His first item is all about a Clydeside loon and his mistress, Bella 'the Belle of Dunoon. Lauder makes his lover hardly human. With his rude thatch, squat figure, dependent arms and warped legs, he recalls ancestral boughs. The actor insists wilfully upon this, executing between the verses a jocund step in parody of our father, the ape. It is not until the next song that you size up the artistry of the man. It is a different Lauder who, in the garb of an old salt, puts on the tenderest humanity. The verse is pure doggerel, the tune reminiscent of Mr. Chevalier's 'My Old Dutch'. Yet such is the intensity of the emotion conveyed that the whole house, simple and hypercritical alike, fall a-singing:

> There is somebody wai-ai-ting for me
> In an old cabin down by the sea.
> In the land where I wish I could be
> There is somebody wai-ai-ting for me-e-e,
> There is somebody wai-ai-ting for me.

The composition is all Sir Harry's own, and I am to admit that it would seem to be the singer's proper, unsimulated emotion which produces the spontaneous and magical effect. And yet the man's an actor. Shades of the Frenchman and his accursed paradox!

Lamb was wrong when he said that the school of Munden began, *and must end*, with himself. Lauder is in the direct line of Munden. Can any man 'wonder', like Lauder? Can any man 'see ghosts', like him, or 'fight with his own shadow', as he does? 'She'll be full of surprises, In the morning when she rises, To hear I'm in the town', he sings, and as at the word 'surprises' he drops his voice to a whisper Lauder conjures up a poet's vision of first rapture. So Lucy thinking on Richard Feverel. So, too, if you will permit, the greatest of all writers. 'She laid on my waistcoat, close to my heart', contains the core of 'Hang there like fruit, my soul, Till the tree die!' Mundenish in its quiddity is the picture of Doughie the baker, ruminating on the jealousy of his spouse. Doughie describes the two houses, and the narrow passage between them, as graphically as you would want to describe them to a child. He makes you see the two houses as they were the painted arks of twin Noahs. The baker is coming home to his tea just as his neighbour, Mrs. McCulloch, emerges upon an errand. They meet in the passage 'like two trams'. 'Mind ye', says Doughie with superb irrelevant insistence, 'I canna tell ye what Mrs. McCulloch was going oot for!' The whole of this patter is crowded with particularities which give it credibility. Old favourites followed, and then Sir Harry showed us that doubling of the artist which, on the stage, is least pleasing. He gave an unaccompanied maudlin song, and a little homily on the blessings of peace. His performance had lasted an hour and a half, and it was ten minutes too long. This is a great achievement.

It must not be supposed that Lauder does not calculate his effects. He does. Each verse is more elaborate than the preceding one, so that the effect is both cumulative and culminative. This actor has an exceedingly fine feeling for character. Soldier, sailor, yokel, God's innocent are all to their several manners born. They are true to nature, yet transfigured. Even Doughie, the loutish baker, his face covered with flour, his brow bound with a ragged bonnet, wears about him something elfin, something of Pierrot. Once or twice the daft fellow will cock a malignant eye, and in such a moment the great actor is revealed. Lauder can make a face of horror like the mask of Irving's Dante confronted with the starving Ugolino. These qualities of pathos and tragedy are not what the generality look for. To them Lauder is a figure of pure fun, with a modicum of sentimental alloy. They love that description of bonnie Wee Jean with her velvet arms round her father's neck, but they adore still more that rueful 'But she's got ma nose and ear-r-r-s!' Here again the comic idea is given an ingenious twist. The gist of it is not the superimposing of absurdity upon plain sense, but the discovery of the rational in lunatic or sentimental disguise. When all is said and done the man remains an evangelist whose tidings are of pure joy.

GEORGE CARNEY

THE first of Mr. Carney's two 'song-scenas' is a study of grandeur and decadence, of magnificence on its last legs, dandyism in the gutter, pride surviving its fall; in plain English, a tale of that wreckage of the Embankment which was once a gentleman. He wears a morning coat which, in spite of irremediable tatters, has obviously known the sunshine of Piccadilly, has yet some hang of nobility. The torn trousers still wear their plaid with an air. *Enfin*, the fellow was at one time gloved ·and booted. There is something authentic, something inherited, something ghostly about this seedy figure. Trailing clouds of glory he haunts the Embankment. The ebony cane, the eyeglass with the watered ribbon, the grey topper of the wide and curling brim — all these fond accoutrements of fashion bring back the delightful 'nineties, so closely are they the presentment, the counterfeit presentment, of the swell of those days. 'Bancroft to the life!' we mutter. And our mind goes back to that bygone London of violet nights and softly-jingling hansom cabs, discreet lacquer and harness of cheerful brass — nocturnes, if ever such things were, in black and gold — the London of yellow asters and green carnations; of a long-gloved *diseuse*, and, in the photographer's window, a delicious Mrs. Patrick Campbell eating something awesomely expensive off the same plate as Mr. George Alexander; of a hard-working Max with one volume of stern achievement and all Time before him; of a Café Royal where poets and not yet bookmakers forgathered; of a score of music-halls which were not for the young person . . . But I am getting away from Mr. Carney.

The matter is not very much above our heads — something about a Count who has 'taken the count'. The purest stuff of the music-hall, as a music-hall song should be. 'There's a n'ole 'ere!' pipes with fierce glee the cherub boot-black, bending over the broken boots and abating the deference to the broken swell no jot of his Trade Union rate of 'frippence'. How it hurts, the contempt and raillery of this pitiless infant! *Enfant goguenard* if ever there was one, a capitalist in his small way, and with all the shopkeeper's scorn of failure. 'There's a n'ole 'ere!' he insists, and we are reminded of Kipps's tempestuous friend, 'a nactor-fellow'. 'Not a n'ole — an aperture, my dear fellow, an aperture', corrects the noble client, 'the boots were patent, but the patent's expired.' Here the Count drops his cigar and indulges in unseemly scuffle with the urchin. 'No, you don't', says the riper smoker, regaining possession, 'that's how *I* got it.' But the child has yet another arrow. 'Landlady says as 'ow you've got to share beds wiv a dustman.' But the shaft fails to wound; clearly our hero is of that mould to which social distinctions are as 'piffle before the wind'. 'Want a pyper?' goads the boy, and his client expends his last remaining copper. He unfolds the sheets and instinctively his eye runs over the fashionable intelligence. 'Know Colonel Br'th'l'pp?' he inquires. And at once we recognize the delightful touch of the man of the world anxious to put a social inferior at his ease. Something after this manner, one imagines, Royalty. 'Doing very well in Russia. Was up at Cambridge with his brother, the *elder* Br'th'l'pp, don' cher know.' And so to babble of the day's gossip to the scornful child at his feet. The courtesy, I submit, of one man of polish to another.

Night falls, the river puts on its jewels—the result of a cunning arrangement of n'oles and n'apertures in the backcloth — it draws very cold. More pitiful than the accustomed heir of destitution, but with stiff upper lip, our *déclassé* shivers, draws his rags more closely about him, and moves on.

But it is the second song which brings down the house. Here the actor appears as an Army cook, and we in the audience have all been cooks in our time. A couple of dixies, the stew in which is discoverable last week's 'Dickey Dirt', talk of 'jippo' and 'the doings' — all the familiar traffic of the camp rises to the mind's eye and sets the house in a roar. We are not, we gather, in any theatre of war, but safely at home in halcyon, far-off training days. Almost you can hear the cheerful clatter of the canteen, the thud and rattle of the horse-lines. The wording of the song is in no sense precious.

> What was the tale the Colonel told the Adjutant,
> What did the Adjutant say to Major Brown?

There is a chorus, also serving as *corps de ballet*, and consisting first of the inveterate grumbler who objects to the presence in his coffee of so harmless a beastie as a 'drahned mahse' — the accent is a mixture of Devon and Berkshire with a dash of Cockney. Then comes the superior youth of ingratiating, behind-the-counter manner, the proud possessor, we feel sure, of a manicure set in ivory — does he not abstractedly polish his nails with the end of the towel? After him the 'old sweat' who will neither die nor fade away, and lastly our rosy boot-black, now the dear brother-in-arms of the immortal Lew and Jakin. This nucleus of an Army has but a single mind: to know what has become of its blinking dinner. Many and various are their ways of putting it, and it appears that they are no more than messengers or forerunners of the cohorts pressing on their heels. But the orderly beguiles their impatience.

> What did the Major whisper to the Captain?
> The Captain told the Subs to hand it down.

The orderly is the slipshod, inefficient, imperturbable 'bloke' we know so well; with him we are to rise to what Mr. Chesterton calls 'the dazzling pinnacle of the commonplace'. (I am not sure that this is not the best of all this author's fireworks; it is so stupendous a rocket that the stick has cleared the earth, never to return but to go on whirling around us for evermore.) Mr. Carney is the embodiment of the commonplace civilian turned warrior. He is the cook who will drop into the stew all manner of inconsidered trifles: cigarette ash, match ends, articles of personal attire. He is the hero who will be up to all the petty knavery and 'lead-swinging' that may be going, who will 'work dodges' with the worst of them, and, on occasion, join with the best in such deeds — he would still call them 'dodges' — as shall put terror into the hearts of a ten times outnumbering foe. Of that order of heroic cooks which held Ypres. But it is part and parcel of this actor's generalship that he will have no truck with heroics. Tell Mr. Carney that he raises tears and he will make a mock of you. Or more probably he will continue his song.

> What did the Quarter-master tell the Sergeant?
> The Sergeant told the Corp'ril, it appears;
> The Corp'ril told the Private and the Private told his girl,
> Now she's looking for Mademoiselle from Armenteers.

Have I over-glorified my subject, whose talent is not more remarkably expended than on a dixie and a soldier's ration of stew? Ah, but is not the greatest of all tests for comic acting the power to throw a preternatural interest over the commonest objects of daily life? 'What', say you, pricking your ears at the familiar phrase, 'surely at this time of day you are not going to dish up that old stuff about kitchen tables and constellatory importance, joint-stools and Cassiopeia's chair?' Oh, but I am, and let appositeness be my apology. 'So the gusto of Munden antiquates and ennobles what it touches. His pots and his ladles are as grand and primal as the seething-pots and hooks seen in old prophetic vision.' Why should I not elevate, an it please me, Mr. Carney's pot and ladle to the same high category? I do not ask you to see in this actor an image of primeval man lost in wonder of the sun and stars, but I do ask you to believe that a tin of 'bully' contemplated by him amounts, or very nearly amounts, to a Platonic idea. Grant at least that he understands a dixie in its quiddity. It may be that in my estimate of this conscientious comedian I have overshot the just mean. Well, granting that my appraisement is an error, it seems to me to be an error on the right side. I have a comfortable feeling that Islington at least is with me, that I have a solid popular backing. Collins's pit and stalls, gallery and circle would have borne me out that the actor diffused a glow of sentiment 'which made the pulse of a crowded theatre beat like that of one man'; would have probably agreed that he had 'come in aid of the pulpit, doing good to the moral heart of a people'.

I do not think that in expanding Islington's approval I have misread it. Its ecstatic hand-clapping and shouts of 'Good ole George! Good *ole* George!' cannot deceive an ear attuned to shades of applause. The civilian on my left with the wound-stripes on his sleeve is dumb with appreciation. His lips are parted, his breath comes in short gasps, his eyes are fixed on the stage seeing and not seeing, his whole soul in some setting of the past. I am sure he hears once more the clatter of the canteen and the cheerful rattle of the horse-lines. The soldier on my right, still in the Army's grip and not yet victim of the nostalgia to come — a very small fly in demobilization's ointment, but there it is — is drunk, simply, uncomplicatedly drunk, with the lilt and swing of the tune. He rises half out of his seat, puts a steadying hand on my arm, and with the other wildly conducts the house now singing in chorus:

> What was the tale the Colonel told the Adjutant?
> What did the Adjutant say to Major Brown?
> What did the Major whisper to the Captain?
> The Captain told the Subs to hand it down.
> What did the Quarter-master tell the Sergeant?
> The Sergeant told the Corp'ril, it appears;
> The Corp'ril told the Private and the Private told his girl,
> Now she's looking for Mademoiselle from Armenteers.

There is a limit to the number of recalls even the most grateful servant of the public may permit himself, and at last Mr. Carney is allowed to retire in favour of the next turn. But my friend on the right takes some little time to simmer down. 'Good ole George!' he continues to mutter under his breath. 'Oh, good *ole* George!' And as the tumblers who come next are a dull pair, I wend my way out.

VESTA TILLEY

There's a tune in my head to-night,
   As I walk, as I talk,
And it swoons in a whirl of light
   (While the day fades away).
And I hear my heart as it beats
   A refrain, and again
I am splashed by the mud of the streets,
   And again feel the rain.

— ARTHUR SYMONS

IT could be wished that poets and philosophers were not such cozeners. To make the best of a bad business is a form of worldly wisdom, a policy and no more. But where the business is so bad that no amelioration is possible, your poet and philosopher will have it that it cannot be such a bad business after all. Necessary evil, be thou my good! they cry. But like the essayist who was honest with himself, I take death to be the capital plague-sore. Like him I can in no way be brought to digest that 'thin, melancholy *Privation*'. Yet those others will tell me that since no man has aught of what he leaves, 'tis naught to leave betimes; that he must be very impatient, who would repine at death in the society of all things that suffer under it; that no man can be living for ever, and we must be satisfied. Well, I am not satisfied and there's an end on't. One of the great dissatisfactions of my life is the retirement of actors. *Partir, c'est mourir un peu.* To say good-bye is to die a little. To bid farewell to the stage is to depart wholly; these ceremonious leave-takings are only one degree less chillsome than the last adjurations. I dislike all partings, adieux, valedictories. I hate to pray for Buckingham, and have a distaste for the slow decline. I would leave ships to sink and dying men to die; the pity's too abominable. I would pretend that age and death are not, and on the stage that players remain what they have always been. Let the retired actor live in our memories if it be of comfort to him; 'tis none to us. To comfort me must Ellen T——y be a goblin?

Actors should die in harness. I open my paper o' mornings and, turning first to the column of theatrical advertisements, still look to see *Olivia*, Miss Ellen Terry; *Susan Hartley*, Mrs. Kendal; *Quex*, Sir John Hare; *Old Songs and New Favourites*, Miss Vesta Tilley. It is with this little lady that I am concerned here. I will not say that appreciation in volume of applause has not been deep enough. Palms may wear out with clapping, voices hoarsen through cheering, curtains part again and again to give yet one more glimpse of that trim, taut little figure with the boyish hair, boyish manner and proud, boyish smile — and yet leave something unexpressed.

I remember as though it were not more than a year ago the first time I saw Vesta Tilley. It was my first pantomime, and I recall to this day her clearness of enunciation and tiny modicum of voice. In recollection I breathe again the 'tart ozone' of her distinction. She was not content with being just Aladdin or Dick, Sinbad, Robinson or Prince Charming. She was the 'masher' of those days, and how long ago those days are you best can tell by entering the snuggery of some theatrical house of entertainment and examining the faded photographs on the wall. There you will find beauty long since faded with the rose — simpering, wistful memories. Belle Bilton and May Yohé, Letty Lind, Harriet Vernon, Lottie Collins, Maggie Duggan. Among these melancholy pictures you will of a surety espy one of a trim little figure in a dress-coat curiously rounded and curved, with what is obviously a red silk handkerchief — the note of the period — in the shirt-front. Other images there will be of that long succession of 'Midnight Sons', 'Piccadilly Johnnies', 'Sea-side Sultans', heady youths all, with an amazing selection of waistcoats, gloves, ties

and canes. They are the embodiment of the bucks the most
modest of us in our hearts knew ourselves in those far-away days
to be. Let others talk contemptuously of the transmogrification
of the toga'd citizen into terms of boiled shirt, dove-tailed coat,
black-cloth clothes, white pocket-handkerchief and diamond ring.
Vesta Tilley has always known better than to be contemptuous of
clothes. Her waistcoats have had both a devastating and a moral
effect upon the young man. Her visits to provincial towns were
occasions for extravagant launchings-out on the part of the
'cards' into suits of clothes they could ill afford; but never, on
the other hand, did these visits fail to lead to a more regular
pressing under the mattress of workaday trousers. To what vain
comparisons, to what emulations did we not surrender ourselves?
But the influence was all to the good. You have only to read
Mr. Arnold Bennett to realize that well-creased trousers, even if a
trifle worn, have more influence on a young man's career than a
verbatim knowledge of the poets. And didn't hearts beat soundly
beneath the creases? Weren't the hearts of the gay and giddy
young 'clurks', as Miss Tilley has always called them, in the right
place in their bodies if not in my prose? Didn't they volunteer for
the South African War? Not 'arf! *Welcome, welcome, C.I.V.s!*
Has she not cheered in greater circumstance the children of those
earlier heroes? Of all the songs, 'Jolly Good Luck to the Girl
Who Loves a Soldier' was perhaps the best. It had the most of
heart in it. It showed the 'rookie' puffing behind his big cigar, his
heart swelling with pride and just a little too full for words. The
suspicion of a tear brushed away upon the pipeclayed cuff, one
more roll and lick of the cigar, one more tug at the belt, and with
swagger-stick under arm the boy would march away, the heir to
all our military glory.

'Dost thou think, though I am caparisoned like a man, I have a
doublet and hose in my disposition?' Yes, we do think this. Vesta
Tilley was ever a boy whom nothing could unman. Master of her
characters, she was mistress of herself. Was there ever such
triumphant storming of an audience, such dignified acceptance
of their fealty? Has ever actor since Irving so proudly proclaimed

himself the public's 'loving, grateful and obedient servant'?

Recently, in an old lumber-room, I came across a fretwork frame, made in the days when boys did that sort of thing, containing five photographs of Vesta Tilley. Two of them were illustrative of Happy Hampton and the Sad Sea Waves, the others showed a recruit, a Piccadilly Johnny, and an amazing young gentleman, presently to enlist in the C.I.V.s, and now clad in a waistcoat quartered into the emblems of England, Scotland, Ireland and Wales, and having at the end of his gold-mounted cane the flag of Empire. Is the lumber-room a fitting shrine? *Nenni!* Not in that sad repository but in the storehouse of the mind shall she be preserved. But it will take more than Shakespeare, Synge, or the gentle Elia, with whose trite philosophies I began, to persuade me that she should have departed at all. It may be true that no one can be acting for ever. I am not satisfied.

'MARIE'

WHEN, in the Tottenham Court Road, I saw the sheet which announced that Marie Lloyd was dead, everything around me became still. The street lost its hubbub, and for a space I was alone with a sharp and personal sorrow. In moments of emotion one is apt to notice the little things, and at once I remarked that, on the poster, the artist's name was prefaced with the word 'Miss'. Death, laying his hand upon her who was known over the English-speaking world as 'Marie', must use more ceremony. 'Marie' — pronounced with the broad vowel beloved of the Cockney — was in everybody's mouth that day, in club and barrack-room, in bar-parlour and in modest home. On the high seas 'Marie's dead' would be droned from ship to ship. Returning from Kempton a party of bookmakers fell to speaking of the dead artist. One said with tears in his eyes, 'She had a heart, had Marie!' 'The size of Waterloo Station,' another rejoined. Her abounding charity was a commonplace of the profession. That night, at Blackfriars Ring, a bruiser with the marks of many fights declared: 'We shan't none of us see the likes o' Marie again. She was a great artist.' Those who know that soundness must underlie a boxer's brilliance before he receives the title of 'artist' will recognize the force of this tribute. If the music-hall singer, embodying a social stratum to those who know it like their hand, had deviated from truth by so much as a finger's breadth, she would not have received this highest meed of praise. To those whose verdict is based upon the most positive of evidence such fancy things as implications are without meaning. Facts are facts, alike in the New Cut or in Leicester Square. Marie Lloyd's characters knew no parishes but these; they were born in one and rose to the other. 'Sank', the moralist will exclaim, true to his eternal preoccupation and for ever beside the point. Morality is a philosophy of life; this realist presented types of human character and drew no moral.

It was not, however, from a world of bullies or the lower deck that Marie Lloyd drew her chief support. She was enormously popular with the class which lives in villas and makes a fetish of respectability. To placate these, would-be apologists have pleaded that 'whilst many of the songs were in themselves offensive, the manner of their delivery took away the offence'. This is the purest nonsense. The genius of this *diseuse* consisted in the skill and emphasis with which she drove home the 'offensive' point. She employed a whole armoury of shrugs and leers, and to reveal every cranny of the mind utilized each articulation of the body. Frank in gesture as Fielding was in phrase, her page of life was as outspoken and as sure. Hottentot and Eskimo knowing no English, the respectable burgess priding himself on his ignorance of the way of the saloon-lounge, would yet recognize from the artist's pantomime the burden of her song. 'No one was ever the worse for her performance.' Everything depends, surely, upon what these squeamish critics mean by 'offensive' and 'worse'. It will not be claimed, I think, that 'A Little of What you Fancy does you Good' turned the young men out of the heated music-hall into the Strand determined to look neither to the right nor to the left. Marie Lloyd sang, as Rabelais wrote, for good Pantagruelists and no others, and chastity had to look elsewhere for a minister.

> Inside the Horsel here the air is hot,
> Right little peace one hath for it, God wot,

was the last reflection conveyed from that Hill of Venus which was the stage of the Tivoli Music Hall. Hoxton's daughter was as much the embodiment of her period as some more pretentious folk. She reduced to the comprehension of butcher's-boy and clerk the poet's limbs moving 'as melodies yet' to quite unpardonable music, all that meaningless tosh about 'curing the soul by means of the senses'. Little patience, we may be sure, had the comédienne with the original form of these nostrums for sick minds. She translated them into tonics for the healthy body; she preached the world and the flesh, and gloried in their being the very devil. None ever left the theatre feeling spiritually better for her songs. From that blight, at least, one was free.

Free, too, from a poison even more deadly. Flaubert, you remember, makes one of his characters conjure up the red lamp of a brothel with the reflection that of all life's experiences this youthful one was the most truly happy. Marie Lloyd's honest spirit would have disdained so pitiful a philosophy. The sailor of whom she sang might, as the result of an encounter in Piccadilly, miss his ship. But a mere incident would not turn him, like Flaubert's sentimental fellow, eternally adrift. There was no decadent Latin taint about Marie; she was most saltily British. Villadom accepted her in the way it accepts the gay dog who makes no secret of his gaiety; it will have nothing to do with the sad fellow whose pleasure is furtive. There was nothing sad or secret about this idol. She knew that the great English public will open its arms to vice, provided it is presented as a frolic. This idiosyncrasy is one with the tradition of English letters, which has always envisaged the seamy side of life with gusto rather than with deprecation. Yvette Guilbert harrowed the soul with the pathos of her street-walkers; Marie Lloyd had intense delight in her draggle-tails. She showed them in their splendour, not in their misery; the mopishness and squalor of their end were not for her.

And that is why, when she came to the portrayal of elderly baggages, she refrained from showing them as pendants to her courtesans. A French artist would have insisted upon the inevitable descent to the procuress, whereas the English artist rejected even Mother Peachum. Instead she gave happy life to battered harridans ludicrous in the sight of man, if not of God; diving into their very entrails for the unstilled riot which made old Jenny steal from her husband's bed to dance at the ball. Again she proved herself an infinitely greater realist than others more highly esteemed. She depicted the delight of humble life, the infinite joy of mean streets. When some jovial crone, emerging from the wings, flung at an unseen, routed foe a Parthian, 'And it wouldn't take me long, neither!' you settled in your stall to listen to a reading from the Book of Low Life. There was unction here, and a smack of the lips over a Vulgate the accuracy of which, divined by the boxes, was eagerly checked by the gallery. Was Marie Lloyd vulgar? Undoubtedly. That great quality was her chief glory. She relished and expounded those things which she knew to be dear to the common heart.

Marie had the *petite frimousse éveillée*, the wideawake little 'mug' which Sarcey noted in Réjane. Her 'dial', as the Cockney would put it, was the most expressive on the stage. She had beautiful hands and feet. She knew every board on the stage and every inch of every board, and, in the perfection of her technical accomplishment, rivalled her great contemporary of another stage, Mrs. Kendal. Briefly, she knew her business. But it is not my purpose to talk now of technical excellence. Rather would I dwell on the fact that she was adored by the lowest classes, by the middle people, and by the swells. 'I hope', she said in a little speech before the curtain at her last appearance at the Alhambra, 'I hope I may, *without bigotry*, allude to my past triumphs.' Poor soul, it is we who should ask to be delivered from that vice. She broadened life and showed it, not as a mean affair of refusal and restraint, but as a boon to be lustily enjoyed. She redeemed us from virtue too strait-laced, and her great heart cracked too soon. The hymn which she sang will not be repeated in our time. *Explicit Laus Veneris.*

GROCK

G ROCK is always at his best when it is obvious that he, too, has taken a seat at the banquet of folly of which he is the host. Lamb, we remember, strongly opposed the notion that a man must not laugh at his own jest. 'This', said Charles, 'is to expect a gentleman to give a treat without partaking of it; to sit esurient at his own table and commend the flavour of his venison upon the absurd strength of his never touching it himself.' To-night this great clown laughed as heartily at himself as we at him.

Grock's fun, when he is at his best, seems begotten of the occasion. It is as though he had never before had that little trouble with the keyboard-lid, and had that evening, for the first time, conceived the notion of sliding down it to the floor. In this little manœuvre we see all the art of the well-made play — the art of preparation. The lid will keep tumbling on to the player's fingers, and therefore demands removal. Partner behaving obstreperously, what more natural than that Grock should snatch up that lid as a medium of remonstrance, or that, melting in his own good humour, he should lean it up against the piano ready for that piece of virtuosity in sliding? This is play-making as it is immemorially understood, and practised by none better than Grock's compatriots. There is a whole comedy by Scribe or Legouvé, Halévy or Labiche in that manipulation of the keyboard-lid.

Looking, recently, into one of those humourless guides to the psychology of laughter, I wondered how it was that none of the authorities quoted, from Descartes to Freud, explains the whole of Grock. Some, so far from explaining him a little, would seem to negative him altogether. Take, at hazard, Immanuel Kant. 'Laughter', says that unfunny philosopher, 'is an affectation arising from the sudden transformation of a strained expectation into nothing.' As if Grock did not *fulfil* expectation and beyond our wildest hopes! He is not one of your comedians who are reasonably funny; with him performance outruns promise to a

quite unreasonable degree. Bergson more nearly explains him
when he says that many a comic form, which cannot be explained
by itself, can only be understood from its resemblance to another,
which only makes us laugh by reason of its relationship with a
third, and so on indefinitely.

We can perhaps explain the comicality of Grock's walk
up-stage in those immensely baggy trousers by that view of an
elephant which they suggest. But why is a retreating elephant
funny? Probably from the incongruity to be established between
our idea of size — implying moral as well as every other sort of
grandeur — and those drooping quarters and humiliating tail.
As Grock retreats behind the screen he is exactly like a tail-less
elephant, and thus we arrive at Hazlitt's definition of the ridiculous — 'that which is contrary not only to custom, but to sense
and reason'.

Note how, before reaching the backcloth, and still with his back
to us, our friend has deposited bow and fiddle on the floor, the
bow to his right and fiddle to his left. Returning, he takes them up,
only to find that he must now attack his instrument left-handedly.
This is relativity, and so pure Einstein. And thus you may go
through Grock's bag-of-tricks. They are all pure Somebody-or-
other in the philosophic world. But it is never the wise men who
explain him; it is always he who elucidates them. This clown
'surprises by himself' all the philosophies. Or say that one touch
of Grock makes the wiseacres kin.

Watching this supreme genius the lines come to mind:

> 'Cherchez les effets et les causes,'
> Nous disent les rêveurs moroses.
> Des mots! des mots! cueillons les roses.

In other words, a live Grock is a better mentor than all dead-
and-gone theorists. Let us, then, desist from arguing and take
tickets for the Coliseum. The little poem might, one thinks, have
been as fittingly dedicated to our subject as to Adolphe Gaïffe.

> Jeune homme sans mélancolie,
> Blond comme un soleil d'Italie.

Perhaps 'young' is not quite the word, and our friend is not more than morally blond. Yet there is something golden about that dome of his which recalls a shaven field glistening in the Italian sun. 'Sans mélancolie' is, perhaps, not perfect felicity. Like Leno and like Chaplin, Grock has pathos, and pathos is akin to melancholy. But

Garde bien ta belle folie

is entirely fitting.

The philosophers may have their sense on condition that Grock is allowed firm hold of his lovely nonsense.

KATE CARNEY

THERE is a great deal of fun in reviving old memories. I have no doubt they did it in Greek and Roman days, although the fashion in this country seems to have received fresh impetus with the generation which could vaguely remember Cremorne. You will remember how Mr. Galsworthy's old Heythorp went on about four-in-hands and Mario and Grisi. To-day we have taken to sentimentalizing over the jingling hansom. Piccadilly without the roar of the motor 'buses or the scream of the sky signs, the old Empire, Marie Lloyd. All these things we see, alas, in the mind's eye only. This week at the Alhambra Miss Kate Carney re-creates an old vision in a manner which is palpable to feeling as to sight. She presents the past in the round and is herself a very noble and satisfying monument to it. This highly talented artist is probably the last of the great *lionnes comiques*. If she should retire, which one hopes will not be for a long time yet, there must disappear from our stage the last of that grand manner which was the sum of so many small perfections. Kate Carney, like all the great in her kind, can do absolutely nothing and yet hold the stage, or execute a trivial gesture of the hand or meaningless flick of the heel and rivet your attention as upon something vital. Her superbity is such that you can no more take your eyes off her than you could off a Roman gladiatoress.

Kate Carney deals authentically in all that material which our puny modern aesthetes deem it amusing to reproduce in their thin, cold-blooded way. By throwing a scarf over her be-diamonded person she will ask you to believe that she is an East End widow. From the wings there emerges a piping child of ten who in shrill tones declares:

> Mother, I love you; I can work for two.
> Don't let those tears roll down your cheek;
> I'll bring my wages to you every week.
> Mother, I love you; what more can a loving son do?
> You have worked for me a long, long time,
> So now I can work for you.

Now what on earth is the good of chattering about high art in connection with such matter as this? Did not the thunders of applause the other evening indicate the presence of hundreds of sons and daughters who know of their own experience the matter of this ditty? That being so, all other babble is purely impertinent. Are there in an audience lovers who have quarrelled? If so, then I commend to them a lyric which may not possess the beauty of Tennyson's 'As thro' the land at eve we went,' but has at least as much sense:

> Are we to part like this, Bill;
> Are we to part this way?
> Who's it to be, her or me?
> Don't be afraid to say.
> If ever it's over between us,
> Don't ever pass me by;
> For you and me
> Still friends will be
> For the sake of the days gone by.

To the makers of *vers libres* I recommend 'The Mouth-Organ Brigade' as model. It goes as follows:

All round the houses we'll roam each night,
Kids all hurrahing when we are playing
Tanner Mouth-Organs; they sound all right,
For they knock all your big brass bands.

But Miss Carney's best song is entitled 'Alice's 'Ouse'. It appears
that the singer, having been 'treated' by the highest in the land,
desires to 'return the compliment'. So:

Let's all go round to Alice's 'ouse;
Alice's 'ouse is like a Palis', is Alice's 'ouse.
    Carpets on the Floor,
    A Knocker on the Door.
I've never seen so many people knock at the door before.
Free and Easy, Bright and Breezy,
When you get in they say it's go as you pleas'y.
So let's all go round to Alice's 'ouse;
Alice's 'ouse is like a Palis', is Alice's 'ouse.

Hear this — sung to a rollicking tune which puts swing in its
proper place — and you are back again in the palmy days of the
Oxford and the Tivoli.

NERVO AND KNOX

BOSWELL happening to mention Miss Burney's *Cecilia*, Johnson
said: 'Sir, if you talk of *Cecilia*, talk on.' Happening upon
Nervo and Knox at the Palladium the critic, willy-nilly, must
write on though conscious that the writing will avail him little.
It is the old business of explaining ecstasy. Every man knows
ecstasy; the commodity is to be encountered at Derby finishes and
Cup Finals. Jazz bands evoke it equally with Mr. Bobby Jones.
At the race for the Schneider Trophy it will be as much in the
air as the machines, and possibly more so. The difficulty is not
to recognize ecstasy but to account for it. In the happy far-off

times there came a Wednesday when Mr. Walkley set himself out to account for Grock. Benedetto Croce, Peacock, Jean Paul Richter, Aristotle — all the familiar fogeys were laid under handsome contribution. But the essayist could only arrive at the blank wall which confronts every critic. 'One comes in the end to the old helpless explanation of any individual artist. Grock pleases because he is Grock.' So let me confess at once the impossibility of trying to explain that individual artist which is Nervo and Knox, first positing boldly that twice one do not always make more than one. Nervo and Knox are one unity, inseparable as German verbs, unsunderable as twin stars. 'You will never', Mr. Shaw is said to have postcarded to the late James Welch, 'be as funny as the Brothers Griffiths.' Which is like saying that an earthquake cannot compete with flood plus famine. For the Brothers Griffiths were never one entity but two entities, as unlike and as decipherable as the fore and hind legs of Pongo, their horse. Whereas Nervo and Knox are indissoluble. They are a single tonic, and were I in the patent-medicine business I should shyly announce upon all convenient hoardings 'Nervonox, the Unique Recuperator'.

'But', an Esquimaux might object, providing the Behring Straits have a corresponding word, 'you have not told us what it is that these philosophers achieve.' Well, one would say that they are the supreme parodists. Let the point be moot how often Mr. Jimmie Nervo and Mr. Teddie Knox have attended at that mystery known as the Russian Ballet. In view of their duties it is probable that their vigil has not been persistent, and that only on comparatively rare occasions have these twain made·one at such séances. Yet our parodists' attendance, though intermittent, has been sufficient to enable them to suck all the melancholy out of those rites and present it as something else. At the Palladium we behold half our pair semi-swathed in leopard-skin but otherwise décolleté. This moiety pursues the other, whose description calls for a fresh sentence. Imagine a haphazard assemblage of arms and legs, crowned with an auburn mop, invest the trunk with wisps of clothing from the Nellie Wallace collection, endow the whole with all that 'joy and gladdery' of which Beachcomber's Miss Violet Cork alone has the secret — achieve this ideal portrait and embellish it with the leaps and lollings, pirouettes and prancings of the classic dancer's repertory, and you will have some poor notion of the 'winsome madcappery' of this superb droll. May I put it this way, that whereas I can suffer that Massine and Karsavina should visit other capitals, it is unbearable that our parodists should peregrinate even as far as Golder's Green? In plainer English still, Messrs. Nervo and Knox are extremely funny fellows. Only, whenever we think of these nonsensical arms and legs, let us do their owners the justice to remember what Dr. Johnson said of Mr. Barry's paintings: 'Whatever the hand may have done, the mind has done its part.' Nervo and Knox are one body and one mind.

TOTO

THERE is a story about a beautiful but not good actress, an incapable divinity who, in Sardou's fustian, used to play second parts to Bernhardt. But in Sardou only, for when it came to the classics the great actress had compunctions and would excuse the goddess. Now the goddess had a mother who watched over her offspring from the wings and at the end of each inefficient tirade would cry: 'Mieux que Sarah!' This innocent tale came to mind when I was asked to believe by rumour, telephone, and other means of communication that Toto, the new clown at the Palladium, was better than Grock. Belief, as everybody knows, is largely a matter of practice. Was there not once a lady in a monumental work of fiction — to wit, the White Queen in *Alice* — who succeeded in believing six unbelievable things before breakfast? Holding that seeing is the better part of believing I sallied forth, 'utterly purposed' not to belie either artist with false compare.

It is possible, however, that a generation has arisen which knows not Grock; and to recall what Grock was like is to go some way towards describing Toto. It is not idle, then, to recall Grock's *size*, the impression he created of a gorilla-man who, when he put on that absurd dress-suit, crept under the skin of a beetle. Obviously he was possessed of immense strength and could at will have broken as many notes in his piano as Rubinstein. He had the agility of the giant, the physical reflection of that nimbleness which characterizes the master-brain. The intellectuals were conscious that he played down to them, and even the simple recognized one who could have made metaphysical mincemeat of Coleridge and had probably mastered Kant in an afternoon. Everything about the man was super-human. Asked if he could play the piano, he would roar in contempt. Of course he could play the piano just as he could take a ship's bearings, compose sonnets, solve chess problems, or head a Royal Commission — because he was the man to do anything. Could he have written dramatic criticism? Walkley said Yes. 'He would blandly thrust his feet through the seat of his chair and then write his criticism with them.' And went on to say, joking only a little, that the criticism thus written would have been better than Sainte-Beuve.

The important word is 'blandly', since it exactly describes everything that Grock's successor is not. Toto is not bland, but busy. Instead of discarding, as Grock did, from intellectual strength that we may be amused, Toto patently and industriously bends up each corporal agent to entertain us. For note that his prowess is almost entirely physical. Grock impinged upon the mind — that is to say, he first subdued our brains and was then graciously pleased to tickle them. Toto does not impose his mentality upon us because he is not concerned with mentality. His antics are visual. You can 'get' the quality of Toto's art by noting the number and variety of accessories it demands, including dogs, a perambulator, and a mechanical baby. He will give an imitation of Pavlova which has none of the wit of Nervo's — or is it Knox's? — classical ballerina, and depends rather upon the acrobatic use of Little Tich's long boots. Incidentally, one submits that maximum ugliness of motion is not a good parody of maximum grace. Or he will give you an 'impression' of an

American film-star in *The Merry Widow*. But take away the
chrome-yellow wig, the Gaby Deslys headgear, the dress of
glittering silver-foil — take these away and the comic idea has
evaporated, since these were the trappings and the suits of a mirth
which never really existed. The imitation of a mechanical doll is
tumbling *à la* Lupino Lane — first-class tumbling, but no more.

Last, one has the uncomfortable feeling that Toto is a young
man, whereas the folly of clowns should always be the bouquet
of long and slowly gathered wisdom. Cleopatra's 'Though age
from folly could not give me freedom, It does from childishness'
perfectly presents the resemblance between Empress and Clown.
For every perfect clown suggests, or should suggest, Lear's head on
the Fool's shoulders. If there is any hint of disparagement in the
foregoing it is because an extremely clever young artist has been
praised for the wrong qualities. 'There are clowns and there is
Grock' was a happy pronouncement. One would say that the
world has many clowns, among whom, for sheer indefatigableness,
Toto stands high. But for those who remember him, Grock still
remains: 'last, loneliest, loveliest, exquisite, apart'.

NORA BAYES

EVERYTHING comes to him who knows how to wait, including
Miss Nora Bayes. To judge from this artist's reception you might
have thought that she was Judic, Nellie Farren, Yvette Guilbert,
and Marie Lloyd all rolled into one. She is not all these, but is
possessed of a very genuine and undeniably individual talent.
To begin with, Miss Bayes sang a song about returning to
London, which was the purest — pass me the word — drivel.

> I've been counting the days
> *Annoyed with delays!*

Surely not even our operatic translators can do worse? And
again:

NORA BAYES

Tears in my eyes
Breaking many home-ties.

But had not the paragraphists been busy telling us that what
the artist had broken, by arrangement, were expensive home-
contracts? Even genius should stick to the same tale. Yet this
nonsense, droned to the most dismal of tunes, was delivered in a
geranium-coloured mantle and a pose, neither of which a Sargent
would have scorned to paint.

An admirable song followed, in which, by the simple conduct
of a fan,

Every way the wind blows
This sweetie goes

was made to conjure up all the airs of heaven. For a while each
song, and each line of each song, seemed like a new conquest over
dullness. This artist has tremendous *brio* and a presence like that
of Brünnhilde. She makes something of jazz and almost redeems
its rhythms from idiocy. She can, with a single gesture, bring a
whole world before you — the world of the New York midinette
or the Kentucky negro. And she can look as magnificent as the
centre figure in a composition by Leighton.

Yet, if Miss Bayes aspires to be something more than a popular
success she should get some better material. Her song about a
dead nigger, with the guying, in the accompaniment, of a well-
known funeral march, seemed to me to be distressing. I cannot
understand the liking for 'Sweetie' and 'Samson'. Ditties like this
would seem to show that there is something in what the scientists
call 'katabolism', 'destructive metabolism', or 'retrogressive meta-
morphism'. In other words, the white man's brain is giving way,
the negroid strain is coming to the top, and Kentucky is become
the capital of the once civilized world. Half-way through Miss
Bayes's repertoire became more than tedious, not through any
fault of the artist, but because there were no brains in her material.
But the audience, self-intoxicated, would certainly not have
agreed with me. Towards the end Miss Bayes undertook to rebuke

Mr. Melville Gideon, who, it appeared, had parodied her, by singing one of his songs in her own way. I can only say that the better is the enemy of the good, and that, in my opinion, Miss Bayes came off distinctly second-best.

WILL FYFFE

WILL FYFFE's daft loony is a masterpiece of tragi-comedy. For a time the fellow rambles on, recounting the minor victories of witlessness over wit. And then the note changes. The boy is to draw from the savings bank his seventeen treasured pounds. Jim McGregor — who gave him shoes and stockings, who never called him daft, and brought blood to the faces of those who did — Jim McGregor is dead, and the money is for his bairns. The exquisites of the 'nineties made great fuss over Flaubert's burying of M. Dambreuse — 'of whom there shall be no more question on this earth'. Seven people, and seven alone, declared George Moore, were capable of appreciating this great passage from *L'Education Sentimentale*, and they met once a year in the Champs-Elysées to read it aloud to each other under the lilac trees. But there must be nearly seven million people in London capable of appreciating Fyffe's burying of Jim McGregor. He does it with so much passion. This wonder-wit shows something of that awe which even those who possess their souls most tightly must feel in the presence of annihilation. For the idiot as for the reasoning there looms but the horror of the shade. And with the expression of this dread comes the loosening of all that has been pent up in the crazy prison of his mind — natural grief, resentment even. He is not to be allowed to go to the funeral lest he should make the villagers laugh! Fyffe has a sob here of which Garrick had been proud. I use the great name to give this piece of acting its scale. Let there be no mistake. I do not say that Will Fyffe is as great an actor as Garrick. But I do say that the older actor could not have bettered that mingling of pathos and grotesquerie. If one may use the word genius of a performance of our day, here is genius.

224

BILLY BENNETT

BILLY BENNETT

Is mind a disease of matter? At one of those amateur Brains Trusts which enliven the countryside on Sundays, the question was asked: Are dirty jokes permissible, and where should the line be drawn? The reply was given that jokes which have to do with the natural functions of the mind and body are permissible, whereas jokes which palliate and condone the infiltration of the normal and healthy by the abnormal and unhealthy are impermissible. This answer, understood, shall I say intermittently, by the South Loamshires, would seem to let in Rabelais, Montaigne, Swift, Sterne, Smollett, and the Restoration dramatists, while letting out the writers of 'shockers' obnoxious to the police. It would equally keep in the great succession of British music-hall comedians from Arthur Roberts to George Robey, while excluding the modern exploiters of the innuendo and the leer.

Billy Bennett — I speak of the artist — was forthright, bawdy and wholesome. He knew that what sailors and soldiers on leave look for is not a rock bun, a symphony concert, or a lecture on T. S. Eliot. He knew that a Saturday-night audience is a crowd of clerks and shop assistants on leave after being pent up for the week in warehouse or store. He was a wiser man than Burke, who ought to have known that vice which loses its grossness doubles its evil. Bennett's grossness had that gusto about it which is like a high wind blowing over a noisome place. He never meant more or worse than he raucously proclaimed. Sometimes you said to yourself in half-delighted, half-fearful apprehension: 'Surely he isn't going to suggest . . .' Which was foolish of you, because Bennett never suggested anything. He said what he had to say, and emptied his mind of the matter very much as our eighteenth-century caricaturists would show viragoes at upper windows emptying their wrath and other things on the heads of those below.

Bennett will live in the annals of the music-hall. Nobody who ever saw him is likely to forget that rubicund, unaesthetic countenance, that black, plastered quiff, that sergeant-major's moustache, that dreadful dinner-jacket, that well-used dickey and seedy collar, the too-short trousers, the hob-nailed boots, the red silk handkerchief tucked into the waistcoat, the continual perspiration which was the outward and visible sign of a mind struggling for expression — these things will not be forgotten. His best witticism was that in which he deplored his permanent non-success at Huddersfield — 'They take me for a baritone.'

On the death of Elliston, Leigh Hunt wrote: 'The death of a comic actor is felt more than that of a tragedian. He has sympathized more with us in our everyday feelings, and has given us more amusement. Death with a tragedian seems all in the way of business. Tragedians have been dying all their lives. They are a "grave" people. But it seems a hard thing upon the comic actor to quench his airiness and vivacity — to stop him in his happy career — to make us think of him, on the sudden, with solemnity — and to miss him for ever.' Let it be said of Billy Bennett that he raised every night in the week to the level of Saturday night, and never uttered a word at which sensible people could take offence. Off the stage he had a manner quiet almost to shyness, and in keeping with his gentle and wholly nice mind. We shall miss him ever.

GRACIE FIELDS

I AM cross with the Palladium. For why? — as the vulgarians, but also some of the writers in the Bible, ask. Simply because the Palladium posters still show the old enticement of a Gracie Fields flashing gipsy eyes under a mop of unruly black hair. What we are now offered inside the theatre is the same picture in a gold frame, a Gracie with blond hair and gold finger-tips, excessively *soignée*, and until she begins to speak as lacking in significance as mannequin or marchioness *à la mode!* This actress, who could have looked and played and sung you Carmen, Ortrud, or any darkling rôle, has been transmogrified. Now the point is not whether an actress changes her personality for better or for worse. The point is that she is married to it, and that if a divorce has been arranged the theatre posters should announce it. There is the old complaint of the man who, when asking for bread, is given a stone. It is not generally realized, perhaps, that the man who asks for a stone and is given bread is cheated just as much.

Talking about the Carmen that our Gracie might have been sets me thinking about the one part which I should like to see her play. This is Mr. Shaw's Joan. How admirably the two would fit! Joan, in Mr. Shaw's own words, is 'the most notable Warrior Saint in the Christian calendar, and the queerest fish among the eccentric worthies of the Middle Ages'. Gracie is the queerest fish among the eccentric comédiennes in the belated Middle Ages in which we are still living, and I see no reason why she should not play this notable Warrior Saint. Indeed, I see every reason why she should.

The task would be easy. Easy because, if and when the physical resemblances gave out, Miss Fields is a fine enough actress to bridge discrepancy. I hope before these lines appear in print to have spent a few days in Blackpool, in which town I shall have put my hand on a dozen Joans, if looking like it and speaking like it and stretching harking ears with an ineffable rapt glumness were the whole of the business. But then I am a lover of acting and not of mere casting to type. Your cinema magnate wanting a 'Cromwell sends to a casting agency for all the stockish men with warts on their noses. I prefer an actor, lean and tall as a lamp-post, who can make you think that he has breadth of shoulder, will-power, and the wart if you want it. I haven't the least desire to see a young woman play Joan merely because in her own person she is rather like Joan. It is possible that not many members of the Palladium audience the other night were instantly struck with the notion of Gracie as Joan; I saw it in a blinding flash.

However, one must leave voices and get back to what one actually beheld. It is fair to say that one's disappointment at the change of hair was short-lived. Even pictures in gold frames must tell their story, and Miss Fields had only to open her mouth and the old riot came tumbling forth. She began with two sentimental songs, and then burst into the well-known 'Poor Little Angeline'. I do not know who wrote this, but it is the kind of tune which Haydn would have transmogrified into a symphony and for which German mechanics would have built musical boxes. One would very much like to see how much fun M. Balieff would get out of it, and there is always M. Massine, to whom the tinkle might presage a new Choreartium! The next song, purporting to be about a visit to the cinema, was all about mill-hands and shawls in the days when the artist first knew them. That is to say, before the days of the super-cinema, when mill-hands came away from unsophisticated little pictures and, like the description of Doll Tearsheet, 'blubbered'. To-day's millhand does not bawl her emotion as Gracie suggests. If she has any tears at all, they are whisked from a mascara'd eyelid with a vermilion talon. This incomparable artist wound up with a song about sticking to her man, a silly sentimentality void of any artistic merit whatever. And this is where the artist and the actress come in. No other performer that I know — always excepting, sempiternally, and for ever, whichever is the more forcible, Miss Ivy St. Helier! — no other music-hall artist could invest this howling, defiant drivel with such exquisite and unerring pathos and sincerity.

GEORGE ROBEY

'I LOVE everything that's old', says Mr. Hardcastle, 'old friends, old times, old manners, old books, old wine.' To these I would add, old actors. On another aspect of this subject Mr. Somerset Maugham has said: 'It is not only that we grow to see the beauty of things as we know them better; it is rather that the delight that succeeding ages take in them somehow adds to their beauty.' It is a far cry from the Odes of Keats to the sallies of Mr. Robey.

But surely these too are 'enriched by the emotion of all who have found solace and strength in their loveliness'. No, I do not hesitate to apply Mr. Maugham's word to the quips of the greatest artist in his kind since Leno. This loveliness has now a patina which previously it had not, something half polish and half incrustation, Henry James's 'tone of time' all over again, and perhaps something more. A connoisseur of the right sort will see in the beauty of these ageing Widow Twankeys and Mrs. Crusoes 'a beauty wrought out from within upon the flesh, the deposit, little cell by cell, of strange thoughts and fantastic reveries'. For strange and fantastic to a quite Paterish degree, judging from the samples intermittently vouchsafed, have been the meditations of Robey's beldams and harridans.

Of this true descendant of the Commedia dell'Arte Montague wrote: 'Mr. Robey's patter is everything now, and yet he says, altogether, wonderfully little; first a word, and then he seems to detect some misplaced laugh in the audience, checks, bridles up, passes in pantomime from tantrum to tantrum, the gusts and squalls of temper coming and going in him visibly. You may call the topics outworn and trivial, the mere words insignificant, the humour metallic, rasping, or worse, but the art, within its limits, is not to be surpassed in its gleaming, elliptical terseness, the volumes it speaks in some instants, its suddenness, fire and zest.' Are the fire and zest something diminished? 'Old, old, Master Shallow,' replied Falstaff, when asked whether a certain *bona roba* still held her own. And we remember Shallow's corroborative: 'Nay, she must be old; she cannot choose but be old; certain she's old; and had Robin Nightwork, by old Nightwork, before I came to Clement's-Inn.' And how Silence must needs choose this moment to break in with his 'That's fifty-five year ago'. That which befell Robin's mother equally befalls Robinson's; she cannot choose but be old.

Must the hey-day in the blood of every actor with more than fifty years' experience behind him be tamer than it was? Alas, yes. Is it possible that where formerly one recognized participation in the riot, one has now the sense of pranks recollected in tranquillity? It is possible. But the law of compensation works here as everywhere else. What Mr. Robey has put off as homely philosopher he has put on as abstruse metaphysician; the exposition of 'here' and 'there' at the Bristol Hippodrome the other evening was pure Einstein.

It is a matter of forty-five years since I first saw this great player assume bonnet and dolman. I saw him 'just above the horizon, decorating and cheering the elevated sphere he just began to move in, glittering like the morning star, full of life, and splendour and joy'. And never, as Burke didn't say, were these optics dazzled by a more delightful vision. In those far-off days an elephant used to call for the star at his lodgings and squat on the kerb till a sufficient crowd had collected, when a frock-coated figure, collarless but with brow circumspectly cinct, and carrying an odd little cane, would mount on to the animal's back and ride down to the theatre indifferent to the mob, wrapped in his own thoughts, and as if this were his usual mode of conveyance.

I remember that in this early pantomime there was a cow alleged to be ten years old, that the Principal Boy said, 'Isn't she a picture, mother?' and that George, wearing a blue and white check apron, said, 'Yes, a picture by Teniers!' Did I miss, the other evening, some of the old exuberance? Possibly. But will anybody insist that Beethoven in his Third Manner retained everything of the frolicsome First or tempestuous Second? To Robey, too, must be allowed his third period. After the storm comes the calm, and it is conceded that those over-the-wall squabbles with Mrs. Moggridge belong and may now be relegated to the order of happy, far-off things and battles long ago.

SOPHIE TUCKER

THE key to Sophie Tucker is to be found in the use she makes of her vocal resources, the method being to spill them all at once. So generous is the spilling that it seems impossible that exhaustion should not be reached. There is something respectworthy in recklessness of this kind, as there is in all magnoperations. No one has any regard for the niggard, the small bankrupt, the pettifogging adventurer, and it has been well said that of all gamblers the man who gambles within his means is the meanest. Miss Tucker's lavishness demands the opposite censure. Every movement of her performance is an orgy of expense like that banquet which Fouquet offered his royal master. But even ministers of *le Roi Soleil* could not continue in that strain, and we feel that the same fate must attend Miss Tucker. It is here that the miracle presents itself. For just as appetite grows with what it feeds on, so this artist's waste of energy creates more. And, indeed, you might liken her to an engine getting up steam, full pressure being attained at the fall of the curtain and not a second before. When she permits herself occasional indulgence in a *pianissimo*, it is only to show possession of the faculty to ration exuberance. Otherwise, she scorns equally the *piano*, the *mezzo-forte*, and the *forte*, nothing less than four *f*'s sufficing. Wagner's Elizabeth screaming welcome to the Hall of Song, Senta drowning Atlantic breakers with a ballad, Weber's young woman apostrophizing the mighty ocean and looking as though she had swallowed it, Isolda describing a dying faintness through an obliterative orchestra one hundred and twenty strong, Salome shrieking farewell — all these strident ladies are, compared with our subject, the brides of quietness. Miss Tucker is wedded to Sound, to all-shaking thunder striking flat 'the thick rotundity o' the world'. Even her grace-notes might be described as 'vaunt-couriers to oak-cleaving thunderbolts'.

But no artist can do this who lacks physical correspondency. Miss Tucker's appearance has the necessary courage. Since this artist in the most familiar of all her numbers has bid us know 'how fat girls can love', there can be no harm in saying that she owns that physical quality for which Lady Jane chose the word 'massive'. But in the coming by-and-by there can never be too much of this artist, for the reason that the peculiar property and genius of her treasure is its wealth. Indeed, the opposite calamity is the more greatly to be feared, and I am not at all sure that Miss Tucker is not a little thinner than she was. It is an accident that this vaudeville performer was not an operatic singer, since she is, to adopt Mr. Shaw's description of Janet Achurch and Marie Brema, 'of the broad-browed, column-necked, Germanic type . . . the type distinguished by great voices, busy brains, commanding physical energy, an untamable impetuosity and originality'. Miss Tucker has this outstanding attribute of the great player, that when she is on the stage you can no more take your eyes off her than you can off the sun when it is rising. Or you might put it that she is like one of those mountain-tops which the rising sun with sovereign eye has flattered, for her crowning glory is not only gold but like something newly and startlingly gilded. Nimbus and aureole are pale words to describe that heavenly alchemy, and her hair is always faultlessly 'done'.

This artist has one other attribute which always goes with genius: that of never appearing to do wrong. Away from the theatre your cold-blooded analyst might object that intonations and gestures celebrating the fearless new fashion of being the universal red-hot momma are not those which should accompany invocations to discretion. In the study one asks how the same envelope can be apt to the flaunting extravagant quean and to the maiden thrifty of her virtue. The answer is that the cold-blooded and the studious have no business in the theatre, and that when they get there they become something else. Miss Tucker is perhaps a little too big for the comedy, which proves how childishly wrong Euclid was when he denied that the part could be bigger than the whole. Certainly the artist's best moment occurs when voluminous and velvet folds descend to blot out the play, a piano emerges, and for a good half-hour it is our pastime to be bound 'within the Lyric's scanty plot of ground', as Wordsworth very nearly wrote, such lyrics being distinctly un-Wordsworthian and inclining, indeed, to the Rabelaisian. The lyrics in question are, the programme informs me, uniformly the work of Mr. Jack Yellen, and I am divided between wondering whether

I always caught the exact drift of Mr. Yellen's meaning or whether great art has the further quality, that it excuses the seeming unpardonable. Miss Tucker has many things in common with poor old Jack Falstaff, and among them is the knack of turning diseases to commodity.

PANTOMIMES

THE SLEEPING BEAUTY
(Drury Lane)

PUSS IN BOOTS
(Lyceum)

THE BABES IN THE WOOD
(Scala)

'Aloof in its refinement', was a famous wine-list's description of a certain Château Léoville. This is what is wrong, or if you take the modern point of view, what is right with Miss Lilian Davies's Prince Florizel at the Lane. Obviously your verdict upon this charming lady's 'interpretation' of the Prince must be swayed according as you incline to the fleshly or idyllic school of Principal-Boydom. In the old days Principal Boys were swaggering gallants ready to drive a coach-and-four 'to happy Hampton' or down the Duke of York's Steps, though with these magnificences went a positively uncanny knowledge of the phenomena of humble life — the opening-times of public-houses, the beguiling of pawnbrokers and bailiffs, the whole complicated machinery of widows' houses. In matters of the heart these bucks combined constancy to the Principal Girl with the lyrical exploitation of a Don Juan-like temperament. 'None but thou shalt be my paramour', they would declare to their sweetheart, yet seizing the occasion of this divinity's absence to chant other praises. 'I have been faithful to thee, Cinderella, in my fashion', sums up a philosophy in which every mood was explored except moodiness.

234

If, then, it be possible to define something in terms of the qualities which it does not possess, here is Miss Davies's Principal Boy. He 'has a leg' but does not slap it; he carries no riding-whip, and the jewelled garter is not honoured even in the breech; we know that the pint-pot will not be honoured in its quiddity. Miss Davies looks enchanting, and she sings some musical-comedy numbers very prettily. But she chants no joys of street and bar, racecourse and gaming saloon, preferring to paint the town a chastened mauve, and in a succession of nostalgic ditties confess the spell of moon and allegiance to the rose. 'You have a highly respectable reference for everything, have you?' asked Mrs. Wititterly of Kate Nickleby, and we feel that this unraffish Prince would have had that faint lady's sanction.

But if the new orientation of pantomime tends to over-refinement in the sentimental direction, it leads also to a greater subtlety in the comic. Now, Drury Lane's humour, even in its palmiest days, was never entirely of the bull-necked order. The point about Dan Leno was that beneath the grotesque envelope you felt that there was a spirit to be hurt. This was the quality which made him a great actor in that small and very select category which includes 'Little' Robson, James Welch, and Charlie Chaplin, though it is doubtful whether he was conscious of that quality. But there can be no doubt about Mr. G. S. Melvin's consciousness. He is, to begin with, a very brilliant character-actor, whose versatility has long been his bane. The British music-hall public likes to see a buffoon who is always recognizably the same buffoon; Mr. Melvin will give you in the course of twenty minutes a Professor of Mathematics, a Clyde-side riveter, and a Girl-Guide Mistress, each performance true to type and each owing nothing to what one might deem to be the actor's proper countenance, accents, or gait.

There is not, so to speak, any Melvin, though there is a wonder-ful gallery of portraits all signed by the same artist. As the Queen in the first part of this pantomime he presents three or four of those hard, fortyish, admirably-tailored women of the world, at once a little mannish and a little *maniérées*, whom one may meet in

Bond Street any afternoon. These clever sketches — for with each change of costume another woman appears — are as different from the old pantomime dames as the cocktail-drinking *ingénues* of to-day's stage differ from the cup-and-saucer Misses of Tom Robertson. In the second half Mr. Melvin appears as some devastating heroine from the centre-court at Wimbledon. If the skit were a shade less good the house would be rocking with laughter; as it is, it holds its breath so as not to lose the least of the actor's subtle cruelties. Mr. Melvin's performance throughout is a masterpiece of irony, and in finesse he has certainly no equal on the lighter English stage.

The chorus may be said to set the seal on the new school of pantomime. These eighty-four young ladies wear lovely clothes designed by Mesdames Doris and Anna Zinkeisen and Dolly Tree, and are equally at home in a ballet reminding us of *Les Sylphides* and in the choreographic inanities designed to illustrate some poverty-stricken musical-comedy theme. They are gracious decorations to the scene, but a century away from the simple Corydons and Phyllises who, in the old-time opening Village Scene, while the principals were mustering, were wont to sway backwards and forwards with engirdling arms. The scenery is the very last word in sophistication, and one feels that nothing better than M. Marc Henri-Laverdet's 'Beauty's Boudoir' could be thought of for a full-fledged performance of *Rosenkavalier*. There is a backcloth to this scene which is exactly in the spirit of the first illustrations to *Les Liaisons Dangereuses*.

It is true that later on there are some elaborate suggestions of Toyland. But these, I fear, are 'amusing' only for grown-ups, and in the sense of that word which Mr. Aldous Huxley so strongly deprecates. That is possibly not a very strong objection, since on the first night there was not, so far as I could see, a single child in the entire huge audience. I am afraid I must adhere to the view that *The Sleeping Beauty* is, in setting, dresses, spirit, and acting, essentially a musical comedy. Even the programme conforms to the musical-comedy fashion of printing a table of Musical Numbers. If my case wants any further proving it is here, for a Pantomime Hit is not, never was, and never can be a Musical Number. In case the foregoing should appear grudging, let me say at once that, considered as a musical comedy, *The Sleeping Beauty* is everything that could be desired. Or so I am informed by the initiate in that mystery.

It might be said of the pantomime at the Lyceum that, aesthetically speaking, there is 'no damned merit about it'. Everything in it proceeds handsomely, cumulatively, and finally cataclysmically according to the good old-fashioned, or, if you prefer, bad old-fashioned plan. Villagers gather and, heedless of minor cometary visitors, await the effulgent coming of first that luminary which is Princess Rosamund, and second that orb-in-chief, Jack, the Miller's Son. Presently we arrive at Mrs. Tickle's Cottage, Mrs. Tickle being the widow bearing up hilariously against immemorial weeds and woes. To her enters a Broker's Man, so that at last one can satisfy the shrill piping voice at one's side which at every new entry asks: 'Is this George Jackley?'

Mr. Jackley's chief asset is his voice, of which Pistol might have said: 'There roar'd the sea, and trumpet-clangor sounds.' Mr. Jackley makes more noise than Stentor, Bully Bottom, and a Marseilles tenor in *Wilhelm Tell* put together. In more *piano* moods he will imitate a canary, but the dulcet temper does not last long, and presently we find this noble actor bellowing in imitation of a sea-lion. Match him against a Welsh-dresser full of crockery, and this Carnera among comedians will crack each cup and platter as though they were the jaws of mortal men. 'With' Mr. Jackley, as they say in the Law Courts, are Messrs. Naughton and Gold, a superb pair of natural drolls who, after demolishing the theory of relativity with some such sentence as 'To-day was to-morrow yesterday', put up a display of back-chat question and answer to disconcert Socrates. There is a long and excellent cast, and I shall have only space to mention the admirable Dame of Mr. Andy Andrews, and the at least well-intentioned Principal Boy and Girl of Miss Gwladys Stanley and Miss Kitty Reidy.

PANTOMIMES

The scenery is of the staggering representational order which to the child-mind conveys so much wealth of illusion, an illusion which is not defeated when, it becoming necessary to move the Tower of London, a very obvious scene-shifter haled it from one side of the stage to the other, again in Pistol's phrase, 'by most mechanical and dirty hand'. The infant who honoured me with his company was far more upset when the King, having promised to knight Puss in Boots, failed to carry out that promise. There was the usual Transformation Scene, though here, I think, it was illegitimate to draw occasional curtains, and thus obviate the greater perils of that complicated business. Something to one's horror, too, the early part of the transformation took place in a lighting so crepuscular that the glade which it failed to illumine reminded one of Borrowdale in the rain. Presently, however, a thousand-candle-power sun came out, and the young ladies of the *corps de ballet* were seen disporting themselves in the manner beloved of Sir E. J. Poynter.

These solemnities over, the real fun of the afternoon began, and we had immense doings at an Ogre's Castle, after which there was a troupe of Chinese acrobats who alone were worthy the money. In fact, the whole pantomime is to be recommended for its quality of luscious glamour kin to that of the best solidified brilliantine. Every song in it is a song which belongs definitely to pantomime and nowhere else. In the matter of the dresses blue is blue and red is red, and it may be that the mingling of the colours is in the nature of a mechanical mixture rather than a chemical compound. But what does that matter so long as the whole company come down to the footlights at the end, the humblest first, and so in order of transcendence?

To the charming pantomime at the Scala Punch speaks the Prologue, and Titania the Epilogue. The dresses are sufficient, the setting is adequate, and the scene entitled 'The Depths of the Wood' is a good corrective to any modern notions as to how *A Midsummer Night's Dream* should be produced. That the comedians sing the right kind of songs is proved by a glance at the titles — 'What are you going to do about Mary?' Mary being the cow, and

238

PANTOMIMES

'Mucking about in the Garden', an excellent skit upon the town-dweller's makeshift for a rural existence. There was a scene in a kindergarten in which a small child, being asked to name the favourite wives of Henry VIII, replied: 'Mary Pickford, Gracie Fields, Sybil Thorndike, and Nellie Wallace.'

December 29, 1929

ROBINSON CRUSOE

(Lyceum)

ALADDIN

(Dominion)

THE pantomimes at the Lyceum Theatre have the considerable merit of being newly minted. The mould of one Christmas may bear a family likeness to that of another, but we have glistening assurance that the coins which the Melville Bank issues each year are being put into circulation for the first time. This is the happy result of having a mint on the premises. Other impresarios, other habits. To the pantomime-producer who knows not where next year he will lay his head, new creation is obviously an impossibility, and that is the reason why London must sometimes take her delight in that which pleased Manchester last Christmas or Glasgow seven years ago. Whether you like your pantomime to be old or new largely depends upon whether you prefer the tag about old friends being the best to the cliché embodying the charm of novelty. If you are a child the distinction ceases, and for the highly metaphysical reason that for anybody who has not yet learned to read, Defoe has not yet written his masterpiece.

Uncles desiring a peaceful afternoon would perhaps be well-advised not to take to the Lyceum a nephew too recently conver-

239

sant with that work. Otherwise they will be exposed to a rain of questions impossible of answer. Why is there so little in the book about Will Atkins and Mrs. Crusoe? Were the boatswain and mate on Crusoe's ship really so funny? When is the story going to begin? To this one vaguely replies that we shall probably land on Juan Fernandez in the second part. Questions resumed:— How does Crusoe manage to shave? Who gave Man Friday his signet-ring? Whence comes it that that savage, two minutes after conversing by signs alone, should show an intimate knowledge of the Cockney language? Why, after a desperate battle on two sides of a stockade, which I agree is like the one in *Masterman Ready*, should the cannibal chief be found dancing a hornpipe with his so recently intended victim? These questions, and the lack of any possible answer, prove what the priggish would call the educational value of *Robinson Crusoe*. This admirable pantomime certainly stimulated one young mind as well as entertained it.

The second part was largely given over to Mr. George Jackley and Messrs. Naughton and Gold, who, after the deplorable manner of the best fiddlers, made their individual cadenzas more important than the concerto they adorned. There was a scene in which Mr. Jackley and Mr. Naughton, having contrived to get themselves invited to a box on the dress-circle level, thence exchanged discourtesies with Mr. Gold remaining on the stage. After this Mr. Jackley conjured, still with the same unhelpful assistance, and then Mr. Jackley, who seemed to be in better form than ever, invited the house to go into committee on the important question: 'Does a Puff-Puff Go Choo-Choo?' Not by Honegger.

Afterwards 'The Marvellous Max Theilon Troupe' performed, not on this occasion very successfully. A wit has said that people who jump to conclusions rarely alight on them, and the result of much of this hurtling from a spring-board was that the somer-saulters frequently failed to alight on shoulders prepared to receive. Perhaps, as Dr. Johnson nearly said, these young gentlemen will be more marvellous by-and-by. For the rest, everybody voted the Crusoe of Miss Kitty Reidy and the Principal Girl of Miss Constance Carpenter to be huge successes, the show was nicely sprinkled with envenomed allusions to the Income Tax, Council houses, and common informers, there was a great deal of service-able magnificence, and the usual number of spry young ladies whose function it is to carry banners did so in loyal adherence to the sheepish tradition.

I approach the subject of *Aladdin* at the Dominion with some diffidence, since, frankly, this show did not quite come up to my personal expectation. Perhaps the theatre was responsible for something of this. Whoever built the Lyceum knew that the old horseshoe model, with boxes at each end, is the best in this respect — that it enables actors to pour their performances into a cup specially prepared to receive it. Things are quite different in theatres which, like the Dominion, are built with more than half an eye to the screen. Here there are no boxes to speak of, the horseshoe diminishes to a semicircle, and a good deal of the performance escapes, so to speak, into the wings. One knows quite well what Miss Nellie Wallace can do, and there was the evidence of one's eyes that she was giving heroically and exhaustively of her superabundant energy. Yet she did not 'get over' in her usual fashion, since, in addition to the acoustic difficulties, it would appear to be impossible for a player to hold both sides of this huge house at once. Mr. Wylie has obviously been conscious of the difficulty, since he has tried to diminish the size of the stage by an inner proscenium, and in this show to concentrate principally upon spectacle.

Here again I don't quite know what to say, for though some of the stage-settings were good, the design and colouring of the costumes struck me as almost uniformly hideous. To my considerable astonishment the programme attributed these costumes to Mesdames Calthrop, Zinkeisen, and Dolly Tree, who have done such marvels for Mr. Cochran. Perhaps, before deciding whether these ladies have run completely out of form, one should be told the exact date of their efforts. The programme announces the music as having been 'composed, selected and arranged by Jas. W. Tate and E. W. Eyre'. Now, since the former died some seven years ago, this would seem to date not only the pantomime but possibly the efforts of the costume-designers. I have already alluded to Miss Wallace who, with the handicap of appearing to be acting over the way, did valiantly. Mr. Lupino Lane had not many opportunities to be funny, though he tumbled as well as ever.

The Principal Boy was that firm favourite, Miss Ella Retford, whose performance, if a shade less nimble than of yore, retained the old warm-heartedness. If archness be a virtue in Principal Girls, then Miss Stella Browne acquired inordinate merit; she certainly sang very well. But I shall on this occasion divide first marks between Mr. George Atterbury for that captivating animal, Bonzo, and some forty children for their captivating little selves. Half-way through the show the supply of original music seemed to run out, and we were entertained with Bishop, Rossini, and lots and lots of Grieg, jazzed up according to the fashion of some years ago. It is only fair to add that the normal spectator did not appear to endorse any of my views on this production. But then the normal spectator presumably did not arrive at this theatre in the same condition as the exhausted dramatic critics, who necessarily approach the last of many Christmas entertainments, in the words of a lamented poet, 'as sobbing runners breast the tape'.

December 28, 1930

PANTOMIMES

DICK WHITTINGTON
(Hippodrome)

MOTHER GOOSE
(Daly's)

ROBINSON CRUSOE
(Scala)

CLEARING our minds of cant, let it be said that the London panto-mime has never been a patch upon its provincial brother, a fact which would have been recognized aeons ago but for the astound-ing pathos of Dan Leno and the fatness of unfunny Herbert Campbell. I may know nothing about Plautus, and Mr. Carroll will aver that I know less about parody. But I would defend my knowledge of provincial pantomime, with which I first made acquaintance exactly fifty years ago. I remember the first appear-ance of Lily Elsie at Manchester in 1897 in the title-rôle of Little Red Riding Hood. I remember Phyllis Dare's appearance in the same town and part in 1900. This was at the Royal, while over the way in the same year George Graves appeared as the Emperor of China in *Aladdin*. I can just recall Bessie Bellwood, Bessie Bonehill, and that female Atlas, Harriet Vernon.

Manchester was always fortunate in its Principal Boys, of whom the best, in my considered opinion, was Maggie Duggan. This great artist not only knew her job, but knew what her job was, which is something the present-day chit wearing her dimples at the wrong end knows nothing at all about. In the galaxy were Ada Reeve, Ada Blanche, and Queenie Leighton, all of whom not only played the game but knew what it was about. Thereafter the *bel canto* of the flesh became a tuneless rhapsody of spirit. The comedians of those days came not in single spies, but in battalions. Thus I have seen in one and the same pantomime George Robey and George Graves; G. P. Huntley and George Graves; Malcolm

Scott and Eugene Stratton; Little Tich and the Sisters Levey. Remember, too, that to a great pair of comedians would be added a great Principal Boy, and if you are the right period you will realize that those were the days!

Decay, or at any rate change, in the matter of the Principal Boy began when the curtain first rose on *Peter Pan*. Henceforth the strapping thigh, sicklied o'er with the pale cast of thought, wilted to nothing, and the rollicking lay gave place to mawkish ballads about megrims. Take those songs which have to be sung by Miss Fay Compton at the Hippodrome. They may be very good songs. But the point is that they are drenched with as much nostalgia as if they came out of Delius's 'Brigg Fair', and I should not like to print what Maggie Duggan would have said if she had been invited to let the gallery have them. How Miss Compton gets the better of these crooning, sagging, maudlin dithyrambs I cannot tell, because on the night of my visit to the Hippodrome she was indisposed and did not appear. Nor can I tell what kind of Principal Boy she makes, though I must surmise that he is a wistful, eerie, fey Dick Whittington, like Mary Rose in trews. Turning up things which have been said in this column about this charming actress, I find that I have been so far moved out of reason as to find analogies in lambs grazing above Rydal Water, distant waterfalls, and elves weeping under the moon.

But there is little that is lamb-like about Prince Charming, who should be driving a coach-and-four down the Duke of York's steps. Neither can you, with riding-whip or anything else, slap a distant waterfall, and the last thing a Principal Boy, my school, should be like is an elf weeping under anything. Now either Miss Compton is a Principal Boy of the old style or the new. If of the old style, then she is that extraordinary genius the artist who, having consistently stood for one set of qualities, now stands forth as the embodiment of their antithesis. If she is of the new style, then obviously we have to welcome the exquisite substitution of something else.

Alas, too, that on this occasion Mr. Leslie Henson, 'through swallowing emery-paper at Christmas', must confess to almost total loss of voice. Yet, as Stevenson very nearly said, a spirit goes out of the man who means execution which outlives laryngitis and other untimely interruption. But there are pleasures other than aural, and it was sheer delight to mark the disgust on Idle Jack's countenance when somebody proposed that he should look for work, and in our own minds to fill out the bellying sail of his emphatic: 'Don't be so *utterly* absurd!' One conjectures, too, that the book is not wholly untitivated, and, following the manner of your Shakespeare commentator, I shall attribute to Mr. Henson the remark on being sacked: 'And may I ask the reason, if it isn't a rude *answer?*'

I speak with diffidence of Mr. Tom Newell's Martha, who, with a mask exactly like Tenniel's Carpenter, has every attribute of your pantomime Dame except the essential one of being funny, I could sense the audience admiring Mr. Newell's art, but unless my ears deceived me, there was never the roar which goes with side-splitting. There can, however, be no two opinions about Mr. Johnny Fuller's Cat; whoso holds that there could be a better Cat lies, and whoso thinks there can be as good risks lying.

There was at least one other absentee on this unfortunate evening whereby some acrobatics, which I hear are wonderful, could not take place. Also, one of the six Catherine wheels which formed the apex, apogee, and apotheosis of the whole affair refused to work, as against which the Plaza Tiller Girls performed miracles of align-ment, while it would be heresy not to acclaim in Beam's Babes some two dozen geniuses in embryo. At least, that is what their parents, who all sounded as though they were present, probably thought of each of them while throwing scorn on the other twenty-three. It is only fair to add that, with Miss Compton restored to the firmament and the return of Mr. Henson's normal voice, the show will be some 200 per cent. better than one could suppose it on Thursday night.

No reservations of any kind are, however, to be made for *Mother Goose* at Daly's. This is the first pantomime ever staged at this theatre, and it is also the only pantomime I have ever seen in London which at all approaches provincial rank. There is about it what Mr. Curdle called 'a completeness, a kind of universal dove-tailedness, a sort of a general oneness' in all that should constitute a pantomime. Miss Cora Goffin — heavenly and Dickensian name! — is the Principal Boy here, and though the flesh is a little weak the spirit is indubitably willing. Miss Goffin has looked upon principal and boyish majesty, and at least knows what it should be if she cannot quite reproduce it.

But the thing that makes this show is the astonishing genius — and I do not think the word too strong — of Mr. George Lacy, in my view as entertaining a Dame as Huntley and the lawful successor, lustres hence, to Robey. I do not know where Mr. Lacy comes from, or how old he is or isn't, or anything at all about him. I only know that he has the gift of making an audience laugh without reason, which is the best kind of laughter, since every member of the audience must join in it. Even those blighted mugwumps who cannot smile till Bergson has ratified the occasion must capitulate and laugh at this effortless droll, who has taken care, moreover, to supplement drollery with high technical accomplishment. The number of things a pantomime Dame can do is limited, and perhaps cannot now be added to; Mr. Lacy brings a new virtuosity to them all, and perhaps his skill is best shown in this — that he can amuse in an impersonation of a Fairy Queen without descending to the idiom of effeminacy. There is a chubby, likeable quality about a comedian whom, on the whole, I take to be young, though in discovering him I am probably declaring that of which the provinces have known for years. Such is Metropolitan nitwittery.

At the Scala is Miss Ella Retford, who is to be approached with awe, since she embodies both the Grand Style and Perpetual Youth. 'What makes a Principal Girl a good one, in the judgment of special connoisseurs of pantomime, is a mystery hidden from mere common playgoers. When and where Principal Girls should be pert and when and where refrain from pertness; how close they should come to being what the uninstructed might call minxes and yet how they should differentiate themselves from minxes in the eyes of the experts; to how many affairs of the heart they should make lyric reference while adhering like gum, in their prose passages, to their respective Sinbads, Princes Charming, and Little Boys Blue — all these are deep and hidden things, for ignorance of which, let us trust, we shall not be rebuked, as a-Kempis says, at the day of judgment. But, going simply by last night's applause, we should guess that a competent committee of bloods would mark Miss Retford's Ruby *alpha plus.*'

The above, which I would give my ears to have written, was dashed off by Montague on a snowy, pre-war Christmas Eve. It shall stand without alteration for Miss Retford's Robinson Crusoe since, in pantomime, sex is what the Mad Hatter would describe as much of a muchness. This first-class artist is well supported in a very charming show.

December 31, 1932

CINDERELLA
(Drury Lane)

DICK WHITTINGTON
(Lyceum)

ROBINSON CRUSOE
(Lewisham Hippodrome)

ROBIN HOOD AND THE BABES IN THE WOOD
(Victoria Palace)

'EVERYBODY in our land', wrote Stevenson in a famous passage, 'everybody in our land, except humanitarians and a few persons whose youth has been depressed by exceptional aesthetic surroundings, can understand and sympathize with an admiral or a prizefighter.' He might have added a Principal Boy and a comedian red-nosed, loud-voiced. According to this school the book of a pantomime should be written by, say, Lord Dunsany, with lyrics by a Bridges or a Yeats. The spineless *décor*, backed by Delius's wilting ecstasy, must convey the green thought in the green shade, and this goes equally for Robinson Crusoe's tropical brake and for Cinderella's wood.

Reader, don't you believe it! 'If you told them [the frequenters of ale-houses] about Germanicus and the eagles they would very likely fall asleep, but tell them about Jem Belcher, or about Nelson and the Nile, and they put down their pipes to listen.' Offer the youngsters the new, lymphatic fudge and they will pipe their eye; give them the old stuff of pantomime and they pipe in chorus. The oldsters too!

Julian Wylie was not much of an outdoor man, and presumably in the outdoor scenes of *Cinderella* at Drury Lane left Nature and his scene-painter to look after themselves. His woodland glade is entirely successful, and bears a singular resemblance to a shortened fifth hole at Woking, so that you find yourself wondering whether you would run your approach shot or pitch it and take J. H. Taylor's awful and historic risk, which in this case means the road along which Cinderella's coach will presently trundle. Indoors the continuous glamour ends by winning that adjective which Hazlitt applied to certain kinds of poetry — 'working'. The Enchanted Lake set is neither within doors nor without — it is really a palatial bathroom, with constant warm water, open to the sky. Smilingly each naiad immerses herself, remaining by ingenious device dryad as to the upper half. Like Henley's barmaid, 'her head's a work of art', and not to be endangered. The last scene, all in white, is a dazzling affair evocative of antimacassars, confirmation frocks, and wedding-cake.

On the score of fun this pantomime at the Lane might be deemed a trifle short, though as Buttons Mr. Billy Danvers in the second act has his moment, and a very long moment it seems to some of us. This actor is not without a touch of pathos, and Mr. Dan Leno, junr., is, as 'twere, a trifle o'erparented. Most of the laughter is imported by The Three Sailors, who repeat two music-hall turns which in their new setting keep this august house rocking perilously.

One feels that before the antics of these superb buffoons the Walls of Jericho must have fallen down. Yet an earnest colleague has called their humour 'not very spirited'. This makes me wonder for the mental stability of the entire first-night audience whom this trio rightly convulsed. In my view, it is like saying that Miss Phyllis Neilson-Terry lacks dignity, or that June is without grace.

Is it permitted to say that the first of these distinguished ladies is principal without being boyish? That she is faultily faultless, icily regular, and therefore, alas! splendidly null? That she never gets on terms with the gallery, and wants the warm good-nature of a Bellwood, Barlow, Vernon, Duggan? That so much of aloofness and majesty is not the wear? That so many inches of upstage scorn forbid the insinuating approach of a Vesta Tilley or an Ada Reeve? That trilling like a Trebelli or a Tietjens is all very well, but that grand-opera manner is here a beautiful thing out of place? That the voice is not big enough for so vast a house? That when to this small rill of song is added June's tiny rillet the result is no more than the dulcet tinkle of a woodland stream? But can June dance? Oh, boy! I grant I never saw a goddess go, but it must be after Cinderella's style. As for Prince Charming the verdict shall be: The statue, but not the bust! As the Ugly Sisters Mesdames Ethel Revnell and Gracie West give raucousness its due and are liked, and as Dandini Miss Clarice Hardwicke is pertness itself. A good pantomime which is never quite a panto.

There is no nonsense about *Dick Whittington* at the Lyceum. Or, rather, it is all nonsense, and anybody who can resist the scene in which Messrs. George Jackley, Charlie Naughton, and Jimmy Gold retire to bed during a storm at sea should immediately consult a doctor. Two questions have long assailed me: Where does Mr. Jackley's voice go to in the summer time, and by what means does he keep it so miraculously hoarse? The verse is of the sort the right-minded want to hear at this season:

> And as for you, you idle apprentice,
> You make me quite *non compos mentis*.

There is a ballet in which a great many young ladies persevere to no particular ends, and of the transformation scene it may be said that *plus ça change....*

At Lewisham, which is in itself an adventure, there is an all-black pantomime. This is at the Hippodrome. Perhaps 'all-black' is an exaggeration; one would say, however, that the artists are, as to 90 per cent. of their number, coloured, and ranging from pure coal through coffee to the lightest of creole tan. The twelve piccaninnies who delight by their dancing seem, for some odd reason, to be painted green, and I will swear that two of the comedians are sons of no sultrier a clime than Bow. The pantomime is *Robinson Crusoe*, and surely, if logic prevailed, Man Friday, in a cast of coloured artists, should be white! He is, however, of the kettle's hue. Logic, ever the white man's burden, is not the strong point of his Christmas entertainment; if it were we should not have Miss Alberta Hunter, as a dusky belle of Juan Fernandez, hankering after a sweetheart marooned on the Isle of Capri. But this is good, honest entertainment, and worth the money.

All things considered, the best pantomime that has come my way this year is *Robin Hood* and *The Babes in the Wood* at the Victoria Palace. 'That's two of your pantomimes' would probably have been Hamlet's snub to Osric had he brought him such a tale. To which Mr. Laidler is entitled to retort that his show is twice as much in the pantomime tradition as any other, and I for one shall support him. This manager gives terrific measure of his good things, and how after the matinée he gets his curtain up again by half-past seven is a mystery.

Mr. Douglas Wakefield is the tower of strength here — a long, lean gawk of a fellow with the long upper-lip of the born comedian and a nose like the jut of a cliff undermined by the sea. He acts like the bright spark of an amateur dramatic society who has modelled himself on a composite recollection of Mr. George Arliss and Mr. Ralph Lynn. But his tumbling, in which he is ably impeded by Mr. Billy Nelson, is very professional indeed.

There is a capital scene in which Mr. Wakefield attempts to tell those two sophisticated Babes, Mr. Ivor Vintnor and Miss Patricia Shaw-Page, the story of Dick Whittington. The children insist upon nailing 'once upon a time' to a particular day and hour, and these are finally agreed as Monday morning and 9 o'clock. Why did Dick leave home? Where were his parents that they allowed it? After argument Mr. Wakefield is driven to the position that Dick's mother is dead. But how about his father? 'Gone out!' says Mr. Wakefield. 'What for?' persists the Girl Babe. 'A drink,' says Mr. Wakefield, catching at a straw. 'What!' shrills the Boy Babe. 'At 9 o'clock in the morning!' Out of such slips is made the reputation of a born liar. Mr. Mark Daly is a very good second to Mr. Wakefield.

Miss Gwladys Stanley knows what Principal Boys should be and do and vouchsafes a little of each. With a little encouragement she should warm up famously. Miss Margery Binner is a Maid Marion nearer perhaps to the Staffordshire than the Dresden model, but a comely and credible product of Sherwood Forest. The prettiest thing of the opening afternoon was the sight of the children in boxes and stalls; two little mites were studies in flaxen absorption. I hasten to include the circles and balconies; children's beauty is no respecter of tiers. The tots gave ample evidence of their relish for what, I repeat, is the best show of those I have seen this year.

December 30, 1934

THE FORTY THIEVES

(Lyceum)

In Irving's home laughter is become Man's solitary function, and you have to think hard to recall what the costumes and the scenery are like. In the house that once was Kean's the attitude on both sides of the curtain is ceremonial, and it was only when I got home the other evening that I realized how indefatigable had been Mr. Shaun Glenville as Mrs. Hubbard. Indeed, it is typical of the august Lane that old Mother Hubbard goes to no cupboard, bare or otherwise, for the sufficient reason that there is no dog needing a bone. But Christmas being no time for bones of contention it shall be said that that pantomime was excellent. Now to our Lyceum muttons.

I will resolutely say that I do not remember any pantomime at this theatre quite so heartening as the present one. The curtain rising on *The Forty Thieves* finds everybody treading the tinselled road to Samarkand, and for a long time we are occupied with the unravelling of a considerable plot. The story is closely followed and told in good honest couplets which, however, cheat a little here and there, as when 'neighbour' is made to rhyme with 'favour'. But it is a poor stomach that cannot warm a cold potato, and a poverty-stricken one that cannot enrich a rhyme. Possibly — though I intend to start no disputatious hare! — Morgiana's: 'I must go, though parting is such pain!' is inferior to Juliet's expression of the same sentiment, but this only leads us to reflect that Messrs. Walter and Frederick Melville are not quite so poetic a playwright as Shakespeare, who here confutes his own saying about the hand of little employment having the daintier sense.

The first part of this pantomime happens largely under the ægis of Miss Florrie Forde, who makes me feel Tauberishly. She, and all Principal Boys of her kind, are my heart's delight. But, alas! Miss Forde has let discretion become the better part of valour. Without impoliteness to Miss Kitty Reidy, who makes a delightful Gamen, I could have wished Miss Forde had taken her courage in both hands and realized that valour may still be the better part of discretion. When in *Patience* Bunthorne calls Lady Jane a pretty damozel, that ripe enchantress tartly says: 'No, not pretty. Massive!' There is a school of thought, and I belong to it, which insists that a Principal Boy cannot be too massive. Why, then, should Miss Forde go over to the enemy and tacitly hold that the main prop and pillar of a pantomime should be, in Bunthorne's words, not 'a wild, weird, fleshly thing', but something 'very tender, very yearning, very precious!' Yet this great favourite of an older day still holds us in the hollow of her hand, and it is good to hear the old songs reminiscently sung even when the singer, discarding boyish livery, presents them from a matronly ambuscade of puce and gold draperies surmounted by a confection of obsequious and heliotrope plumes. Let it be put down in black and white that, unlike the Principal Boy *à la mode*, Miss Forde can sing, that when she opens her mouth the issuing sound is not a rillet but a spate, and that you can hear without effort every word and every syllable of every word. This artist still has the power to dominate, and when she is on the stage you cannot look anywhere else even if there be room! This joke is not so good as it would be if Miss Forde had not been before one in virtually making it herself, since she devotes a whole verse of one of her songs to celebrating her figure's broad champaign.

Now how about the comedians? These hardly get their chance until after the Transformation Scene, in which Miss Euphan MacLaren attempts to transform a number of domesticated ladies into the semblance of Eastern houris pirouetting lusciously in a stalactited grotto apparently situate at the foot of the Himalayas. While this is in process a pair of adagio dancers perform whatever it is that adagio dancers perform to the music of Chopin's most hackneyed nocturne played *lentissimo*. At the opening performance one reflected that it was a good thing the dancers made fewer slips than the wood-wind, which hardly escaped with its neck! But when the comedians' chance comes, how finely the quintet take it! Mr. George Jackley leads, and were his performance to divagate one thousandth part of an inch from previous performances the assembled children would be the first to resent it.

Mr. Jackley's first lieutenant is Mr. Charlie Naughton, if possible more mercurial than ever, and — not to be niggling in comparison — more than ever like Coquelin in the flick of his terrier-like nose! What a superb comedian this is! How he *draws* sympathy towards him! He is partnered as devotedly as ever, and Mr. Naughton, faithful on his side, has probably long ago realized that in the matter of foils all that glitters might not be Gold. Mr. Naughton may be the front legs of comedy's stalking-horse; he could not get on without that other pair. About Monsewer Eddie Gray, attired in a costume partaking equally of the ringmaster and the professional golfer, whole tomes could be written.

To-day's workaday world lacks a Walkley to explain this delirious artist in terms of Croce and Jean Paul Richter, Sainte-Beuve and Peacock: 'The creature looks more simian than human, but is graciously affable — another Sir Oran Haut-ton, in fact, with fiddle substituted for Sir Oran's flute and French horn.'

This is perfect, except thàt Monsewer Gray affects the trombone. Perhaps, if nobody will produce a play for six months or so, I shall have leisure to write a small volume on the supplementary art of the Monsewer's unnamed assistant, a second fiddle which comes dangerously near to eclipsing the first. Last in this catalogue are the Liazeed Egyptian Troupe, a company of tumblers in whose virtuosity I find an echo of Sarah Bernhardt in Byzantine mood. So much for the pantomime at the Lyceum, a Boutique Fantasque in the sense that if you are out for touch-and-go jocularity this is the shop for it.

December 29, 1935

IN SEARCH OF PRINCE CHARMING

SOME talk of Dan Leno and some of Herbert Campbell, but for me pantomime has always centred in such artists as Harriet Vernon, Ada Blanche, Marie Loftus and Maggie Duggan. Youngsters sometimes ask with wonder in their voice: 'And did you then see Maggie plain?' In the mind's eye I see these 'Principal Boys' as though it were but yesterday that they trod the boards, golden visions with their cockades and their diadems, modish riding-whips and jewelled garters. I have loved them all, without distinction or faithfulness; captivated now by a bunch of lace pinned at the throat by a diamond the size of a pheasant's egg, now by an elegant phrase of the hand, now by a particularly handsome turn of the heel. About comedians there could be dispute: *quot homines tot* funny-bones! All Principal Boys were adorable in their own right.

And then a change came over them which it is hard to define — a leaning to circumspection is, perhaps, the nearest. At any rate, the Boys became less dashing. They lost the art of slapping their thighs, and executed that spanking manœuvre, when indeed they did not omit it altogether, with diffidence. They became introspective, sicklied o'er with the pale cast of thought; and one I encountered who was positively morose. I confess that when, last Christmas, I set out on a round of the pantomimes it was with the intention of re-discovering not only my lost youth but a lost young man, the Prince Charming of long ago. I began with *Cinderella* at the Hippodrome, and found Miss Clarice Mayne doing exquisite and dainty things, but hardly those which I wanted her to do. She annihilated all that the scene-painters had made to a pink thought in a pink shade. In the ballroom scene she struck a magnificent attitude, black and silver against a world of rose. Yet, soliloquizing mutely over the slipper, she reminded me less of Prince Charming than of Lawrence's painting of Kemble's Hamlet. 'Alas, poor Cinders!' she might have been saying, 'get you to your Ugly Sisters' chamber', and so on. This is not Miss Mayne's fault, but her librettists'. Do they not know that in such a costume — black velvet with a rake to it like a cutter's bowsprit — Harriet Vernon sang 'He's a rider'?

There were two admirable pieces of pantomime. To be strictly accurate these were dances, executed with maximum felicity by Messrs. Nervo and Knox, the 'Brokers' Men'. In possession of the Baron's kitchen these lively fellows engaged in a wrestling match, which they then reproduced after the fashion of the slow-moving cinematograph. You would have said that the minds of the dancers had conquered the matter of their bodies, or that they had compounded with gravitation for a full minute in which to execute a fall of sixteen feet. Their deliberate convolutions gave the impression of a resistant atmosphere supporting the body as water supports a fish, and the house watched with the curious tension which the slowing down of pictures always evokes. Later, the dancers gave a happy imitation of the classic performers, of a Nijinsky, in admirable poise, making the best of an incredibly clumsy and big-footed partner, a Mordkin *à rebours*. Here the law was not defied but fulfilled, since the dancers made it manifest that they had attained to the grotesque in motion by an under-standing of the poetic. It is a pity that the occasion was not seized to poke a little legitimate fun at the music of the modern ballet. Mr. Stanley Lupino showed an engaging personality, but hardly that of a great droll. He was at his best in a kind of pin-pricking, deflatory criticism, a reduction to the point of view of the fellow in the street. He would ridicule the precious with a glib 'You are under a misapprillusion!' Or he would take a good look round the Royal Ballroom and exclaim, 'So this is the Corner House!' Whereby all sorts of untoward magnificences, including those of Messrs. Lyons, became one with Nineveh and Tyre. Apart from these three performers the success of this pantomime was impersonal. The costumes were very splendid. The scenery was of considerable grandeur and elaboration, and sometimes touched beauty. There was a pretty wood which had a carpet of apparently real moss, and an Enchanted Lake, which the programme certified as containing eighteen tons of real water. Real steam assured us that the nymphs who descended into its depths ran no risk of pneumonia, and a decorative touch was added by the real ducks which, in one corner of the lake, signed the picture in the same way that the terriers sign 'George Stubbs' in the Welbeck portrait of the third Duke of Portland. But I did not find here the Principal Boy of my heart.

Next I sought out *Robinson Crusoe* at the Lyceum. There was plenty for the children here. There was an ogre of such size that his mustachios were human arms. There were marionettes made of gauze interiorly lit up who, on a darkened stage, gave admirable representations of Pip, Squeak, and Wilfred, and lesser celebrities. There was an old-fashioned Transformation Scene, which in-cluded a magnificent ballet called the Wonders of the Deep, and the whole ended with a harlequinade. The book too was in verse, which see-sawed quite properly between the heroic couplet and some such lilt of expedience as:

> I regard that man as a wily opossum,
> And whenever I can, I put it across 'im.

'Don't be so familiarity!' said an exuberant crone, and the

audience roared. Well, we have authority that the centuries 'kiss and commingle', and it is interesting to recall Mistress Quickly's 'Didst thou not desire me to be no more so familiarity with such poor people?' Perhaps only those who remembered Vesta Tilley's exquisite Crusoe and Bert Gilbert's pathetic Friday realized that the possibilities were insufficiently explored at the Lyceum where, indeed, there was a drollery of things rather than of men. But alas! no Principal Boy of my dreams.

Again, it was not Miss Nancy Benyon's fault. She did all that in Mr. Leedham Bantock's view became a Principal Boy. But it is in my mind that in the scene of the stockade the Robinson of long ago doffed goat-skin for a moment to tell us how 'All of Us Played the Game'. In this same pantomime the idol sang, 'Down at Happy Hampton' in a fawn Melton overcoat, brown bowler and whanghee cane, and 'By the Sad Sea Waves' in a dinner-jacket, red silk handkerchief, and straw hat. *Eheu fugaces!* Does this great little artist really think that in 'Lady de Frece' we can ever forget Vesta Tilley?

In my search I turned to ways less elegantly trodden — to wit, the Elephant and Castle, where, in *Babes in the Wood*, I encountered a capital smell of oranges, a good old-fashioned advertisement curtain, the information that Septuagesima Sunday is the second after Ascot, but no Prince. Robin Hood may, or may not, have reproduced the atmosphere of Thomas Hardy's green wood-landers, but was in no wise the he of my quest.

At the Kilburn Empire I found *Dick Whittington*, whose hero was eclipsed by the most human thing in cats I have ever known. 'Dog conscious of dog, attains to Man', says Mr. Lascelles Abercrombie in some erudite volume. Mr. Hallatt's gentlemanly Tom was very human. There was another admirable feline in *Puss in Boots* at the Brixton Theatre, Wee Wally Walters proving that by taking philosophic thought Boy can attain to Cat. It would seem that such an actor and the chief of the tribe of Felidæ are brothers under their skins. I saw this pantomime in the afternoon, and enjoyed it enormously. The audience was composed almost entirely of children, who took the choruses out of the mouths of the singers and sang them with full-throated glee. It was a little disconcerting to find how apt these mites were at the most sophisticated allusions. Let me instance a song which they took up at the first hearing. You must imagine a good, swinging tune to the words:

> Are you working?
> No. Are you? (*bis*)
> Oh, oh, everywhere you go,
> When you meet a pal you shout —
> Are you working?
> No. Are you?
> Three cheers for the red, white, and blue,
> Tell me the old, old story,
> Are you working?
> No. Are you?

I thought I detected a shade of double-edged raillery in these babes — a hint that, whilst the work-providers may be wholly lax and iniquitous, brother Tom, if not Dick and Harry, is not doing so badly out of his enforced idleness. Hundreds and hundreds of tiny tots took up the choruses as though they would burst their little lungs: they roared when the man with the shiny black bag and the worn top-hat tried to get into the Ogre's Castle on the pretext of mending the telephone, or 'on behalf of the Prudential': and when finally the doorkeepers were seduced from their post by a piece of cheese artfully placed within sniffing distance, the mites — whereby I mean the human ones — set up such a yell as would have done credit to their elders at a Cup Final.

At this moment I noticed that the little old lady sitting in the next stall was silently wiping her eyes. She had never had children, she said. This being no time for sentiment, I bade her admire that accuracy of natural observation which enabled the Dame to describe rhubarb as 'celery gone bloodshot'. At once my little lady cheered up. 'He's very right, sir; indeed he is!' There were a number of masks here worn by the minor ogres, some of which had the hideousness of Gustave Doré's untempered imaginings, whilst others were simply like the members of my Bridge Club. And still no Prince.

And then I hied me to Kennington. There, in *Cinderella*, I found a wonderful quartette of finished pantomime artists. First, Albert le Fre who made the Dame something between Betsey Trotwood and Mr. Albert Rutherston's view of Mrs. Gladstone. Then Harry Claff as the Baron, in well-trained singing voice, and Jack Barty as Buttons, with a speaking voice like all the foghorns of the P. and O. On the night of my visit the stage-box was full of Mr. Will Evans. Now to play the fool to that austere mentor would seem to be almost as intimidating an experience as when Duse had to let fly at Salvini, in one box, and Ristori in another. But the trio minded it not.

And there I found him whom I sought — the fair, the not too refrigerative, the inexpressive he of long ago. This was Ouida Macdermott, born to orris-root and patches, ruffling it with inimitable grace and swagger. She was the fellow who had driven four-in-hand along the midnight front at Brighton and upset the Regent returning from a carouse. She was the chap who, in a former incarnation, had put on the gloves with an earlier Harry Preston. This was the lover who

> hath Dian's wit,
> And in strong proof of chastity well arm'd,
> From love's weak childish bow doth live unharm'd.

She, in short, was Prince Charming. For all that, I fancied I detected a shade of uneasiness in Miss Macdermott's gesture. Might it not be out of date to slap a thigh? No, dear lady and dear boy! Slap on! Slap ever! One heart, at least, beats for you.

INDEX

INDEX

INDEX

INDEX

INDEX

264